D1071798

Birth Quake

POPULATION AND DEVELOPMENT
A series edited by Richard A. Easterlin

Previously published:

BIRTH QUAKE

The Baby Boom and Its Aftershocks

DIANE J. MACUNOVICH

THE UNIVERSITY OF CHICAGO PRESS
CHICAGO AND LONDON

Diane J. Macunovich is professor of economics at Barnard College of
Columbia University.

The University of Chicago Press, Chicago 60637
The University of Chicago Press, Ltd., London
© 2002 by The University of Chicago
All rights reserved. Published 2002
Printed in the United States of America

11 10 09 08 07 06 05 04 03 02   1 2 3 4 5
ISBN: 0-226-50083-7 (cloth)

Library of Congress Cataloging-in-Publication Data

Macunovich, Diane J.
    Birth quake : the baby boom and its aftershocks / Diane J. Macunovich.
    p. cm. — (Population and development)
    Includes bibliographical references and index.
    ISBN 0-226-50083-7 (cloth : alk. paper)
    1. United States—Population—History—20th century.   2. United
States—Economic conditions—1945–   3. Overpopulation—History—20th
century.   I. Title.   II. Population and development (Chicago, Ill.)

    HB3505 .M33 2002
    304.6'2'2'0973—dc21

                                                        2001052756

⊚ The paper used in this publication meets the minimum requirements of the
American National Standard for Information Sciences—Permanence of Paper
for Printed Library Materials, ANSI Z39.48-1992.
This book is printed on acid-free paper.

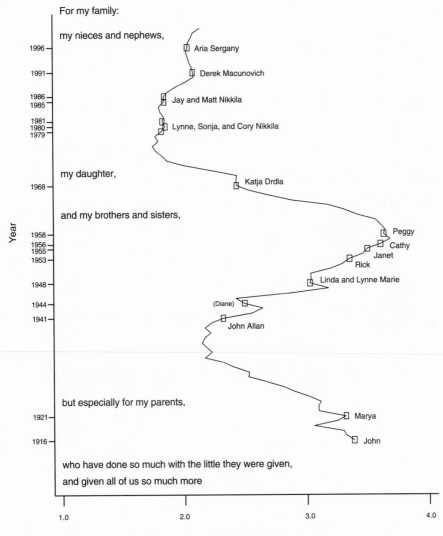

For my family:

my nieces and nephews,

Aria Sergany

Derek Macunovich

Jay and Matt Nikkila

Lynne, Sonja, and Cory Nikkila

my daughter,

Katja Drdla

and my brothers and sisters,

Peggy

Cathy

Janet

Rick

Linda and Lynne Marie

(Diane)

John Allan

but especially for my parents,

Marya

John

who have done so much with the little they were given,

and given all of us so much more

1996
1991
1986
1985
1981
1980
1979
1968
1958
1956
1955
1953
1948
1944
1941
1921
1916

Year

Total Fertility Rate

1.0   2.0   3.0   4.0

Contents

In the space of one hundred and seventy-six years the Lower Mississippi has shortened itself two hundred and forty-two miles. That is an average of a trifle over one mile and a third per year. Therefore, any calm person, who is not blind or idiotic, can see that just a million years ago next November, the Lower Mississippi River was upward of one million three hundred thousand miles long. . . . And by the same token any person can see that seven hundred and forty-two years from now the Lower Mississippi will be only a mile and three-quarters long. . . . There is something fascinating about science. One gets such wholesome returns of conjecture out of such trifling investment of fact.

Mark Twain, *Life on the Mississippi* (1883)

Sometimes we lose sight of the fact that an economy is just *people*—working, playing, eating, sleeping, loving, learning, and dying—because of our tendency to focus on mergers, acquisitions, IPOs, dot coms, and the stock market. But what would happen to stock prices if the population were suddenly halved—or doubled? An economy is ultimately a mechanism for satisfying the wants of a population, and its performance in the long run will be a direct function of that population—its size and composition. The purpose of this book is to demonstrate this relationship using the post-WWII baby boom, tracing the profound effect of that gigantic fluctuation in marriage and birth rates throughout our economy. My hope is that even if readers don't "buy" all of the arguments presented here, they will still come away convinced that any economic model that doesn't include population factors is bound to produce misleading results. Those who ignore the effects of population change tend to extrapolate current trends into the future in a linear fashion—much like Mark Twain's "science"—instead of recognizing the cyclic variation introduced by fluctuating population age structure.

This is not intended to be a monocausal argument. In many cases population change may be neither a necessary nor a sufficient condition for the events discussed. Nevertheless, it keeps emerging as a theme, an undercurrent running through many of the baffling changes we experienced as a society and an economy during the twentieth century and even earlier. Perhaps demographic change tends to be omitted from economic models precisely because it is so ubiquitous: we take it for granted.

The work presented here identifies common trends in population age structure underlying not only social changes, such as evolving women's roles and fluctuations in fertility, marriage, and divorce, but also tumultuous events, including the market crash of the 1930s, the "oil shock" of 1973, and the "Asian flu" of the 1990s. Significant economic dislocations seem to occur in the aftermath of a "birth quake," a disruption in what had been a smooth and seemingly predictable pattern of birth rates. For example, the crash of '29 was preceded in the industrialized nations by what demographers call the "fertility transition"—the decline from high to low fertility rates that accompanies modernization. The dislocations of the 1970s were preceded in those same nations by the end of the post-WWII baby boom. The crises in Brazil, Mexico, Korea, Thailand, and Malaysia were preceded by their own "fertility transitions"—some of the first to occur in the developing world. It seems plausible that these demographic shocks destabilized economies by confounding producer and investor expectations and undermining financial systems that had become overextended in response to preceding patterns of demographic change. We like to think that we can use monetary and fiscal policy to stabilize our economies, and perhaps we can, but we need to be aware of the potentially destabilizing effects of demographic change in order to make proper use of these tools. In complexity theory there is a crucial point—a tipping point—when many factors come together to generate change. I would suggest population change as not necessarily answering the question, Why? but rather the question, Why *then*?

Some will question the results presented here, pointing out that, for example, the entire Western world experienced an economic slowdown after 1973. My response is to refer to the pervasiveness of the post-WWII baby boom—at least in English-speaking countries—and to suggest that the massive fluctuations experienced by the United States during this period affected markets around the world. Look at the stock markets in other countries, how they tend to mirror changes in the Dow Jones Industrial Average. Given the volatility of investment behavior, that tendency alone could have made the ramifications of the U.S. baby boom contagious. Add to that the rapid fluctuations in the United States' demand for imported goods in an increasingly global economy, and it seems disingenuous to suggest that the U.S. baby boom would not have had a significant effect on markets in other countries.

In an attempt to understand the experience of the second half of the twentieth century, this book traces what appear to have been interactions between population age structure and the economy. We need to understand that past before we can ever hope to predict the future. Any "predictions" in these chapters are intended only to show the strength of population effects: they show what would occur if nothing other than demographics were to change in the future. Other potentially mitigating factors haven't been included in the models developed here. That's a shortcoming of this work, but one meant to restore balance in a world of models that focus on those other factors without ever considering population change. I don't mean to imply, with this work, that there will be some kind of mechanical "cookie cutter" repetition of past experience in the future. People aren't machines. We gradually learn the "rules of the game" and adapt to them, and in doing so we inevitably alter them. The curse of a good model is that it aids in that learning process, thus almost guaranteeing its own obsolescence.

Birth quakes appear to mimic earthquakes: it is impossible to predict the resultant landscape, but inevitable that the terrain will be indelibly altered in their aftermath.

Acknowledgments

I'd like to acknowledge the people and institutions associated with my move into academia: Robert W. Macaulay, Q.C., who took a chance on me as an independent consultant, giving me the opportunity to work on projects which led me to the baby boom; the University of Southern California, for taking a chance on a "mature student" with no previous training in economics; Williams College and Barnard College, for their support and encouragement; the Maxwell Center for Policy Research at Syracuse University and the Population Reference Bureau, for supporting me while on academic leave when the bulk of this research was conducted; Lee A. Lillard, for giving me my first opportunity to work with large data sets; and of course, Richard A. Easterlin for his inspiration and support. I also take this opportunity to extend heartfelt thanks to my editor, Geoff Huck, my copy editor, Jenni Fry, and two anonymous reviewers for their many thoughtful suggestions.

Parts of the present volume have been adapted or excerpted from my previously published work. Portions of chapter 2 are from Macunovich 1996a. Portions of chapters 5 and 6 are from Macunovich 2000a. Portions of chapter 8 are from Macunovich 1997a. Portions of chapter 11 are from Macunovich 1996a and 1999b. Portions of chapter 12 are from Macunovich 2000b.

The Birth Quake and Its Aftershocks

> Nevertheless, one cannot repress the thought that perhaps the whole
> Industrial Revolution of the past two hundred years has been nothing
> else but a vast secular boom, largely induced by the unparalleled rise
> in population.
>
> John R. Hicks, *Value and Capital* (1939)

Birth quake: a totally unexpected, earth-shattering, and ground-breaking event experienced not just in the United States, but in virtually the entire Western industrialized world during the 1950s and 1960s, as birth rates erupted and the number of babies born annually in many countries nearly doubled within just a few years. "Totally unexpected" in that fertility rates had been falling in all of these Western nations since the late 1800s and had in many cases dipped below replacement level[1] by the mid-1930s (fig. 1), causing gloomy prognostications among demographers and economists alike of a continued decline that many felt would weaken the West's position in the global community. "Earth-shattering" in that the birth quake produced continued upheavals—aftershocks—in the economy and in social structure from its earliest days. The epicenter of many of the most notable of these upheavals has been the transformation of women's roles, as Rosie the Riveter watched her daughters and younger sisters being pulled back into the home and then her granddaughters bursting forth once again into the labor force, in large part to ameliorate some of the disruptive effects of the birth quake. "Ground-breaking" because the birth quake has forced on our society and economy, demo-

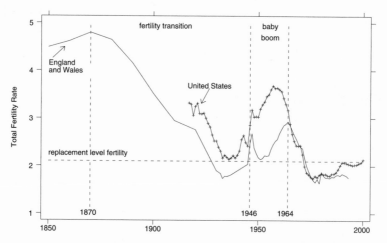

Figure 1. Fertility rates in the United States and in England and Wales, 1850–2000. The total fertility rate (the number of births a woman would have if she experienced current age-specific rates throughout her lifetime) for the United States is available only since 1917 but, based on available crude birth rates (births per 1,000 total population in a given year) for the preceding years, probably followed a time trend not unlike that in England and Wales. These rates are typical of the general pattern of fertility in the industrialized nations: a long period of demographic transition (when both fertility and mortality rates declined from high to low levels) from the late 1800s to the 1930s followed by a baby boom and a baby bust. Sources: Coleman 1996 and Glass 1967 for England and Wales; National Center for Health Statistics 1997b, 1999, 2001a,b for the United States.

graphic conditions never before experienced in modern history—changes in population age structure that no previous economy has had to accommodate. One of the most notable of these changes is the increase, since about 1994, in absolute numbers of young adults in the household formation stage, while the proportion of young adults in the total population has remained constant: a combination that may have contributed to the strength of the "New Economy."

As with an earthquake, the effects of a birth quake seem to show up everywhere one looks. Trying to explain the resultant landscape without reference to the baby boom's tumultuous effects will never convey a full understanding of the genesis of all those rifts, peaks, and gullies. This overview presents a summary of the evidence accumulated thus far—laced with a smattering of speculation—that appears to explain how so much of the social and economic change over the last fifty years has been related to the post-WWII baby boom and that generation's passage through the life cycle, and how the baby boom itself was probably triggered.

Relative Cohort Size and Male Relative Income

"Relative cohort size" is a basic demographic concept central to all of the explanations presented in this book. The word "cohort" originally denoted a type of Roman military unit, like a platoon, but is now used to refer to a group of people who have banded together in a common cause or who share some common statistical characteristic. This book focuses on "birth cohorts": individuals who were born in the same year or period and who will thus experience all of the various stages of the life cycle at about the same time. A crucial aspect is the size of a given cohort relative to that of its parents' cohort—hence "relative cohort size."

Although relative cohort size may have significant effects at many points in the life cycle, much of the focus here is at the point of labor market entry, when members of a given cohort are in their late teens and early twenties, just emerging from high school or college. In the United States over the past fifty years, relative cohort size at labor market entry has been halved (during the 1950s), then doubled (in the 1970s), and then halved again (in the 1990s), and currently—looking at the cohort just entering the labor market in the beginning of the twenty-first century—relative cohort size is about 1:2. Relative cohort size is a direct function of fertility rates at any given time: high (low) fertility produces a large (small) relative cohort size. As a result, the time trend in the general fertility rate (GFR: the number of births in a given year relative to the number of women of childbearing age) provides a fairly close approximation of the pattern of relative cohort size over the years and is therefore a good indication of relative cohort size at labor market entry up to twenty years in the future.[2]

The other essential concept underlying the analyses summarized here is "relative income," intended here to refer to young adults' earnings relative to their material aspirations—their desired standard of living. Although one's material aspirations might be the product of many different factors, it is assumed in the analyses summarized here that for young adults (those just entering the labor market), material aspirations will be significantly affected by the standard of living—determined largely by total income—enjoyed in their parents' homes.

In the historical context—even today, many would argue—young couples viewed the man's earnings as the primary component

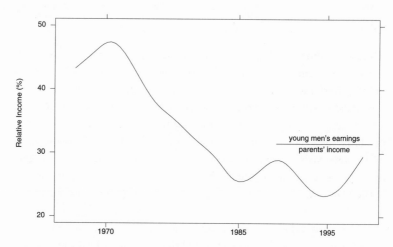

Figure 2. Stylized history of male relative income in the United States.

of their total income, the basic determinant of their standard of living. As a result, most of the analyses presented here focus primarily on *male* relative income, defined as young men's earnings relative to the material aspirations of young adults. A stylized version of average male relative income in the United States—as measured by young men's earnings relative to the total income of young adults' parents—is presented in figure 2.[3] The pattern is characterized by a sharp decline from 1970 to 1985 followed by a brief increase and another decline, with some improvement occurring again after 1995. During this period young white men experienced, on average, a 40 percent decline in their relative income, while young African Americans experienced a 60 percent decline.

The following sections of this chapter provide a summary of relative cohort size effects, divided into three categories:

1. Direct or "first-order" effects of relative cohort size on male relative income; male unemployment, hours worked, and labor force participation; men's and women's college wage premium (the extra earnings of a college graduate relative to those of a high school graduate); and levels of inequality generally.
2. "Second-order" effects of relative cohort size operating through male relative income, especially the demographic adjustments people make in response to changing relative income, such as changes in women's labor force participation and their occupational choices; men's and

women's college enrollment rates; marriage and divorce; fertility; crime, drug use, and suicide rates; out-of-wedlock childbearing and the incidence of female-headed families; living arrangements; and retirement behavior among the elderly.

3. "Third-order" effects, on the economy generally, of changing relative cohort size and the resulting demographic adjustments, such as changes in average wage growth; the overall demand for goods and services in the economy and hence the growth rate of the economy; inflation, interest rates, and savings rates; stock market performance; industrial structure; measures of gross domestic product (GDP); and productivity measures.

Although most of the analyses presented focus exclusively on U.S. experience, there is also some discussion of what appear to have been related experiences in other nations, both developed and developing.

First-Order Effects of Relative Cohort Size

The primary effect of relative birth-cohort size is on the earnings of young men relative to their material aspirations, working through changes in the ratio of young men's earnings relative to their fathers' earnings. This effect, analyzed in chapters 5 and 6, occurs largely because young, less experienced workers are not perfect substitutes in the labor market for older, more experienced workers, and the "production function" is sensitive to the balance of these two types of workers.

If there is an oversupply of one type of worker relative to the other (think of it as an oversupply of assembly-line workers relative to management), the wages of the oversupplied group will tend to go down relative to the wages of the undersupplied group. (In addition, there will probably be an increased demand for managers to train and supervise the inexperienced workers, relative to the supply of older men capable of working in management, perhaps increasing the wages of those managers.) This disparity will occur even in a period of strong economic growth, in which case the wages of both groups might rise, but on average the wages of the oversupplied group will not rise as rapidly as those of the undersupplied group. In addition, the age group in greater relative supply will experience increased levels of unemployment and part-time employment, leading—through the "discouraged worker effect"—to reduced labor force participation rates among those in the oversupplied group.

In the first paragraph of this section, I used the word "largely" in describing imperfect substitutability as the source of declining relative wages of younger workers because a number of other effects, including overcrowding (in the family, leading to less parental time with each child; and in schools, leading to higher student-teacher ratios and half-day sessions and hence to lower average performance), have been suggested as contributing factors.[4] Each of these other effects would tend to decrease the productivity and hence the wages of younger workers relative to those of prime-age workers, all other things being equal.

Labor economists have hypothesized that imperfect substitutability between prime-age and younger workers will be more pronounced for college graduates than for high school graduates: as skill levels increase, it should become more and more difficult to substitute a young, inexperienced worker for a more experienced one.[5] Thus, the negative effects of large relative cohort size would be stronger on relative college wages (the wages of younger relative to prime-age college graduates) than on relative high school wages, leading to a deterioration in the college wage premium—the additional wages an individual earns in return for obtaining a college education.

In addition, the very oldest and youngest workers tend to be *good* substitutes for each other (think of the jobs in fast food restaurants and behind checkout counters that are alternately filled by teenagers and senior citizens). As a result, large cohort size among young workers also tends to depress the relative wages of workers approaching retirement age—their wages relative to those of prime-age workers and also relative to their *own* earnings at younger ages (in constant dollars).[6] The pattern of relative wages for men nearing retirement is very similar to the pattern depicted in figure 2 for young men's relative income. Workers nearing retirement in the early 1970s were enjoying wages 15 percent higher than what they had received five to ten years earlier, but thanks to the baby boom, those facing retirement in 1985 were taking home 15 percent *less* than they had five to ten years earlier, in real terms.

The effect of imperfect substitutability—and close substitutability between the oldest and youngest workers—has been documented by labor economists.[7] However, because relative wages and employment prospects did not begin to improve when relative cohort size declined (i.e., after the peak of the baby boom had entered the labor market in 1979/80), labor economists began to assume that they had overestimated relative cohort size effects and so turned to other factors for analysis. Recent work, however, demonstrates that relative cohort size effects on male relative wages continue to be very strong, once allowance is made for asymmetry in those effects and for lack of closure in the U.S. economy (due to immigration, international trade, or both).[8]

More detailed analyses (presented in chapter 6) demonstrate that these relative cohort size effects are felt throughout the entire wage structure, affecting not just wage levels, but factors such as hours and weeks worked and the proportion of the population working full time. As a result, general levels of inequality rise with relative cohort size, with more marginal workers (those with less experience or skill) hurt disproportionately by its effects. Even workers with six to fifteen years of experience suffered a 20–25 percent decline in their relative wages, and their hours worked fell markedly.[9] Analyses presented in chapter 5 suggest that relative cohort size increased the overall unemployment rate by more than 50 percent between 1960 and 1980, providing a plausible explanation for past increases in what economists term the "natural rate of unemployment"—the outward shift of the curve economists have used to depict the trade-off between unemployment and inflation—as well as its apparent decline in recent years.

The same analyses described in chapter 5 also show the pattern of pressures that will be exerted by relative cohort size over the next twenty years. We can look forward to high levels of male relative income and returns to college in the future, and a continuation of the current low levels of unemployment, based on expected changes in relative cohort size. The simulations presented in chapter 5, prepared using data only up to 1988 or 1993, accurately predicted the low levels of unemployment in the late 1990s, as well as the current upturn in male relative income.

Second-Order Effects of Relative Cohort Size

Researchers have repeatedly demonstrated that people evaluate their income in *relative* as well as absolute terms. For example, one recent study found that, given a choice between a world in which survey respondents have more income than everyone else and one in which everyone (including the respondent) has more but the respondent has less than everyone else, half of the respondents preferred to have *50 percent less* real income, but high relative income.[10] Similarly, other researchers have found that subjects in experiments involving cash prizes are willing to pay out of their own winnings in order to reduce the winnings of others, and that this decision to "burn" others is relatively insensitive to the "price" of burning.[11] Consistent with this, recent work based on the General Social Survey of high school seniors between 13 and 19 has identified a strong relationship between individuals' subjective evaluations of their own happiness and measures of relative income that compare own to parents' income.[12] And in 1999 the *New York Times* devoted several pages to descriptions of the angst experienced by middle income families because they couldn't "keep up with the Joneses."[13]

As is described in chapter 2, economist and demographer Richard Easterlin has hypothesized that individuals tend to evaluate their earnings relative to some internalized desired standard of living, and that this standard will be strongly affected—especially when one is young—by that experienced in one's parents' home.[14] When young men's earnings decline relative to those of older workers, they also decline on average relative to the total income of their own parents, and thus relative to their own material aspirations. What happens in a society when these relative earnings decline sharply? Chapters 3 and 4 discuss various ways of measuring relative income, but in general it declined by close to 50 percent from the 1960s to the 1980s, by 60 percent for African Americans. Among young African American men, relative income fell by 50 percent for college graduates and nearly 85 percent for high school dropouts.

It seems reasonable to assume that in an attempt to close the gap between income and aspirations, members of relatively large cohorts will tend to make a number of adjustments, including increased female labor force participation and delayed or reduced marriage and childbearing.[15] In addition, because young women in large cohorts will anticipate higher levels of labor force participation, they will also tend to enroll in college at increased rates. Similarly, there will be increased motivation for young males to achieve a higher level of education, one method of raising their earning potential relative to that of their parents. This increased supply of young college graduates, however, will tend to lower the returns to a college education.

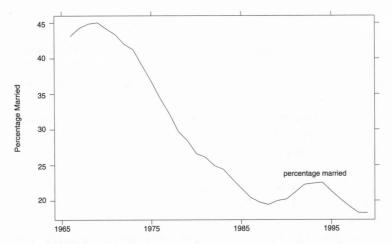

Figure 3. Percentage married among young men working full time in their first three years of work experience. This trend and others presented in chapter 9 appear to mimic the pattern of male relative income in figure 2. Source: author's tabulations of data from the March Current Population Survey public-use tapes.

Individuals, it is assumed, are ultimately concerned with *per capita* disposable income relative to their desired standard of living. An individual evaluates his or her earning potential as dictated by the market: how much he or she can earn by and for him or herself. Given this level of personal earnings, an individual then decides how many people can be supported on that income: self only? self plus spouse? Self and spouse with children? Per capita disposable income is the amount available to the individual and his or her dependents after making these demographic choices.

Individuals are assumed to focus on this per capita disposable income and make the necessary adjustments to keep it on a par with material aspirations. Thus the time trend in the proportion of young men who have married over the past thirty-five years has followed closely the pattern of their relative income, as illustrated in figure 3. The percentage married among young men working full time in their first three years out of school fell from 45 percent to less than 20 percent between 1970 and 1985, rose briefly to about 23 percent, and then fell again to about 20 percent, closely mirroring the pattern of male relative income in figure 2.

My colleagues and I have conducted analyses of pre-boom and baby boom cohorts and found that their male relative income—

individual earning potential of baby boomers relative to that of their parents—was significantly lower than the individual earning potential of *pre-boom* cohorts relative to that of *their* parents. After making the type of demographic adjustments indicated above, however, the boomers managed to bring their per capita disposable income on a par with that of their parents.[16]

This explains the paradox of the yuppie phenomenon occurring among the supposedly economically stretched baby boomers: sometimes these demographic adjustments will result in overcompensation. For example, average statistics notwithstanding, couples can't choose to have a fraction of a child—it's all or nothing. A couple able to support 2.5 children may well choose to have only two children and the extra disposable income rather than stretch their earnings to support three children. Similarly, the couple might need only part-time earnings from the wife to bring them up to their desired living standard, but she may be unable to find, or unwilling to limit herself to, part-time work in her chosen profession. Her full-time earnings might cause the couple to overshoot their earnings target. Surplus income—relative to the desired standard of living—produced the yuppie generation.

The psychological stress associated with these demographic adjustments has been put forward as a source of strain on marriages when they do occur, leading to an increased incidence of divorce, and as a possible reason for increases in the age-specific rates of other forms of anomie, such as juvenile delinquency, crime, drug use, and suicide.[17] The pattern of divorce for young married adults has followed closely—in the inverse—the pattern of male relative income in figure 2: the percentage of young ever-married women who were divorced nearly doubled between 1970 and 1985, declined for a few years, increased in the early 1990s, and then declined again.

Relative cohort size—more specifically, male relative income—is also a likely factor in the rise and then spectacular decline in crime rates over the past thirty-five years. In addition, because delayed or forgone marriage does not mean delayed or forgone sexual activity for males (increasing relative cohort size creates an abundance of younger females relative to older males), levels of out-of-wedlock childbirth and proportions of female-headed families also increase.

Marriage, Divorce, Fertility, Female Labor Force Participation, and College Enrollments

The theories presented here have not been popular with feminists, who see them as overly focused on relative cohort size effects on young males, implying a very passive role for young women. However, this is an extremely narrow interpretation of the relative cohort size model. The analysis presented in chapter 7 demonstrates that young women were hardly passive in the face of these changes. Their actions were shaped by the norms of the society they lived in, but they were not passive.

They, too, had material aspirations that were largely a function of the standard of living experienced in their parents' homes. Because societal norms focused on a "traditional" family with a male breadwinner and a female homemaker, women looked first at the potential earnings of men in order to determine the likelihood of achieving their own material aspirations. As male earnings alone became increasingly unlikely to support these aspirations, women anticipated that they, too, would enter the labor market—whether because they foresaw a lower likelihood of marriage or because they realized the need to supplement their husbands' earnings.

To prepare themselves for greater labor force participation, young women enrolled in higher education programs at increasing rates. Then, partly to maintain their desired level of per capita disposable income and partly because they were postponing marriage and family until after achieving college and career goals, fertility rates decreased. Figure 4 demonstrates the close correspondence between young women's fertility and the pattern of male relative income in figure 2. As demonstrated in chapters 7 through 11, all four of these effects—declining fertility and marriage rates and increased female college enrollment and labor force participation—together with increasing divorce rates, appear to correspond with an economic model based on the female wage and on male relative income and the college wage premium, all of which are in turn a function of relative cohort size. Based only on data through 1979, the models presented in those chapters correctly predict values for the following fifteen years.

This strong statistical relationship is hardly surprising, given even a cursory comparison of the historic trends in marriage, divorce, and fertility rates with the pattern of male relative income

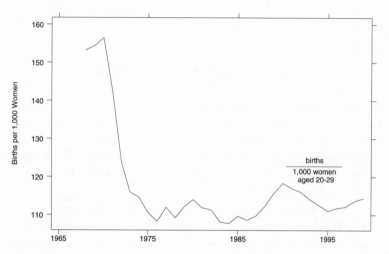

Figure 4. Fertility rates of women in the United States, aged 20–29. The pattern follows that of male relative income in figure 2, suggesting a direct relationship. Sources: Ventura et al. 1997; Peters et al. 1997; National Center for Health Statistics 1997–2001b.

presented in figure 2. Age-specific marriage and fertility rates followed relative income's precipitous decline through the 1970s and early 1980s, with the same "hump-shaped" recovery at the end of the 1980s—a pattern closely matched in the inverse by female labor force participation rates and divorce rates among young men and young women. Similarly, the college enrollment rates of young men have clearly responded to relative cohort size effects. As set out in chapter 8, a model based on relative cohort size closely tracks the long-term trend in male enrollment rates with its sharp dip in the 1970–1980 period caused by the baby boom.

The Emergence of the "Career Woman"

Another important manifestation of relative cohort size over the past thirty years has been its effect on young women's occupational choices. Though many consider sharply rising wages to be the most important factor leading to the emergence of the "career woman" in the United States, women's wages have in fact barely risen, in real terms, since the early 1970s. The "observed" average real wage among young women aged 20–24 who are no longer in school has indeed risen, but these increases are virtually eliminated after 1970, once controls are introduced for changing levels of hours and weeks worked, education, experience, occupation, and race. That is, the average real wage for a *given job* increased about 20 percent between 1961 and 1972—but between 1972 and 1985, when women made their dramatic shift into more "professional" occupations, it rose by only 1 percent. It's difficult to argue that women chose to move into career-oriented occupations because of increasing wages if the wages in those particular occupations didn't rise! While it's true that the removal of gender-specific occupational barriers might have given women access to higher paying jobs during this period, only a very small proportion of young women actually moved into formerly restricted occupations.[18] Most of the "dramatic increase" in women's wages that we hear so much about is simply the result of women's own choices: as they became more educated and more experienced in the labor force, their average wages rose.

The work summarized in chapter 7 analyzes women's labor force participation and occupational choices in a number of ways and concludes that one of the most important factors influencing women's occupational choices during the period after 1972 was actually, once again, changing relative cohort size. Prior to the emergence of the baby boom into the labor market, when there was an excess demand for labor in the economy, the market was forced to pay a premium in order to attract workers into part-time and temp positions and other jobs with little prospect for advancement. Thus, for example, in the 1960s (holding all other factors such as education and experience constant), young women just starting out could earn a higher hourly wage, on average, in part-time work than they could earn in full-time work: white women 10 percent more, African American women 30 percent more.

Chapter 9 explains that, prior to the 1970s, this premium appears to have attracted women to part-time work and into the more "female" occupations like teaching, nursing, and secretarial work, where they could have both a flexible schedule and a higher wage. The premium disappeared—became in fact up to a 25 percent *penalty*—as the baby boomers flooded the labor market. The resulting excess supply of labor led even male workers to prefer "dead-end" jobs—those with little prospect for wage growth—to no job at all. (Remember the college grads who ended up driving taxis!) During this time, those women who could moved into more typically "male" professions with better wage growth.

But the part-time to full-time wage ratio—and hence the

premium paid to jobs with relatively flat lifetime wage profiles—began to improve again in the mid-1980s. Younger women began moving back into more "female" occupations, trading wage growth for more flexible work schedules. The share of employed women aged 25–29 in teaching and nursing, after having fallen from 21 percent to 14 percent in the 1970s and early 1980s, began to increase again in the late 1980s. At the same time, the share of women in "male" skilled blue collar occupations and in engineering, science, and math— which had increased from about 2 percent in 1970 to more than 7 percent in 1985—began to fall, dipping to about 6 percent at the end of the century.

It must be emphasized that this analysis does not preclude the existence of longer-term trends in labor force participation, occupational preference, and college enrollment for women—nor is it meant to imply that we're headed back to an Ozzie and Harriet world of the 1950s. The significant changes that have occurred in these areas have altered public attitudes toward women's roles, creating enough inertia to prevent declining relative cohort size from completely reversing the process of the past thirty years. Rather, this analysis is intended to show that in addition to any longer-term trend there has also been a strong effect of fluctuating relative cohort size—and that the "change in attitudes" toward female labor force participation that's often cited as the *cause* of these increases might well have been the *result* of a groundswell of change in response to increasing relative cohort size.[19]

The trends in young women's labor force participation and occupational choice in the 1970s are excellent examples of the Why *then?* issue mentioned in the preface. If a change in public attitude were the primary driving force behind these trends, why weren't they triggered by the acceptance of Rosie the Riveter during World War II, or by the women's suffrage movement in the early 1900s?

Crime, Suicide, and Drug Use

There appears to be strong evidence in support of the hypothesized link between male relative income and the incidence of juvenile delinquency, crime, suicide, and drug use. One study found pronounced effects of relative cohort size on suicide rates between 1948 and 1976, and it seems likely that the relationship would have been even stronger had the authors of that study used relative income in place of relative cohort size.[20] Another study found a strong negative relationship between market wages and crime: "[Y]oung men are responsive to wage incentives. . . . [The] wage gap [between African Americans and white Americans] explains about one fourth of the racial difference in criminal participation rates. . . . [D]ecreases in real wages may have played an important role in the increase in youth crime during the 1970s and 1980s. Finally, wages largely explain the tendency for crime to decrease with age."[21] Unfortunately this latter study focused on absolute (rather than relative) wages: given the even more pronounced movement of relative income for young men over the past thirty years, there is a need to extend that work to consider male relative wages.

A rash of articles has appeared in the popular press recently, pointing out that the United States appears to have "turned a corner" with respect to a wide array of social indicators.[22] One of these chronicles a fall in teen births, abortion and illegitimacy rates, divorce rates, premarital and teen sex, crime, homicide, juvenile crime, teen suicides, teenage drinking, and school dropouts, as well as a slight increase in marriage rates. The data suggest that the turnaround coincides with the leveling and subsequent increase in male relative income after 1985.[23]

Living Arrangements

Whereas parents prior to the 1970s fully expected to become "empty nesters" when their children were grown, the parents of the baby boomers encountered what has been dubbed the "cluttered nest syndrome." Young adult children whose earning potential fell dramatically relative to their material aspirations felt financially unable to set up their own households.[24] My colleagues and I have found a direct relationship between relative cohort size and the living arrangements of older women.[25] The mothers of small cohorts born in the 1930s were responsible for the upsurge over the past few decades in the incidence of older women living alone, but that trend appears to have turned now, with the aging of the baby boomers' mothers. These women display lower levels of independent living in part because they have more children to depend on in old age, but also because baby boomer children are returning—or continuing—to live with their parents. In another study we found that this increased incidence of "intergenerational living" among the baby boomers appears to be a coping mechanism that has improved the economic welfare of the children of single-parent baby boomers.[26]

Retirement Behavior among the Elderly

Although less work has been completed in this area than in others reported in this book, the data are highly suggestive. As mentioned earlier, the relative wages of pre-retirement workers—defined here as their earnings near retirement relative to their own earnings five to ten years earlier—were significantly depressed by the effects of relative cohort size. Their relative wage has followed remarkably closely the pattern shown for young men in figure 2. Whereas workers in the early 1970s could look forward to wage growth of about 15 percent in their final years in the labor market, those who found themselves sharing the market with the baby boomers ended up taking wage *cuts* of about 15 percent in their sunset years.

This pattern of decline in the relative wages of older workers corresponds very closely to the decline in labor force participation among these same elderly workers—the increasing tendency to retire at earlier and earlier ages. The percentage of men aged 60–64 in the labor force fell from about 80 percent to 55 percent between 1970 and 1985, but stabilized thereafter as their relative income leveled out. A very similar pattern exists for men aged 65–69, where the labor force participation rate declined from nearly 45 percent in 1970 to only 25 percent in 1984 and has since recovered to about 30 percent. Researchers have tended to attribute earlier retirement to the availability of Social Security and private pensions, and certainly this "bigger carrot" must be a factor in attracting workers into retirement.[27] But there was a pronounced bottoming out in labor market participation rates of older men after 1985, corresponding with the trend in their relative wage, suggesting that the "stick" was also a factor. Workers had been retiring at increasing rates in part because the financial incentive to remain in the market was becoming insufficient to outweigh the pension carrot. Since 1985, however, rising relative wages for the elderly appear to have at least stemmed the tide, if not actually reversed it. This will of course be a significant factor in determining the future solvency of Social Security: it may be overly pessimistic to assume a (linear) continuation of historic declines in the desired age at retirement.

Third-Order Effects of Relative Cohort Size

Previous sections in this chapter have considered the impact of relative cohort size on the wage structure, and following on that, individuals' responses to that changing wage structure. In this and later sections, however, the concern is with the larger-scale repercussions of the wage changes and of people's responses to them. It becomes increasingly difficult to sort out levels of effects here, as actions and reactions boomerang from the economy to individuals and back again.

Industrial Structure, Gross Domestic Product, and Productivity

What happens when increasing proportions of women enter the labor force, and when increasing proportions of families have two wage earners? Although it is well documented that women do indeed face a "double burden" of market work and work in the home, in most people's experience having two wage earners—or being a single earner in a one adult household—increases the tendency to purchase market replacements for the goods and services traditionally produced by women (or one's self) in the home. Individuals can now order home delivery of groceries over the Internet while at work, hire someone to walk the dog, and contract a "wife"—a commercial service that will take clothes to the dry cleaners, mail parcels, and shop for birthday and anniversary presents.

In considering the effect of this increased consumerism, it is important to recall the U.S. method of calculating gross domestic product (GDP). Government statisticians add together the market value of all new *final* goods and services produced and *exchanged in the market*. This methodology excludes any intermediate goods, such as the windshields and tires a car manufacturer will purchase from suppliers to install in new cars, and any unpaid work, such as housework, since it is not exchanged in the market. In order to calculate productivity, this dollar value of final traded product is simply divided by the total number of paid hours worked in the market.

But over the past thirty years, in conjunction with women's greatly increased labor force participation, our society has experienced a "commoditization" of many goods and services that used to be produced in the home. These are now exchanged in the market and thus counted in official measures of GDP and productivity. When these services were provided by non-wage earners, they were not counted in GDP—and yet their end product, in the form of healthy, happy, and thus productive workers, was certainly reflected in the market value of goods that *were* included in GDP. We were getting a very large bang for our buck in measuring the dollar value of the *result* of all work performed in the economy, but counting only paid workers as having produced that result.

As increasing proportions of women enter the labor force and replace their services in the home with purchased market services, there are three major effects on measures of economic activity. First, many of the goods and services previously treated as intermediate services helping to produce healthy and productive workers begin to be counted as final products. To the extent that this has occurred, measures of GDP growth have been falsely inflated: government statisticians are simply beginning to count more of the work that has always been performed in the economy. This is of course an intrinsic aspect of the development of "modern" market economies—but in this case the change has been telescoped into an extremely short period. The same effect occurred during the United States' period of rapid industrialization after 1850: GDP growth at that time was as much an indication of increased market orientation as it was of increased production.

Second, measures of "industrial structure" begin to skew strongly toward services and retail, away from agriculture and manufacturing. The proportion of jobs in manufacturing declined from 29.9 percent in 1950 to 24.3 percent in 1970 to 16.7 percent in 1989, while the proportion of jobs in retail and service rose from 26.5 percent to 31.4 percent to 41.8 percent in the same periods.[28] This change is not so much due to the fact that we're *consuming* more retail goods and services than our parents did: we're simply *purchasing* more of them in the market than they did, rather than producing them in the home. The low-wage service jobs we lament aren't new: they used to exist in the home, and now they exist in the marketplace.

These goods and services are traditionally "low productivity" in the sense that they are not highly mechanized and thus require high levels of labor input per dollar value of output. This alone will place a severe drag on measured rates of growth in productivity—again, it must be emphasized, not because the balance of work has actually changed, but rather because methods of *counting* that work have changed! It's likely that the process of commoditization has actually made the performance of many of these services more efficient.

So the picture is one of increasing relative cohort size, leading to declining male relative earnings, leading to increasing female labor force participation, leading to increased commoditization of low productivity work. This in turn leads to measured decreases in productivity growth, but only because of very imperfect methods for determining GDP and productivity. These methods work acceptably during times of little change in market behavior, but fall apart completely in the face of the drastic changes in female labor force participation induced by large relative cohort size.

In addition, as the baby boomers entered the labor market, the large influx of inexperienced young workers exacerbated any decline in productivity growth by changing the composition of the workforce to one dominated by inexperienced and therefore lower-productivity workers. And, to add insult to injury, the decline in relative wages of younger workers resulting from their oversupply led employers to substitute cheaper labor for more expensive productivity-enhancing machinery and technology, thus inhibiting the young workers' productivity still further.

But the drastic increase in female labor force participation rates appears to have ended along with the increase in relative cohort size (see chapter 7), and the momentum of the shift toward low-wage, low-productivity jobs therefore will also attenuate.[29] In addition, the baby boom cohort has matured, shifting the composition of the workforce toward higher-productivity workers. These observations are supported by factors such as the trend in the 1990s toward job creation in occupations earning above-average wages and the dramatic increase in productivity growth rates in recent years.

Average Wages

In addition to the effects adding "women's work" into the GDP has had on productivity measures, there has been a third drag on productivity accompanying women's entry into the labor market. This effect has been reflected directly in the pattern of real average wages, for males and females, and tracing it requires a focus on what has come to be known as the "family wage."

In the rapidly industrializing economy that emerged in the late 1800s, males began to be drawn into the industrialized workforce. Prior to this time, mill workers were largely young women and children. Men and their unions, as they entered industrial work, negotiated two things: young women would be laid off once they married (the commonly acknowledged "marriage bar"[30]), and men would be paid a "family wage." These two things are not unrelated. Although Marxist and feminist literature presents this period as one of accession by capitalism to paternalism (men reinforcing other men's rights to the unpaid services of women in the home), it's more logical to assume that capitalism willingly acceded because it was getting its money's worth out of the bargain. That is, these two measures ensured that the vast majority of male wage earners would be supported in the home by unpaid labor, effectively making them more productive in the workplace. Industrialists were simply acknowledging that with each male worker they were in fact obtaining the services of two workers—the man and his wife. This understanding would lead quickly to a form of statistical discrimination in which it was assumed that any male worker would have this home support, and therefore qualify for a "family wage"—whereas female workers would not benefit from such support and therefore would not be capable of producing output worthy of a family wage.

It's a particular shortcoming of the economic literature that in focusing on the male/female wage gap, productivity effects of women's "double burden" have been discussed almost solely in terms of the presumed lower productivity of women in market work due to their responsibilities in the home.[31] Somehow few economists have seemed willing to consider seriously the flip side of this effect: the idea that men with stay-at-home wives will tend to be more productive than men with working wives or no wives. Yet this was the basis of the literature in the 1950s that led to the concept of economic efficiency through specialization and exchange in the home.[32]

But in recent years economists have begun to show more interest in this issue, and the literature on the "marriage wage premium" has begun to grow. Its focus has been on determining whether the premium, estimated to be as high as 40 percent in some times and places,[33] results from true productivity gains from marriage, or from employer discrimination, or whether it's simply a statistical artifact. The statistical artifact would arise if higher earners are simply more likely to marry than are low earners. To the extent that this is the case, marriage would then be just a signal, rather than a cause, of higher productivity and earnings.

Interestingly, this marriage wage premium appears to have declined dramatically since the 1960s: have relative cohort size changes played a role?[34] Chapter 10 reviews this literature and finds increasingly strong evidence that a significant portion of the marriage wage premium reflected real productivity gains from specialization within marriage, but that wives' increased labor force participation has virtually eliminated that financial benefit of marriage for men.

This doesn't seem surprising when one thinks of the distractions inherent in having to take care of errands and household-related personal phone calls during a working day, to name but a few limitations imposed on those who lack a stay-at-home spouse (the source of the working woman's lament, "I need a wife!"). A *New York Times* article reported in 1989 that corporations were "pressuring" their male executives to marry.[35] Although the article speculated that this pressure grew out of homophobia and fears of emotional instability, it seems much more reasonable to assume that the corporations were simply demanding that executives live up to their part of the bargain inherent in a "family wage."

It also seems reasonable to assume that any statistical discrimination by employers in favor of married men would have diminished over the past thirty years, as married men with stay-at-home wives have become increasingly rare. This would account for the fact that the much heralded closing of the male-female wage gap has resulted largely from a lowering of male wages, rather than from a real rise in female wages.[36] Thus we get a gradual disappearance of the family wage, leading to a stagnation of the average real male wage since 1974: any productivity gains from technological change and increasing levels of education have been counterbalanced by the loss of family wage premium for a stay-at-home spouse, as increasing relative cohort size leads to increasing female labor force participation and lower marriage rates.

The real wages of males *have* been rising, but this has been masked by the effect the loss of the family wage premium on married men's earnings. The good news is that, because the increase in female labor force participation and the decline in marriage rates have attenuated since the baby boom's entry into the labor market, the depressing effect of losing the family wage premium should also attenuate. In addition, as increasing numbers of innovative companies spring up to provide "wifely" services, it's possible that the drag imposed on worker productivity by loss of specialization in the home may gradually be attenuated. We're once again moving toward the efficiency inherent in increased specialization.

Inflation, Interest, and Savings Rates—and the Stock Market?

With regard to inflation, interest, and savings rates, evidence in the economic literature is not as strong as that for relative earnings, largely because macroeconomists have until recently tried to ignore effects of changing age structure in the population, dealing only with a single aggregate "representative agent." However, some analysts have begun to discuss the effects of age structure in the context of "life cycle" consumption and savings models. That is, the most commonly accepted models of consumption and savings tend to recognize that individuals vary in their patterns of savings over their life cycle in an attempt to "smooth" overall lifetime consumption. In early adulthood, when individuals face major expenditures on housing, cars, children, and furnishings, and their earnings are low relative to later life, they act as net dis-savers (borrowers). The opposite occurs as their average earnings rise and their average expenditures fall, and they begin to save for retirement.

A widely publicized study estimated a strong effect of age structure on housing prices in the United States (with the entry of the baby boom into the housing market causing the severe house price inflation of the 1970s and 1980s, and the recent entry of the baby bust causing house price deflation).[37] Although some have disputed the magnitude of the effect estimated in that study, most researchers have confirmed its existence. A later study, for example, found significant effects of detailed (single-year) age structure in the adult population on all forms of consumption, including housing demand, and on money demand.[38]

Similarly, another study documents a strong effect of age structure (measured simply as the proportion of young to old in the population) on real interest rates and inflation, because of differential patterns of savings and consumption with age.[39] A higher proportion of young adults in a population will produce lower aggregate savings levels, and hence higher interest rates. In this model, today's lower interest and inflation rates, and booming stock market, are the result of the aging of the baby boomers, as they begin to acquire assets for their retirement years. The flip side of this phenomenon—the potential "meltdown" effect of a retiring baby boom on financial markets, asset values, and interest rates—has been described, as well.[40] These effects are well demonstrated in the work of several researchers who have focused on developing nations, especially the "Asian Tigers."[41]

Savings Rates

Although some analysts maintain that the potential age structure effect of the baby boomers on personal savings isn't large
enough to explain the full drop in our national savings rates over the
past two decades, studies of this phenomenon to date have focused
only on the behavior of the baby boomers themselves. One might
argue, however, that the baby boomers have affected the propensity
to save in age groups other than their own. For example, because
boomers' earnings were depressed and they experienced an inflated
housing market when they went to buy homes (both effects of their
own large cohort size), many parents of baby boomers drew down on
their own savings in order to help with down payments.

The analysis described briefly in chapter 13 explains why this
cross-generational spending has tended to be misinterpreted in microlevel analyses of consumption and also points out the tendency in
these studies to ignore the effects of changing age structure among
children. That is, for all intents and purposes analysts have assumed
that parents spend the same amount on a 5-year-old as on a 16-year-
old, and in many cases have simply lumped the effects of spending
for children together with spending for adults. This could be a very
important shortcoming in analyses covering the period when the
baby boom was passing through its childhood and teen years. In addition, a recent study points out that it has been common practice in
analyses of the effect of age structure on savings rates to treat the
pension payments received by retirees as income rather than as dis-
saving, yet in the aggregate these payments do represent significant
dis-saving.[42]

The analysis reported in chapter 13 attempts to correct for these
problems and identifies a very strong age-related pattern of expenditures and saving, with a tendency for children to induce savings on
the part of their parents between the ages of about 5 to 16, possibly
in anticipation of later educational expenses. When the relationships
identified in that study are combined with the changing age distribution in the U.S. population during this century, they suggest that
holding all other factors constant, such as per capita income, population growth, and immigration, simple changes in population age
structure during the twentieth century account for a 25 percent variation in total consumption demand at the aggregate level. This has
obvious implications not only for savings rates, but also for the

growth rate of GDP. Because children seem to motivate savings in high-income economies, the analysis reported in chapter 13 suggests, somewhat ironically, that one reason for current low savings rates in the United States could be our low birth rates: if Americans are saving less it's because they have less to save *for.*

In addition, the exercise described in chapter 15 produces a theoretically consistent model of the personal savings rate based solely on population age structure. The model fits well enough to forecast the behavior of the economy from 1985–1995 using data just from 1949–1985.

The Demand for Goods and Services and GDP Growth

Population age structure exerts a real effect on GDP growth in addition to its effect on the accuracy of our calculations of that growth discussed earlier. The flip side of the savings effect is spending: whatever we don't save, we spend. Patterns of expenditure as a proportion of income change over the life cycle, and this has a profound effect on the overall per capita demand for goods and services. This effect is demonstrated in the analysis described in chapter 13. The findings there are supported by the exercise in chapter 15, which simply fits a model of GDP growth from 1949 through 1985 using age structure as the explanatory variable. The model is able to predict the course of GDP growth over the following ten-year period, based just on changes that occurred in population age structure during that period.

Inflation

Inflation is considered in many circles to be "always and everywhere a monetary phenomenon"—that is, related solely to the money supply. But there is some evidence that age structure plays a role here, as well. A recent analysis of OECD data identified a "robust correlation [between inflation and age structure] consistent with the hypothesis that increases in the population of net savers dampen inflation while especially the younger retirees fan inflation as they start consuming out of accumulated pension plans."[43] The implication is that if there is "lumpiness" in the age structure of the population sufficient to cause fluctuations in the savings rate, there is also the potential for age-induced fluctuations in the inflation rate.

In addition, some economists have pointed out that, along with the Federal Reserve, private banks exert significant control over the money supply—and hence over inflation—in deciding how much of their deposits to loan out to the public. When demand for loans is strong and banks are optimistic about economic prospects, they will loan out a higher percentage, and through a multiplier effect this increases the money supply. As a result, changing age structure—especially the emergence of the baby boom into the labor market—could have a marked effect on inflation.

Think of a young person who on one day is a student living in his parents' home, supported by their income, and on the next works for an employer earning his own hourly wage. What is the source of the money his new employer uses to pay him? The new worker hasn't yet produced a product that can be sold, thus the employer has no additional revenue. In effect, the employer must borrow on the strength of the potential sale of the potential product in order to pay the new employee. A bank might be hesitant under some circumstances about extending a loan or overdraft to the employer, but in this case the new young employee is also a new consumer because he'll be making a score of purchases in setting up his own household. While he adds to the demand for wages, he also adds to the demand for the employer's product, so the bank will feel comfortable about extending the loan on the basis of projected sales.

Now multiply that one new young worker by three to four million and you have the annual effect, over some fifteen years, as the baby boomers entered the labor market and set up their own households: a tremendous incentive for new loans, supported by the solid prospect of growing revenues. This explains, in large part, the dramatic inflation of the late 1970s: it was simply a temporary imbalance between the demand for wages and merchandise and the actual production of those goods, because of a dramatic shift in population age structure. This could also be the source of the hyperinflation experienced in the past few decades by some of the less developed economies, since those countries were experiencing dramatic increases in relative cohort size at the same time.

Misguided government policy has the potential to exacerbate any effects of relative cohort size on inflation and unemployment rates. For example, in the United States the increased levels of unemployment in the 1970s (brought about by increasing relative cohort size, as discussed earlier) led the government to attempt to stimulate job creation by providing firms tax breaks on investment in physical capital. However, physical capital has been shown in econometric studies of factor substitutability to be a *complement* to experienced labor (that is, the use of more physical capital creates an increased demand for more experienced workers) and a *substitute* for less experienced labor (machinery is used to replace unskilled workers). Thus the government policy of stimulating investment in physical capital led to an inflationary increase in the wages of older workers and at the same time exacerbated unemployment among younger workers. The result was the well-known "stagflation" of the late 1970s.[44]

A cursory analysis described in chapter 15 demonstrates a theoretically consistent correlation between age structure and inflation sufficient to forecast the inflation rate from 1985 to 1995 using an age-structure model fitted just on data from 1949 to 1985.

Age Structure and Economic Slumps

The evidence gathered thus far with respect to GDP growth, savings rates, and inflation suggests a possible connection between changing age structure and some of the severe economic downturns experienced here and abroad this past century. Chapter 14 discusses this idea and presents evidence of strong correlations between the initiation of such slowdowns and changes in the proportion of a nation's population aged 15–24. Why that age group? The hypothesis is that young adults are a major factor in the demand for durable goods, as they set up new households and start families.[45]

As pointed out by economists going back at least to the turn of the century, including J. M. Keynes and J. R. Hicks, one of the most important factors in determining growth is the willingness of investors to commit funds in support of such growth. Most economic analysis has focused on the effects on investment of a declining population, but the argument in chapter 14 centers on the idea of investor confidence and expectations. When the population of young adults is expanding, the resultant growth in demand for durable goods creates confidence in investors, to the extent they expect a continuation of that growth.

Assuming imperfect foresight, an unexpected slowdown in the growth rate of young adults—even a temporary one—could cause cutbacks in production and investment in response to inventory buildups, with a snowball effect throughout the economy. There has been a close correspondence in the United States this century between "turnaround points" of growth in this key age group and significant economic dislocations in 1908, 1929, 1938, and 1974. Similarly, chapter 14 demonstrates the correlation between age structure and economic performance in industrialized nations in the 1930s, and in both industrialized and developing nations during the last twenty years, the Asian Tigers being some of the most recent examples.

A fascinating aspect of population age structure in the United States during the unprecedented run of economic growth in the 1990s is that we were experiencing a demographic combination rarely if ever before seen in economic history. Since 1994 our economy has been enjoying the positive benefits of a rapidly growing absolute number of 15- to 24-year-olds (they exert a high demand for goods and services, relative to their income), but not suffering the productivity drag, high unemployment, low relative wages, and high inflation usually associated with this age group (they remain a relatively small proportion of the total population—that is, relative cohort size is low and constant because of fairly constant fertility rates since 1975). This unprecedented combination occurred because the large baby boom cohorts maintained a fairly constant low fertility rate from the mid-1970s onward: a constant rate applied to a boom in parental numbers has produced a new type of baby boom. Beginning in 2001, however, this growth—especially in the 20–22 age group—levels off for a few years: not a good sign for the economy.

The Relevance of Age Structure in Developing Economies

Historically researchers have invoked the relative cohort size model only to explain fertility experience in the developed nations in the post-WWII period. But there is evidence that the model holds for developing economies, as well. One of the great mysteries in such locales has been the initiation of the fertility transition: the period when a country's fertility declines from premodern levels of six or seven births per woman to only two or three. The inevitability of such a transition is believed to be universal, but neither demographers nor economists have been able to predict when it might occur in any individual country. Data presented graphically and analyzed with simple econometric models in chapter 12 suggest that the fertility

transition has almost without exception begun at the point when relative cohort size first begins to increase in a given country—just as
the baby bust in the Western nations began when the baby boomers
reached reproductive age.

High levels of fertility in less developed nations don't translate
into growing numbers of young adults until traditionally high levels
of mortality among infants and children are reduced. Thus the incidence of increasing relative cohort size, when it does finally occur,
is a unique experience in these countries' histories. The resultant
shortage of jobs and land leaves young adults unable to support
themselves, and their response is fertility reduction (both through
conscious fertility control and through the dampening effects of
postponed or forgone marriage). Whereas earlier generations accepted births as inevitable and uncontrollable, the large cohort's
need to preserve a standard of living in the face of shortages finally
brings fertility within the scope of rational action; it motivates a
change in attitudes that begins to make fertility control socially acceptable. The figures in chapter 12 illustrate the relationship between relative cohort size and fertility rates that can be seen in the
data for country after country in the developing world between 1950
and 1995.

Demographic Influences on the Stock Market

Despite the many effects of the baby boom that have been hypothesized over the past few years, somewhat surprisingly the literature has been fairly silent about the baby boom's *current* effects on
the stock market. An analysis presented in chapter 15 indicates that
the age structure of the population may have had a dramatic effect
on that market over the past decades. A model based only on the proportion of the population at six different ages is able to reproduce
year-to-year changes in the stock market, going back as far as 1934;
and this model, when estimated using data for the years 1934 to
1976, is able to "forecast" the actual market movements that occurred between 1976 and 1995.

A more rigorous analysis also described in chapter 15 makes use
of the full population age structure, by single year of age, to model
the annual percentage change in the Dow Jones Industrial Average
throughout the twentieth century. Here, too, the suggestion is that
population age structure accounts for almost all of the longer-term

cyclicality in that measure—and the model indicates that a continuation of that effect into this century would produce a market dip, similar to the one experienced in the 1970s, in its first quarter. This would be followed by another market rebound in the second quarter of the century. The projection takes into account only the effect of U.S. age structure, however, which appears to have dominated in the past but may well be dwarfed in the future by changing age structure and economic development in the rest of the world, through increasing globalization of trade and the stock market.

The Net Effect: The Big Picture

The theory described here provides a coherent picture of an economy driven not only by the size of its population, but by the age composition of that population. It's an attractive theory in that it appears to explain in a comprehensive way most of the truly puzzling aspects of the U.S. economy in recent years. Forecasts that assumed a linear continuation in declining fertility, marriage, savings, productivity, and wage growth rates severely underpredicted economic conditions for the late 1990s, leaving pundits at a loss to explain the run of good fortune during that period. The theory presented here recognizes that these variables were close to the "bottom" of a cycle driven by population size and age composition, making the economic upturn of the late 1990s unsurprising.

All of the available data indicate that time trends moved in the "appropriate" direction to support a population-based theory as the baby boom moved into the labor market, and once allowance is made for the asymmetry discussed in chapters 3 and 5, they all showed signs of turning around as the baby boom entered its prime years. Thus, for example, young men's relative earnings ended their long descent in the late 1980s, and almost immediately thereafter, the fertility rate in the under-24 age groups began to increase, while the female labor force participation rate in the same group stabilized. Similarly, marriage rates for this group reversed a twenty-year decline, and divorce rates came down. These indicators didn't continue their turnarounds unabated, however; they were following the pattern of male relative income, which took another (temporary) dip due to relative cohort size effects in the early 1990s.

But all the signs turned positive in the late 1990s: fertility rates among young women aged 20–29 began increasing again, unemployment reached a thirty-year low, real household and family incomes rose, and new jobs increasingly appeared in occupations paying above-average wages. This last phenomenon is consistent with the topping out and even decline in female labor force participation rates—and hence a topping out in the creation of new low-wage, low-productivity service and retail jobs. In addition, the sharp reduction in inflation and unemployment in recent years is consistent with the other listed phenomena.

One might be reluctant to credit tests of significance using aggregate data for a period of only thirty-five years if the tests involved only one series of data. But such overwhelming evidence of common movements in all series lends support to the hypothesis that relative cohort size is a significant factor driving all of the aforementioned variables. In addition, to the extent that tests have been carried out using more disaggregated data (as, for example, in the wage analysis reported in chapter 6 and the analyses of marriage and fertility rates in chapters 9 and 11), results are completely supportive of the aggregate-level findings. The analysis of marriage rates is particularly promising. It provides a methodology applicable to a number of socioeconomic variables that circumvents the thorny problem (given lack of data on young couples together with their parents) of estimating relative income at the individual level: making use of regional/state variation in male relative income.

Given the highly supportive initial evidence, we need to put more effort into viewing our past within the comprehensive demographic-economic framework this theory presents. Doing so provides a completely different perspective on socioeconomic phenomena of the last thirty-five years and gives us a key variable for forecasting fluctuations in other variables at least over the next twenty-five years.

A Road Map to the Chapters in This Book

Most of the summary presentations in this overview are supported by work presented in the following chapters, which in turn are summaries of my own published and unpublished articles (all of which are referenced and available in print or online as indicated). I have attempted to present material in the same order as in this overview, beginning with a discussion of population growth and relative cohort size in chapter 1 and male relative income in chapter 2.

Following that, chapter 3 sets out fairly nontechnical descriptions of the most important variables included in the later analyses: quantitative measures of relative cohort size and male relative income. Chapter 3 also contains graphs illustrating historic trends in various measures of relative cohort size and the concept of "asymmetry" around the peak of the baby boom. Some readers may prefer to skim over or skip the material in this chapter and move on to the description of trends in male relative income presented in chapter 4.

Chapters 5 through 15 each address a different component of the substantive ideas presented in this overview. Chapters 5 and 6 examine the first-order effects of relative cohort size, especially the relationship between relative cohort size and male relative income, with aggregate-level analyses focused just on male relative income, unemployment, and returns to college education reported in chapter 5. A microlevel analysis of wages at all age levels throughout the workforce is reported in chapter 6. Along with the wage analysis in chapter 6 is an examination of hours and weeks worked, labor force participation, and levels of inequality generally.

Chapters 7 through 12 address most of the second-order effects, beginning with women's wages, labor force participation, and occupational choice in chapter 7 and young men's and women's college enrollment rates in chapter 8. The closely related issues of marriage and divorce are addressed in chapter 9; the marriage wage premium in chapter 10; and patterns of fertility among young women in the United States in chapter 11. And finally, chapter 12 demonstrates global evidence of a strong relationship between relative cohort size and fertility, even in developing nations during the fertility transition.

Chapters 13, 14, and 15 present some of my preliminary findings on third-order effects of changing age structure: on U.S. patterns of consumption and saving in chapter 13; on overall economic performance across all nations (the incidence of recessions and depressions) in chapter 14; and on the separate measures of U.S. GDP growth, inflation, savings rates, and the stock market in chapter 15. The work presented in chapters 14 and 15 is more speculative than empirical. Chapter 16 concludes and qualifies.

PART 1

Defining Concepts and Terms

Population Growth and Relative Cohort Size

The Easterlin, or "cohort size," hypothesis posits that, other things constant, the economic and social fortunes of a cohort (those born in a given year) tend to vary inversely with its relative size, approximated by the crude birth rate in the period surrounding the cohort's birth. . . . The linkage between higher birth rates and adverse economic and social effects arises from what might be termed "crowding mechanisms" operating within three major social institutions—the family, school and labour market.

The New Palgrave: A Dictionary of Economics, s.v. "Easterlin hypothesis"

The idea behind this book is a deceptively simple one: there are economic and demographic "feedback effects" in which the pattern of population growth is affected by economic conditions, and the economy, in turn, is affected by various aspects of population growth and resultant population age structure. The idea is deceptively simple in the sense that, although there seems to be an intuitive acceptance that such interactions occur—after all, what is an economy but a collection of people?—there is still considerable disagreement about their form and extent.

The economic-demographic feedback model has a long history, going back in most people's minds two hundred years to the 1798 publication of *An Essay on the Principle of Population* by T. R. Malthus. This treatise is often credited with creating the popular perception of economics as "the dismal science" because of its dire predictions regarding the "iron law of wages." Malthus believed there was a direct connection between wages and fertility rates. People

tended to have more children when wages—in the form of crop production—rose: in years with particularly good weather conditions,
for example. But he warned of an inverse relationship between labor
force size and wage rates. That is, increased fertility rates produced
more workers, whose "excess supply" in turn reduced per capita crop
production given the relatively fixed availability of land for cultiva-
tion. This led to the depressing idea that society could never experience long-term economic growth, because as soon as economic conditions improved people would have more children, which would
then make them poorer on a per capita basis.

Malthus's ideas were extremely influential at the time, generating heated debates about society's responsibility to the poor: if the
poor were aided economically, would they simply have more children, thus negating any beneficial effects of society's largesse? But
over the next century, as Europe experienced unprecedented economic growth despite large population increases, analysts came to
feel that Malthus's model was inappropriate in an industrial age,
given the production-enhancing effects of capital (e.g., machinery
and fertilizer) and the potential for technological change. Most came
to accept Adam Smith's notion that population growth enhances economic growth because it enables increased specialization and hence
increased productivity.[1]

Malthus's economic-demographic model fell out of favor and
was later replaced by "growth" models focused on capital:labor ratios, in which population growth was treated as exogenous—that is,
unaffected by economic conditions—and growth depended primarily on the availability of capital and technology. Malthus's model
was revived in the middle of the twentieth century, as fears of "population explosion" were generated by rapid population increases in
the developing world, but this revival was spurred largely by non-
economists, such as Garrett Hardin and Paul Ehrlich.[2] Countering
these non-economists' views, economist Julian Simon has argued
convincingly that technological innovation is actually a function of
population size, both in the sense that a larger population contains
more geniuses than a small one (given adequate investment in education) and that population growth creates increased motivation for
technological innovation as communities find themselves with increasing numbers of mouths to feed.[3] Similarly, some influential
economists have suggested population decline as a significant factor
in economic dislocations like the 1930s Depression[4]—and popula-

tion growth as a factor in the phenomenal economic growth during the Industrial Revolution.[5]

But nearly all of this literature on economic and demographic "feedback effects" concentrates on the rate of population growth, rather than changes in that rate. Changes in the rate of growth—like the "birth quake" of the post-WWII baby boom—cause changes in population age structure, and it's these changes in age structure that are the primary focus of this book. Why? Because people's behavior differs substantially over the life cycle, and if there is any "lumpiness" in the age structure of the population because of "on and off" birth rates, it will emphasize the effects of behaviors associated with some stages in the life cycle and minimize others. The baby boom has often been referred to as the "pig in the python": this is a highly appropriate metaphor. Imagine that pig-digesting python stretched out in the sun along a bumpy road: he'll look fairly normal if the pig's position happens to coincide with a low point in the road, but as the pig passes over a high point, the python's bizarre shape is accentuated. That's been the situation of the Western world during the past fifty years. Given a relatively "flat" age structure, the different behaviors as people age will tend to cancel each other out, with approximately equal proportions of the population in the "spending" and "saving" periods of life, for example. But any lumpiness produces fluctuations between high and low overall savings rates, as well as a host of other economic and social indicators. One group of researchers has demonstrated the marked effect of such changes on the phenomenal rise of the Asian Tigers, as well as the pre-1914 Atlantic economy.[6]

This "compositional" effect is, however, an aspect of changing age structure that's pretty widely known and accepted. Marketing analysts have constantly stressed this issue as baby boomers have moved from mini-skirted, flower-bedecked teens to pin-striped, attaché-toting executives. Even more interesting is the idea that *age-specific behavior* might change if a disproportionately large part of the population passes through a given age range; this is where the work of economist Richard Easterlin stands out.[7] He introduced the concept of "relative cohort size"—the size of a birth cohort relative to the size of its parents' birth cohort—and hypothesized that changes in relative cohort size might produce dramatically different age-specific economic outcomes and subsequent behavior. His very aptly titled book *Birth and Fortune* suggested that members of relatively large birth cohorts might be economically disadvantaged through-out life, leading them to make very different lifestyle choices than those in smaller birth cohorts.

Easterlin—like Malthus, a demographic economist—provided an explanation for the twentieth-century baby boom and bust in more developed economies that put a twist on the old Malthusian perspective. Fertility rates, he said, *do* respond positively to eco-nomic conditions, but not in the absolute sense assumed by the Malthusians. Instead, fertility rates respond to what Easterlin termed "relative income" or "relative economic status." His model in-corporated economic-demographic feedback effects within a frame-work of economic growth by assuming that people's *desired stan-dard of living* increases with each generation as an economy grows and develops. Thus, although per capita income rises with economic development, individuals' consumption aspirations increase, as well. If consumption aspirations rise as rapidly as incomes, people will not feel any wealthier despite their higher incomes (their *rela-tive income* doesn't rise), and fertility will not increase. And if, as some analysts suggest,[8] consumption aspirations rise even faster than income because of the marketing efforts of profit- and growth-oriented firms (*relative income* falls), then fertility will fall even as ab-solute income rises.

And, Easterlin maintained, economic conditions *do* respond negatively to population growth rates as Malthus suggested, but here again, with a twist. The negative effect of an increase in the fertility rate will be experienced approximately twenty years later, as that in-creased fertility rate translates into an increased labor force growth rate, *but will be experienced only by the new labor force entrants,* rather than by society generally. Why? Because new young workers are "imperfect substitutes" for older, more experienced workers: for the most part, they can't take the place of older workers. The older workers perform different types of jobs and are needed to train and supervise the younger workers: the labor market requires both types of worker, but in relatively fixed ratios. Easterlin's concept of relative cohort size describes not just the size of a birth cohort relative to that of its parents, but also the number of younger workers relative to the number of older workers. He suggested that if relative cohort size in-creases, the wages of younger workers—which always tend to be lower than those of older, more experienced workers—will fall even further relative to those of the older group. Thus Easterlin spoke in terms of "relative wages"—the wages of younger relative to older workers—and emphasized that it was these *relative wages* that would respond negatively to increased fertility rates, with about a twenty-year lag.

But perhaps the most intriguing aspect of Easterlin's model was his method of relating these two phenomena—the effect of relative income on fertility and the effect of relative cohort size on relative wages. He suggested that individuals' consumption aspirations—the basis for converting absolute to relative income—are probably influenced strongly by the standard of living experienced in their parents' homes when they were growing up. And the "older workers" against whose wages the younger workers' wages fall are—in the aggregate—the parents of the younger workers. Thus, if relative wages fall because relative cohort size increases, then relative income—income relative to material aspirations—will also fall, leading to lower fertility rates.

In Easterlin's model the large relative cohort size of the baby boomers (born between 1946 and 1964) reduced their relative wages, which in turn reduced their fertility and produced the baby bust. The numbers work out perfectly: Easterlin presented graphs and calculations indicating that the decline in fertility rates that began in the United States in the late 1950s corresponded directly with the entrance of the baby boom into the labor market and family formation stage. And the baby boom itself—the product of fertility rates that had begun to rise in the late 1930s—was produced by the relatively small cohorts that resulted from the decline in fertility rates through the 1920s and 1930s. Baby bust produced baby boom, which in turn produced baby bust.

It is important to note that the twists Easterlin introduced into Malthus's model produced a twist in its prognostications, as well. Although economic growth increases per capita income, it also raises the standard of living and in doing so raises *expectations* regarding future living standards. This tempers any fertility-enhancing effect of rising absolute income.[9] Fertility rates in a developed economy might rise temporarily as a result of some shock to the economic system, but at most this would produce a series of population cycles, rather than any period of sustained fertility increase. Unlike Malthus's model, in which population growth sows the seeds of economic deterioration and then stagnation, Easterlin's model suggested that economic growth sows the seeds of population stabilization.

But Easterlin's model, too, was destined to fall into disfavor. Like Malthus, he seems to have formalized his model on the eve of a turn in socioeconomic trends that was diametrically opposed to the model's predictions. Population growth accompanied by strong economic growth heralded Malthus's treatise, while Easterlin faced declining relative cohort size accompanied by an unanticipated further deterioration in the economic circumstances of young workers. The 1980s constituted a baptism by fire for Easterlin's hypotheses.

As a result, although relative cohort size measures were fairly widely used in analyses by social scientists prior to about 1985, in studies of the U.S. economy and even in fertility analyses, relative cohort size measures are becoming increasingly scarce. Social scientists continue to use absolute measures of income without attempting to quantify or control for the effects of changes over time in material aspirations.[10] In this book I attempt to demonstrate that, once again, analysts may have overreacted in their purge of demographic variables and certainly err in their omission of psychological measures such as consumption aspirations. The world is not as simple as Malthus's model suggested, but neither is Easterlin's model as simple as most characterizations (including the one above) would have us believe. A close examination of historical data suggests that his model provides an excellent framework for interpreting a wide range of puzzling phenomena that have occurred over the past three decades in the United States—especially in the two decades since the first edition of *Birth and Fortune*.

The U.S. baby boom and bust, with its pronounced longer-term fluctuation as well as its occasional sharp year-to-year changes (see figure 1.1), provides an ideal laboratory for testing the economic and demographic feedback effects that are the focus of this book. Unfortunately we have just the one baby boom and bust cycle in the postwar period, but later chapters will show that the characteristic peaks and troughs that mark the otherwise smooth rise and then decline in fertility rates (like those during and after WWII in the 1940s and during the Vietnam War in the late 1960s) provide additional means of identifying economic-demographic relationships. Figure 1.1 presents two of many potential measures of relative cohort size that will be discussed in chapter 3. The population age ratio presented there is

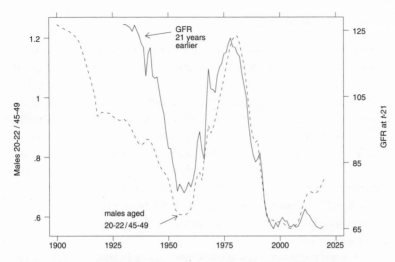

Figure 1.1. Two measures of relative cohort size. The U.S. population ratio (males aged 20–22 relative to males aged 45–49) closely follows the path of the general fertility rate (births per 1,000 women of childbearing age) twenty-one years earlier, 1900–2020. (See chapter 3 for a discussion of these measures.)

formulated specifically to capture the age groups most significantly affected by imperfect substitutability between older and younger workers in the labor market.

The purpose of this book is to show that, when a few more complicated interactions are accounted for, it is perhaps even more true now than when Easterlin wrote that "what is striking is the way in which a variety of developments—developments often regarded as puzzling or surprising—form a coherent picture when approached from this theoretical viewpoint." The sheer weight of evidence across a wide range of variables is simply too strong to dismiss. The strength of the relationships demonstrated here, and the consistent picture they describe, lend a coherence and credibility far beyond the simple sum of the individual parts.

What are these more complicated interactions incorporated in the work presented here, in testing the relative cohort size model? There are four that seem essential: women's changing role in society; immigration or international trade effects (or both); the Vietnam War; and the possibility of asymmetry in relative cohort size effects. Each of these is discussed briefly below, and then in more detail in later chapters.

Women's Changing Role

The relative cohort size model is often thought of, erroneously, as dealing primarily with the economic fortunes of young men because of its emphasis on male relative income, but it is integrally related to women's evolving role, as well. Women's responses to changes brought about by fluctuations in relative cohort size have provided a buffer against some of the extremes that might otherwise have occurred.

The wages earned by young women as a result of their increased labor force participation appear to have had a positive rather than a negative effect on fertility in the 1970s, contrary to the expectations of standard economic models. Young women supplemented the low relative wages of young men during this period, so young couples felt more able to form families.

Of even more importance, women's altered expectations as a result of two decades of significant labor force participation have altered society's perception of the "appropriate" role for women. Even if male relative incomes were to rise to the highs experienced during the 1950s, it is most unlikely that we would return to the gender roles predominant during that period. Women have introduced a measure of inertia in the system that defies the simplistic interpretation of continuing, self-generating cycles that many derived from the relative cohort size model.

In addition, the services women supported as working wives and mothers have transformed our economy, making career and motherhood increasingly compatible. In my own work, I have attempted to quantify the contribution of changing relative cohort size to the trend in female labor force participation and also to incorporate the effects of the changing female wage on women's labor force participation and fertility.

Immigration and International Trade Effects

A crucial factor in producing the post-WWII baby boom was the United States' relatively closed economic system in the 1950s. If an excess demand for young workers can be met easily by an increase in immigration, as in the period before the 1926 immigration law, then young people will not experience the benefits of small relative cohort size. This is an important consideration that has been ignored in attempts to test the relative cohort size model using European data.

And in the past two decades, as international trade flows have increased, many have argued that imports to a great extent mimic the effects of immigration on the domestic market for unskilled and inexperienced labor. This idea has been incorporated in the work presented here, demonstrating a strong effect of both imports and exports on relative wages.

The Vietnam War

It is a sad fact of life that in wartime our combat troops are made up largely of very young men. This has a dramatic effect on relative cohort size in the civilian labor force. During the late 1960s the first wave of the baby boom was already moving into the labor market, but the potential excess supply of labor that might have ensued was minimized because of the large numbers of young men who were drafted during that period.

Educational draft deferments were permitted for several years, enticing many young men, not otherwise motivated, to go to college or to pursue graduate studies. This swelled the already large cohorts of boomer college graduates emerging into the labor market in the early 1970s, depressing college wages relative to those of high school graduates. In addition, young fathers were given draft deferments in the late 1960s, and this appears to have contributed to the 1969/70 rebound in the sharply declining fertility rates that characterized this period. Teen fertility rates, especially, surged at that time. Later chapters will demonstrate significant effects of that fertility rebound on economic outcomes twenty years later.

And finally, another unfortunate aspect of war is that it acts as an economic stimulant. Wartime expenditures boosted the economic growth rate during this period and ensured that those young men remaining in the civilian economy experienced an increase in relative income, rather than the decline they would otherwise have experienced in a peacetime economy as members of a large birth cohort. All of these factors need to be taken into account in explaining fertility, college enrollments, and male relative income during this period. It is likely that similar effects were experienced in the 1950s during the Korean War, but the detailed data needed for wage analyses were not available until the early 1960s.

Asymmetry in the Effects of Relative Cohort Size

First, what does it mean to assume *symmetric* effects of relative cohort size? Look again at figure 1.1, which shows two possible measures of relative cohort size. The traditional focus in studies of relative cohort size effects appears to have been on the troughs and peaks in these measures. Those entering the labor market in a trough period like the 1950s (small cohorts) experience beneficial labor market effects, while those entering in a peak like the 1970s experience the full negative effects of cohort size. But implicit in that assumption is *symmetry around the peak:* persons entering the labor market, say, around 1975 and those entering around 1985 should have experienced identical effects of relative cohort size (all other things equal), since their relative cohort sizes were identical. But they didn't.

It's true that those entering in 1975 had a tougher time than those entering, say, in 1970—but conditions didn't improve as we headed into the 1980s. If anything, they deteriorated further. That phrase "all other things equal" is of course important here: perhaps something *else* was happening in the 1980s that counteracted the beneficial effects of declining relative cohort size. This has been a popular assumption among labor economists, who have since shifted their focus from relative cohort size to factors such as globalization, computers, and other technological change.

But the hypothesis examined in later chapters is that it's too simplistic to assume such symmetry. Why? I have two suggestions, both of which require more testing. The first is what I have termed "bottleneck effects": the congestion that occurred in the labor market as the peak of the baby boom entered. We know that large cohort size did not result just in lower relative wages, but also in higher unemployment and higher incidence of "job mismatch." It took time for the labor market to absorb those largest cohorts, so the negative effects of their large size overlapped onto the smaller cohorts following them.

The second reason for expecting asymmetry is the possibility of aggregate demand effects of changing cohort size. The standard relative cohort size model considers only *supply* effects: the fact that large relative cohort size means an increase in the supply of labor, the number of new workers looking for jobs. But those workers are also consumers, and fluctuations in both the number and the age distri-

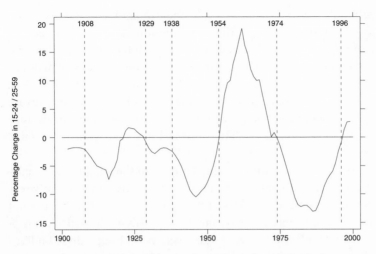

Figure 1.2. Five-year percentage change in the U.S. ratio of population aged 15–24 to population aged 25–59, 1900–2000. The growth rate was large and positive from 1954 to 1974, when US economic growth was strong, and significantly negative between 1974 and 1996.

bution of consumers could have marked effects on the demand for goods (and therefore the demand for workers) in the economy. Those born on what is termed the "leading edge" of the baby boom (those entering the labor market in the late 1960s and the 1970s) would have felt very strong positive effects of such changes in aggregate demand, since there were increasing numbers of baby boomers behind them "in the pipeline," passing from childhood into teen years and requiring increasing amounts of goods and services each day. But those born on the "trailing edge" of the baby boom, who entered the labor market during the 1980s, were followed by rapidly declining proportions of young adults. This demographic difference between the 1954–1974 and 1974–1996 economic regimes is apparent in figure 1.2. We moved from strong positive rates of growth in the proportion of young adults to significant decline in the 1974–1996 period, not unlike the 1929–1954 period. Two different ratios are used in figures 1.1 and 1.2 because the ratio in figure 1.1 is meant to capture supply effects of changing relative cohort size, while figure 1.2 focuses on demand effects. Chapter 3 describes in more detail the ratio used in figure 1.2.

All of this is highly speculative, but my work to date lends support to these hypotheses. Allowing for these additional effects (the

Vietnam draft, international trade and immigration, and asymmetric cohort size), along with the straightforward supply effects of changing relative cohort size that have been the focus of others' investigations, it is possible to explain most of the variation in male relative wages that has occurred over the past three decades.[11] In turn, when the effects of changes in women's labor force participation are included with male relative income, it is possible to explain many of the puzzling changes we have observed in society over those same three decades.

My hope is that the combined impact of the fairly simple analyses presented here will generate a renewed interest in the relative cohort size/relative income model and spur others to join in an attempt to conduct the more intensive microlevel analyses needed to confirm (or reject) findings thus far.[12] And, even more, I hope these findings will cause some reconsideration of the U.S. experience since 1973. Have we observed only long-term trends that analysts are correct in simply extrapolating further, or has there been a strong cyclic component in these time series?

Like Easterlin, I emphasize that "[w]hen I argue that some observers have confused fluctuations with trends, I do not mean to suggest that no real trends are at work." My claim is simply that too little attention has been paid to correcting for cyclic variation that has occurred as the baby boom has passed through our society.

Summary

Following on a long—if sporadic—history of economic and demographic feedback models, most of them focused on effects of population growth rather than age structure, Richard Easterlin proposed a framework suggesting that population age structure might be a critical element in variations over time in age-specific economic outcomes and behavior.

Changes in population age structure occur as a result of "on-again, off-again" patterns of fertility, and the "pig in the python"—the Western world's post-WWII baby boom—is a classic example of a structural effect created by fertility variations during that period. Easterlin introduced the concept of relative cohort size, the size of one's birth cohort relative to that of one's parents, and suggested that its effects on individuals might persist throughout their lifetimes, with the most profound economic effect occurring at the time of labor market entry, when the wages of a relatively large cohort like the baby boom would be significantly depressed relative to their desired standard of living.

Although initially a popular concept among analysts for explaining wage patterns prior to 1980, Easterlin's hypothesis later fell into disfavor when young men's relative wages failed to recover despite the declining relative size of new cohorts entering the labor market after 1980. However, when four additional factors are added into the Easterlin framework, it appears that relative cohort size has indeed had the postulated effects on young men's relative wages, as will be demonstrated in chapters 5 and 6. Those four additional factors are (1) women's changing role in society and the labor force; (2) immigration or international trade (or both); (3) the Vietnam War; and (4) the asymmetry of relative cohort size effects, with negative labor supply effects counteracted by positive consumer demand effects when relative cohort size is increasing, and magnified by negative consumer demand effects triggered when relative cohort size begins to decline. The next chapter explores the significance of male relative income, which acts as the primary mechanism of transmission from relative cohort size to most of the other effects discussed in this book.

2

Male Relative Income and Its Significance

[M]any economists still regard preference formation and change as the business of other disciplines. . . . [T]his intellectual division-of-labor argument [is] unpersuasive. . . . [Because] estimation presupposes a correctly specified model, empirical investigators cannot ignore preference change. If an investigator assumes fixed preferences when in fact they are changing, then all of the coefficient estimates, even those of the narrowly specified economic variables, are inconsistent. Thus, if preference change is taking place, economists cannot ignore it unless they are prepared to abandon empirical analysis and reconstitute economics as a purely deductive enterprise.

> Robert A. Pollak and Susan Cotts Watkins, "Cultural and Economic Approaches to Fertility: Proper Marriage or Mésalliance?" (1993)

Confronted with the prospect of a deterioration in its living level relative to that of its parents, a large young adult cohort may make a number of adaptations in an attempt to preserve its comparative standing. Foremost among these are changes in behaviour related to family formation and family life. To avoid the financial pressures associated with family responsibilities, marriage may be deferred. If marriage occurs, wives are more likely to work and to put off childbearing. If the wife bears children, she is more likely to couple labour force participation with childrearing, and to have a smaller number of children more widely spaced.

> *The New Palgrave: A Dictionary of Economics*, s.v. "Easterlin hypothesis"

The term "relative income" has been used by many social scientists, perhaps most notably James Duesenberry, who emphasized the importance of previous levels of consumption in determining our current desired levels.[1] He wrote of a "ratchet effect," suggesting that while consumption expenditures will increase fairly readily in response to *increases* in income, it is much more difficult to accommodate reductions in income. (Think of trying to reduce one's expenditure on housing during a spell of unemployment, given fixed mortgage payments, or denying your children the college education you enjoyed.)

But economists have been hesitant to address such concepts in their research, relegating them to the area of preferences and preference formation—thought to be the realm of other social sciences—and focusing instead on absolute measures of income and prices. There are increasing numbers of exceptions to this tendency, however, especially with the advent of "experimental economics," an approach that permits the observation of individual choice in controlled circumstances. For example, one recent study found that, given a choice between a world in which survey respondents have more income than everyone else and one in which everyone (including the respondent) has more but the respondent has less than everyone else, half of respondents preferred to have *fifty percent less real income*, but high relative income.[2] Similarly, researchers have found that subjects in experiments are willing to pay out of their own winnings in order to reduce the winnings of others, and that this decision to "burn" others is relatively insensitive to the "price" of burning.[3] And other researchers have been working to identify methods of quantifying individuals' internalized standards[4] and methods of dealing with changing preferences in economic models.[5]

In this book the focus is specifically on preference formation among young adults: those just making initial and often formative decisions regarding labor force entry, household formation, marriage, and fertility. What criteria do they apply when evaluating their own earning potential in terms of its ability to support their desired lifestyle? To what standard of living do they aspire? Although a multitude of influences probably impinge on preferences at this stage in life—those associated with siblings, personal and occupational peers, geographical area, and socioeconomic reference groups, to name a few[6]—Richard Easterlin drew on the literature in sociology and psychology to suggest that an obvious one, and one probably highly significant and fairly easy to quantify, must be the standard of living enjoyed in one's parents' home. The four basic elements of his hypothesis are (1) the concept of crowding mechanisms that transmit the effects of large cohort size to relative wage rates; (2) the notion that individuals' sense of personal well-being derives from a comparison of their own earnings to their material aspirations; (3) the suggestion that individuals' material aspirations will be affected by the standard of living in their parents' home when they were growing up; and (4) the understanding that a sense of relative deprivation will cause behavioral adjustments as individuals attempt to achieve their desired standard of living.[7]

In general, Easterlin postulated a systematic shift in preferences resulting from the fact that each successive generation, under economic development, experiences a successively higher parental standard of living. "In effect, a . . . 'subsistence level' constraint is added to the analysis of [fertility behavior] along with the budget line and production constraints."[8] In other words, an individual's sense of well-being associated with a real annual income of, say, $20,000 will be different if that individual is living in the year 2000, rather than in 1920 because the individual's expected standard of living would be different in the two periods. Because of this "subsistence level" constraint, economic or demographic fluctuations could cause periodic reversals in the secular downtrend in fertility, such as that observed in the developed countries in the postwar period.

According to the Easterlin theory, a large birth cohort meets unfavorable labor market conditions that reduce the earning potential of young males relative to their aspirations. In an attempt to close the gap between income and aspirations, members of such a cohort will tend to make a number of adjustments including increased female labor force participation and delayed/reduced marriage and childbearing. In addition, because young women in large cohorts will anticipate higher levels of labor force participation, they will also tend to enroll in college at increased rates. Similarly, there will be increased motivation for young males to achieve a higher level of education, since this is one way they can raise their earning potential relative to that of their parents. This increased supply of young college graduates will in turn, however, tend to lower the returns to a college education.

Easterlin pointed out that although many different factors might impinge on the formation of material aspiration, in explaining preference changes over time it's only necessary to identify the influential factors that also change significantly through time. In that sense, probably the most important and variable influence from one generation to the next must be the average parental income setting the standard of living in children's homes.

It is important to note that this theory neither implies nor requires a slavish reproduction of parental lifestyles on the part of young adults. It is accepted that many will desire a higher standard of living than experienced in their parents' homes, and perhaps some will be willing to accept or even desire a lower standard. But on average, if the standard of life increases from one parental generation to the next, then on average the standard applied by their children will also rise. This is a point often missed in earlier tests of the Easterlin hypothesis.

Ex Ante versus Ex Post Income

Easterlin introduced a useful concept in understanding this process of adjustment in his epilogue to the second edition of *Birth and Fortune*[9]: the distinction between ex ante and ex post income.[10] It is assumed that individuals are ultimately concerned with per capita disposable income, relative to their desired standard of living. Ex ante income is the level of individual earnings as dictated by the market: how much an individual can earn by and for him or herself. Given this level of ex ante income, an individual can then decide how many people can be supported on that income: self only? self plus spouse? self and spouse with children? Ex post income is the per capita income available to the individual and his or her dependents after making these demographic choices.

A helpful mental image here might be a graph depicting movements over time in the observed levels of variables such as ex ante and ex post incomes, marriage rates, fertility rates, enrollment rates, and female labor force participation rates. On that graph, ex post income approximates a straight horizontal line, while all of the other variables tend to fluctuate in response to any fluctuations in ex ante income.

One might add to that mental graph two more variables—call them "ex ante marriage and fertility rates": the rates which would have been observed in society if young adults had realized the marriage and childbearing plans they formulated for themselves when they were teenagers. It is hypothesized that these variables also approximate fairly straight horizontal lines on our graph—perhaps with a slight negative slope over time, but with nothing like the negative slopes we have observed over the past thirty years. The differences between these ex ante rates and the observed (we could call them "ex post") marriage and fertility rates are the adjustments individuals have made in order to maintain that straight horizontal ex post income line. So there we have it in a nutshell: steady, nearly horizontal ex ante marriage and fertility rates, a fluctuating ex ante relative income and ex post marriage and fertility rates, and a steady horizontal ex post relative income.

Easterlin also postulated that the psychological stress associated with these adjustments needed to achieve the desired level of economic well-being will tend to put a strain on marriages when they do occur, leading to an increased incidence of divorce, and may also lead to an increase in the age-specific rates of other forms of anomie such as juvenile delinquency, crime, drug use, and suicide.

But Haven't Gender Roles Changed?

Objections have been raised to what some have interpreted as the portrayal of young women as able to achieve fulfillment only through marriage and childbearing, the depiction of marital bonds as dependent on children, and the emphasis on *male* relative incomes. Some feel this characterization is no longer relevant—the young women of today no longer treat affluence merely as an opportunity to marry and have children.

But has society today really moved so far from traditional gender roles? Are today's young people really so different from their parents? A 1995 Gallup poll of adults in twenty-two countries indicated a surprising tenacity among Americans, in terms of traditional gender roles: "nearly half of the Americans surveyed said the ideal family structure was one in which only the father earned the living and the mother stayed home with the children."[11] And a more recent study concluded, "Our findings suggest that only the male partner's economic resources affect the transition [from cohabitation] to marriage, with positive economic situations accelerating marriage and deterring separation. Our results imply that despite trends toward egalitarian gender-role attitudes and increasing income provision among women, cohabiting men's economic circumstances carry far more weight than women's in marriage formation."[12]

One might argue, however, that despite the tendency among the population generally, young people's attitudes have become more progressive in the last few decades. Every year I have at least a few students who make this argument and maintain that this will certainly be the case among a career-oriented student body like the one at Williams College, where I taught until recently. Thus, in almost every year between 1990 and 1995, some of my students administered a survey among Williams College undergraduates to identify family and career aspirations. The results have been remarkably consistent over this period:[13]

1. The average desired number of children consistently falls between 2.3 and 2.5 among both women and men, and whereas Easterlin reports that in a "recent survey on young adults . . . three out of every four single women aged eighteen to twenty-one expected to have at least two children,"[14] among Williams College students this figure reaches over 85 percent for women and 89 percent for men.

2. Ninety-six percent of men and 91 percent of women expect to marry, with an average intended age at marriage of 26.7 years for both sexes. These proportions are considerably higher than the 75 percent reported for American high school seniors in the 1970s and 1980s.[15]

3. Average expected age at birth of the first child is 28.7 for men and 28.8 for women: on average these young women do *not* expect to delay childbearing until after they've established themselves in a career. A surprising 85 percent expect to have their first child by age 30; 96 percent by age 33. Perhaps even more surprisingly, the corresponding figures for the men are 81 percent and 96 percent.

4. Respondents were asked to rank the following possible career arrangements for parents in the presence of young children: *(a)* both parents work full time outside the home; *(b)* both parents work part time; *(c)* wife full time and husband part time; *(d)* husband full time and wife part time; *(e)* husband full time and wife at home; *(f)* wife full time and husband at home. Men ranked *(d)* and *(e)* highest and *(a)* lowest, while women ranked *(b)* highest, *(d)* second highest, and *(a)* lowest.

5. Young women indicated that they would on average work about forty-three hours per week before having children, but intended to cut back on average to about twenty-two hours per week when children were under 3 years old. Young men on average shared these expectations

for their wives, although they had a much higher tendency than the women to expect wives to drop out of the labor force altogether, or work twenty hours per week or less when children were young.

6. Among young men, there was a statistically significant difference between those whose fathers had stayed at home full time for some portion of their childhood and those with full-time career dads in the young men's intentions regarding their own participation in child care. Those with stay-at-home fathers (7 percent of the sample) intended to cut back from forty-four hours per week outside the home, to thirty hours per week, while those with career dads intended to cut back only to forty hours per week on average when children were under 3.

These survey results paint a picture of fairly traditional family aspirations among Williams College students in 1995, with the only concession to women's career aspirations being a somewhat later age at the birth of the first child, and the mutual acceptance of mothers' part-time work outside the home when children are young. My experience with individual students is that they seem to ascribe fairly progressive, nontraditional attitudes and aspirations to members of their cohort generally, but that they tend to describe much more traditional aspirations when questioned about their own intentions for themselves.[16]

Cognitive Dissonance and Preferences: "Rationalizing Behavior"

Thus, in the end, despite sometimes vehement objections to Easterlin's portrait of American family values and attitudes toward gender roles, it is difficult to believe that the portrayal is very far off the mark in describing *underlying preferences* in society over the past fifty years. A pivotal factor in the hypothesis, though, is that economic constraints can induce people to make demographic choices that aren't always consistent with those underlying preferences. Doing so can produce what psychologists term "cognitive dissonance," a situation in which people perceive that reality doesn't reflect their own internalized image of what reality "should be."

On an individual basis, this often leads to what is termed "rationalizing behavior." For example, a young high school student might state a preference for three children, but when interviewed ten years later assert that she wants only one. This might well be because intervening economic circumstances limited her ability to achieve the lifestyle she had originally envisioned. Whereas her original statement reflected her "unconstrained" or underlying preferences, her later statement reflected economic realities.

This type of behavior makes it difficult to credit surveys reporting sharp declines in "desired family size" among young women between, say, 1960 and 1985. Surveys of this type provide the basis for prognostications of continuing long-term declines in U.S. fertility. However, most of the respondents in such surveys tend to be women over 20 who have already tempered their underlying preferences based on experiences in the "real world." Because young women during this period were largely baby boomers struggling to achieve a lifestyle slipping rapidly beyond their reach, it's inappropriate to extrapolate their constrained preferences beyond their own generation. It makes more sense to examine young adults' underlying preferences and then assume that their ability to achieve their preferred family size will fluctuate depending on their relative economic status.

However, if over time an increasingly large proportion of the population are forced by economic conditions to make dissonant choices, it must be expected that the principle of "cognitive dissonance" may alter even the underlying preferences. Young people may at a young age internalize what they perceive to be society's preferences. This would be a very gradual process, but, given the twenty-year duration of the baby boom's entry into family formation stage, young people have indeed been influenced by baby boomer lifestyle over a very extended period. To the extent that underlying preferences have been affected, this would create considerable inertia preventing any return to the status quo, even given an improvement in young adults' relative economic status.

For example, consider changes in the public's attitude regarding the labor force participation of mothers with young children. The pendulum has swung from extreme opposition in the 1940s and 1950s to almost unquestioning acceptance as more and more mothers have entered, or remained in, the workforce. Improvements in their relative income may remove some of the economic pressure for these mothers to work outside the home, but it would be foolhardy to assume a mechanical symmetry in relative cohort size effects that leads us all the way back to the attitudes of the 1950s just because relative cohort size declines. It's in this sense that the relative cohort size/relative income hypothesis provides insights into the past that must be very judiciously applied in attempting to predict the future.

Summary

Despite most economists' characteristic tendency to think of preference formation as the domain of sociologists, anthropologists, and psychologists, economist Richard Easterlin drew on these other disciplines to formulate his concept of male relative income—young men's earning potential relative to young adults' material aspirations—and explain how changes in that measure might both derive from and explain birth quakes like the post-WWII baby boom and bust.

Young adults will be less willing to undertake family formation if they determine that their own earning potential is inadequate to support their desired lifestyle, and that desired lifestyle will be a function of the standard of living experienced in their parents' homes. Not necessarily identical to that standard of living, but a function of it: children of a less affluent parental generation will on average have more modest material aspirations. The generation born and raised during the Depression and WWII internalized more modest aspirations than those who grew up in the 1960s, and thus, for any given level of personal earnings, felt more able to take on family formation. And two points must be stressed in response to the argument that the focus on male earnings in this relative income hypothesis is atavistic: first, this focus is entirely appropriate to the extent that we're trying to explain historical behavior; and second, surveys even today indicate that young people continue to view men's earnings as the primary determinant in family formation decisions.[17] Similarly, surveys indicate that underlying preferences regarding women's roles and desired family size appear not to have changed as much as current behavior—constrained by low male relative income—might suggest.

That having been said, however, it's important to acknowledge that the principle of "cognitive dissonance" may over extended periods tend to bring those underlying preferences more in line with current behavior. To the extent that this occurs, it will militate against any tendency for decreases in relative cohort size and associated increases in male relative income to return society to a slavish reproduction of the 1950s.

The next two chapters explore some of the technical aspects involved in attempting to quantify relative cohort size and male relative income, then describe patterns of male relative income over the past thirty-five years, demonstrating the ubiquity of the sharp decline that occurred between 1970 and 1985. Some readers may prefer to skim over or skip most of the technical material in chapter 3 and focus only on the descriptive material on male relative income in chapter 4.

3

Defining Variables

Relative Cohort Size and Relative Income

> [T]he current living level of the parents is a reasonable indicator of the economic origins of young adults. Obviously this does not start to exhaust the influences shaping the material aspirations of young adults. A more accurate way of putting the argument is that the *difference* between the commodity aspirations of the two generations of young adults is assumed to be dominated by the difference in living levels of their parents.
>
> Richard Easterlin, *Birth and Fortune* (1987)

In conducting the analyses presented in this book, the attempt has been to focus on, identify, and test a theory. That might sound self-evident, but in an area like this, where there's very little supporting research, it's all too easy to lose the forest for the trees: to get immersed in data and end up "fishing" for variable specifications that support a coherent story sounding like the Easterlin hypothesis.

Thus, in my work I've tried to be as true as possible to the spirit of the hypothesis presented in *Birth and Fortune:* first, the idea that individuals respond to relative rather than absolute income levels; second, the idea that the income in one's parents' home when one is growing up may be a significant factor in shaping the material aspirations that are a part of relative income; and third, the idea that relative cohort size may be a cogent force affecting the level of one's earnings relative to one's material aspirations.

I emphasize this at the start because reviews of the literature suggest that the earliest tests of the Easterlin hypothesis were severely hampered in their choice of variables, largely because of data availability, and later studies in many cases seem to have adopted these same variables simply because they had been used in earlier work. The variables used have in many cases been very poor approximations of the relative cohort size or relative income concepts.[1] In this chapter I'll review the logic behind my own definition of variables and then, in chapter 4, describe the pattern of male relative income that emerges given these definitions. It should be emphasized, though, that the variables I've used are only a "current best attempt"; undoubtedly they can be improved upon as well![2]

Micro or Macro?

Data limitations plague this area of research, but theory is a problem as well. Because there has been so little research on the formation of material aspirations, the formulation of a relative income measure at the micro level is fraught with hazards. What is an appropriate relative income measure for an unmarried woman? And when looking at married couples, does one need a comparison of earnings of the husband or the wife, or both—and relative to his parents, to her parents, or both? Should one use income, or earnings, or wages—and should these be permanent (lifetime) measures, or observed earnings/income at some specific age?[3] What is the relevant period during which the father's earnings can be said to have affected his child's material aspirations? And should they be corrected for family size? Should one use just the father's income/earnings, or include the mother's? Not only have none of these questions been answered to date, but in general there is a lack of microdata sets that provide information on first- and second-generation income and fertility behavior. Even in data sets that provide such information, it's available for only one of the partners in a married couple.

This combination—of data limitations and the absence of theoretical guidelines—has prompted me to work first at the aggregate level. There at least a few of the theoretical problems melt away: at the aggregate level it's not necessary to associate individuals with their own parents, or with their own spouses, but rather a young generation with its parental generation. Thus average household income in the parental generation, at some point in the past, can be used as a measure of the average desired standard of living for both males and females in the younger generation. For young adults, it's possible to calculate average individual wages, earnings, and incomes both for males and for females (and for other subcategories such as racial groups, if desired). This approach can be applied both at the national and the regional or state level. As illustrated in chapter 4, although male relative income has followed generally similar patterns across all geographical areas of the country, there are enough significant differences—especially in terms of the rebound in the late 1980s—to identify effects on variables such as young adults' marriage and fertility rates. The analyses in chapters 9 and 11 make use of these subregional differences in analyzing the effect of changes in male relative income on patterns of marriage, divorce, and fertility.

In addition, working at the aggregate level of analysis in a relative income context helps address the problem of delayed/forgone marriage as it affects extramarital fertility—something impossible in models of marital fertility. That is, "marriage is losing relevance as a determinant of fertility among . . . women."[4] There is increasing "slippage" between marital and extramarital fertility that makes it difficult to specify the effects of male relative income on women at the micro level. An aggregate relative income model of fertility accounts for such slippage in that low male relative income prompts young adults to delay/forgo marriage, resulting in more young women likely to experience extramarital fertility. Incorporating the average female wage in such an aggregate model, with allowance for changes in its contribution to household income, permits the female wage to exert the primary income effect on fertility in periods of low male relative income: we can model total, rather than just marital, fertility rates.

Similarly, working at the aggregate level enables one to sidestep the question of how decisions are made within the household, since it's not necessary to differentiate between the parental incomes of the two partners. That is, at the micro level one would have to determine whether the strongest effect on demographic variables comes from the young men's comparison of their own earnings with those of their own fathers (and aspirations), or from the young women's comparison of their potential husbands' earnings with those of the young women's fathers (and aspirations). This is a significant point that's been neglected in most cross-section tests of the relative income hypothesis, where it's been assumed that the only relative income comparison made is by the young man, leaving the young woman as a passive participant.[5] The active participation of young women in this decision-making process could seriously weaken tests of the relative income hypothesis using microlevel data. At the aggregate level, it's not necessary to be concerned with identifying different subsets of fathers (or parents) in determining the reference group for quantifying material aspirations in the relative income variable.[6]

However, working at the aggregate level doesn't mean escape from all problems of definition associated with these variables. Which age groups should be used in defining young men's cohort size and average earnings, and parental cohort size and average income? And at what point in their lives should it be assumed that parental income most influences young adults' own desired standard of living? These decisions might affect the time trend and turning points of a relative income measure. In order to make them in a manner guided more by theory than by empirics, I have to some extent treated *Birth and Fortune* as my source: delving there for answers, rather than into the data.

Guidance from *Birth and Fortune* on Age Groups

Easterlin's hypothesis is presented exclusively in terms of "young adults": the relative income, and hence relative cohort size, effects on these young adults as they make major economic and demographic decisions. He discussed in general terms the fact that a cohort can be expected to bear the imprint of these effects throughout the life cycle, but it's only for the cohort when young that he specified a quantifiable mechanism of transmission.[7]

Easterlin suggested that young adults compare their own recent earnings to their material aspirations. These material aspirations are assumed to be a function, at least in part, of the standard of living experienced by the young adults when they were teenagers.[8] He hypothesized that material aspirations "depend not so much on their parents' present income (although this may be of some relevance) as it does on parents' income some years earlier, when [the husband and wife were each] living at home and growing up."[9] He provided in *Birth and Fortune* only one quantification of this measure over time, at the macro level: a seven-year moving average of the income of families with head aged 45–54, four years prior to the date of comparison, as a proxy for the aspirations of individuals currently aged 17–27.[10]

Thus we're interested in the behavior of young adults just entering the labor market and household formation stages, and for this reason the analyses presented in this book focus on young men and women aged 20–24 when dealing with published data on age-specific rates such as those for fertility, marriage, and labor force participation[11]; and on unenrolled young men and women in their first five years of work experience (where the average age is between 21 and 22) when dealing with wages, earnings, and income. For young adults aged 20–24, one might look back at their standard of living four to five years earlier when they were, on average, aged 17–18 and presumably still in their parents' homes.

But how old would the parents have been at this time when the young adults' material aspirations were being formed? The bulk of a woman's childbearing occurs between the ages of 23–34, and assuming the average spousal age difference of about two years, this means that the bulk of a man's fathering of children occurs from ages 25–36. Using the lag of 4–5 years selected above for the 20–24 age group, one is looking, on average, at young adults when aged 17–18, so the fathers of these young adults at the time of observation would be in the age range 42–54.

Alternatively, *Vital Statistics* shows that the median age of mothers at childbirth has varied in a range from 25.3–26.6 from 1940 to 1987, so the median age of fathers at childbirth would have been about 28–29 during this same period and 45–47 when the children were aged 17–18. Both of these estimates (an age range of 42–54 and a median age of 45–47) accord well with Easterlin's frequent use of the parental age group 45–54.

Relative Cohort Size

Researchers often hypothesize that there are three specific types of effect on labor market outcomes of individuals: age specific (are they young and inexperienced, or older and more experienced?), period specific (is the economy growing rapidly, or are we in a recession?), and cohort specific (is this a large or a small birth cohort?). A birth cohort is a group of people born in the same year, or span of years. They thus share, throughout their lives, the same age-specific and period-specific characteristics.

The annual pattern of births in the United States during this century is shown in figure 3.1: here one can see very dramatically the effects of the post-WWII baby boom, when the annual number of

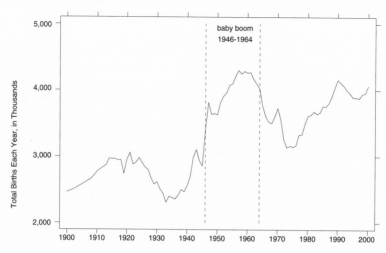

Figure 3.1. Total annual U.S. births, 1900–1998. Sources: National Center for Health Statistics 1997b, 1999, 2001a,b for 1917–2000; United States Bureau of the Census 1975 for 1900–1916.

births shot up from less than 2.5 million in the 1930s to nearly 4.5 million in the 1950s. But when "cohort size effects" are mentioned in this book, the focus is not on the *absolute* numbers presented in figure 3.1, but rather on some *relative* indication of cohort size: how is it to be measured? In *Birth and Fortune* Easterlin regularly refers to "the birth rate," lagged twenty years. When he operationalizes this measure he uses the crude birth rate (CBR)—the number of births in a year relative to the total population in that year. Similarly, when he constructs a corresponding measure using current population figures, he uses a ratio of the population aged 15–29 to the population 30–64—but he argues that the birth rate could be used without any significant bias because of the strong correlation over time between a cohort's size at birth and its size later in life.

The analyses presented here, however, depart marginally from *Birth and Fortune* on this point because Easterlin's choice is not fully consistent with his theory. That is, the focus is on one's income relative to one's aspirations—and these aspirations are in turn theorized to be a function, not of the standard of living in the country as a whole, but of one's parents' standard of living. Thus a measure is needed that best reflects the size of an individual's own birth cohort relative to that of his or her parents. In terms of birth rates, the closest approximation to this will be the general fertility rate (GFR)—the

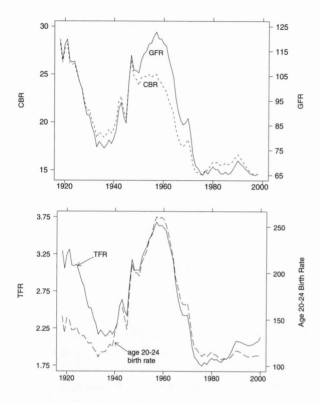

Figure 3.2. Comparison of alternate fertility measures. *Top:* crude birth rate (CBR: number of births per 1,000 total population) and general fertility rate (GFR: number of births per 1,000 women of childbearing age). *Bottom:* total fertility rate (TFR: number of children per woman at current age-specific rates) and age-specific birth rate of women aged 20–24. Source: National Center for Health Statistics 1997b, 1999, 2001a,b.

number of births in a year relative to the number of women of child-bearing age—rather than the CBR.

The top of figure 3.2 presents a comparison of the CBR and the GFR. Characteristic movements of the two measures on either side of the baby boom peak (during the Depression, WWII, and Vietnam War periods, and then in the "baby bust" 1970s) are very similar, but the GFR accentuates the peak of the baby boom much more than does the CBR. This is primarily because the divisor in the CBR—total population—is distorted by the inclusion of the baby boomers themselves during that period. The bottom of figure 3.2 presents two fertility rates that control for changing age structure in the population, and thus, like the GFR, avoid the distortion apparent in the CBR.

Following this logic, and based on the age groups identified in the previous section, the following two relative cohort size variables were selected as best representing the concepts in *Birth and Fortune*. Only the second of these—the lagged GFR—was used in econometric analyses of cohort size effects on wages reported in chapters 5 and 6, however, because unlike current population ratios it is an "exogenous" measure. That is, current labor market conditions might have an effect on current age ratios by inducing inter- and intra-national migration, with workers moving to areas with higher wages and lower unemployment. This is a confounding influence in attempts to measure the effect of age ratios on wages, so it's preferable to use a measure like the GFR that was determined twenty-some years earlier and thus cannot be construed to be affected by current labor market conditions.

1. Males aged 20–22 (to correspond with the average age of young men no longer enrolled in school, in their first five years of work experience) relative to males aged 45–49 (to correspond with the median and average ages of fathers as calculated above). This is intended to be a precise measure incorporating the two age groups where labor market substitutability is expected to be lowest. A broader measure (for example, Easterlin's 15–29 relative to 30–64) would dilute any effects of imperfect substitutability. We know, for example, that workers nearing retirement are often fairly good substitutes for younger workers. But by the same token, what is the labor market relationship between 20–24 year olds and those 25–29, or 30–34? Are they substitutes or complements, on average? A narrower, more precise measure of relative cohort size avoids such problems.

2. The average of the general fertility rate that occurred twenty, twenty-one, and twenty-two years prior to the date under analysis (i.e., a three-year moving average centered on a period twenty-one years earlier). For econometric analyses, this measure is a useful proxy for the 20–22/45–49 age ratio. It provides a method of forecasting conditions at labor market entry twenty-some years in advance and can be thought of as an "exogenous" measure, as explained above.

These two variables are presented on the top of figure 3.3. They have followed a very similar time path in the period under analysis, between 1950 and 2000. For purposes of comparison, the graph on the bottom of figure 3.3 illustrates the differences between the selected age ratio (20–22/45–49) and two less specific ratios: Easterlin's 15–29/30–64 and a "compromise measure," 18–24/45–54. Apart from the height of the 1980/81 peak, the two more specific measures are virtually identical, while the Easterlin measure not only understates the peak but also brings it forward by about five years.[12]

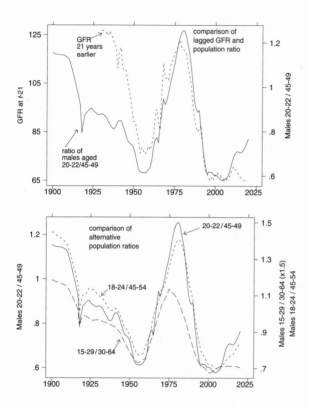

Figure 3.3. Comparison of alternative measures of relative cohort size that are consistent with the concepts in *Birth and Fortune. Top:* a ratio of males aged 20–22 relative to males aged 45–49, and the general fertility rate twenty-one years earlier, when the 20–22 year olds were born. *Bottom:* a comparison of three male population ratios—those aged 20–22 relative to those aged 45–49, those aged 18–24 relative to those aged 45–54, and those aged 15–29 relative to those aged 30–64. Apart from the height of the 1980/81 peak, the two more specific population measures (20–22/45–49 and 18–24/45–54) are virtually identical, while the Easterlin measure (15–29/30–64) not only understates the peak but also brings it forward by about five years.

Considerations of Cohort Position as Well as Cohort Size

Easterlin's hypotheses concerning the various effects of relative cohort size assumed that these effects were symmetric around the peak of the baby boom. As illustrated in figure 3.4, symmetry implies, for example, that the birth cohort of 1950 (on what is termed the "leading edge" of the boom) when it entered the labor market around 1970 should have experienced the same effects of relative cohort size as the birth cohort of 1967 (on the "lagging" or "trailing" edge), since their relative sizes were the same.

When looking just at the experiences of leading-edge cohorts, several researchers have identified effects of relative cohort size as hypothesized by Easterlin, some on wages and others on enrollment and the return to schooling.[13] But wages failed to increase after the peak of the baby boom had entered the market around 1980, despite

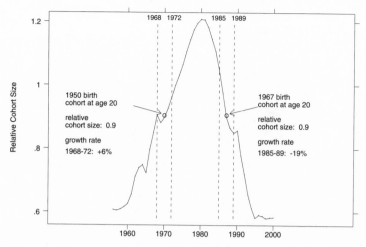

Figure 3.4. Illustrating asymmetry around the peak of the baby boom using the ratio of males aged 20–22 relative to males aged 45–49 as a measure of relative cohort size (RCS). Symmetry implies only supply effects of large RCS (large RCS creates an excess supply of young workers) and implies the same effects of RCS on the cohorts that entered the labor market in 1970 and in 1987, since their RCS was the same (0.9). But the growth rate of RCS in the 4-year "windows" around the two cohorts were very different: +6 percent in 1970 and –19 percent in 1987. Asymmetry implies demand as well as supply effects of RCS (demand for goods and services is rising when RCS is increasing) and thus implies the total effect would be different for each of the two cohorts.

declining relative cohort size. Why? Implicit in all of these early studies was the assumption of symmetry about the peak, which later researchers have come to question.[14]

Cohorts born on the leading edge of the baby boom, it was found, tended to have higher earnings overall than those born either at the peak or on the trailing edge. It was hypothesized that the effects of relative cohort size might be compounded by a "bottleneck effect" on the lagging edge: the peak cohorts glutted the market and caused relatively long-term unemployment, job mismatches, and promotion bottlenecks, outweighing the benefits of smaller relative cohort size for subsequent smaller birth cohorts. This is an extension of what is termed the "supply" effect of relative cohort size: an effect due to the excess supply of labor caused by a sudden influx of large birth cohorts into the labor market. Even more important, however, relative cohort size around this point of labor market entry might have a positive as well as a negative effect on the economy, because at this age young adults are not only entering the labor market,

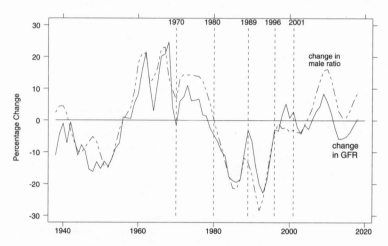

Figure 3.5. Rates of growth related to the two relative cohort size measures presented in the top graph in figure 3.3, showing strong positive growth from the mid-1950s through the 1970s, followed by a long period of decline that didn't recover until the mid-1990s. The pattern between 1970 and 1995 is very similar to the pattern of male relative income during that period.

they're also setting up their own new households, increasing the demand for housing and durable goods. This is referred to as a "demand" effect.

In order to allow for possible asymmetry, the studies presented here (in chapters 5 and 6) use not just a measure of relative cohort size, but also an indicator of cohort position. The position indicator used is the growth rate of relative cohort size at the time a cohort enters the labor market, which is positive for leading-edge and negative for trailing-edge cohorts.[15] Two growth-rate measures related to the relative cohort size variables described above and presented on the top of figure 3.3 are illustrated in figure 3.5. They show strong positive rates of growth from the mid-1950s through the 1970s that helped counteract negative supply effects of cohort size on wages, followed by a plunge into negative growth rates that did not begin to recover until the mid-1990s, coincidentally with the emergence of the "new economy." There is a pronounced correspondence between these growth rates and the pattern of male relative income presented in figures 4.1 and 4.2 in the next chapter, with a long decline between 1970 and 1985, a temporary recovery in the late 1980s, followed by another short decline and then another recovery in the late 1990s.

Absolute or Relative Cohort Size?

There are many theoretical arguments in favor of using a relative—as opposed to an absolute—measure of cohort size, some of which have been mentioned in the preceding discussion. Absolute measures are incapable of capturing the effects of substitutability—or lack thereof—in the labor force, and in the case of aggregate demand effects an absolute measure implies that "bigger is (always) better." That having been said, it's still important to point out that in the period covered by my analyses these two types of cohort size measure have followed remarkably similar patterns, as illustrated in figure 3.6, so that statistically it's difficult to rule out the possibility of absolute effects—either in place of or alongside relative effects. I believe that this is especially true in terms of aggregate demand effects: it may be that producer and investor expectations respond to changes in the absolute number of young adults in the population, more than to changes in their number relative to prime-age adults. This is a question open to further research, and it's a particularly important one given that we've entered a new era in which trends in the

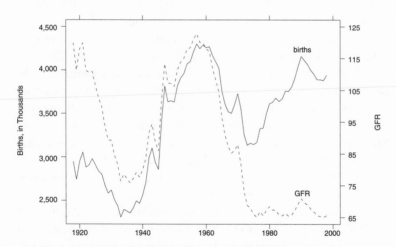

Figure 3.6. A comparison of the general fertility rate (GFR: number of births per 1,000 women of childbearing age) and absolute numbers of births in the United States, showing the increasing numbers since 1975 despite a constant GFR. Because of this divergence between absolute and relative numbers since 1975, we have now entered a "new era" in which absolute and relative measures of cohort size among young adults have diverged as well. Further study is required to determine which of these measures is most appropriate, especially in terms of aggregate demand effects in the economy.

absolute and relative measures have begun to diverge. Relative cohort size is projected to remain fairly constant over the next few decades, while the absolute size of the young adult population grows dramatically—as it did in the 1960s and early 1970s. I suspect that this divergence may have been a factor in generating the "new economy" in the late 1990s—but this hypothesis remains to be tested.

Relative Income: Interchangeable with Relative Cohort Size?

As the reader will quickly appreciate, defining a relative cohort size variable is child's play when compared with defining a relative income variable. Probably for this reason, and also because of data constraints, many researchers have used only relative cohort size variables in their analyses, rather than relative income variables— even in testing models of fertility.

However, it's important to note that relative income is hypothesized to be the relevant factor in demographic decisions—not relative cohort size. Individuals make demographic adjustments in order to improve their ex post relative income, rather than because of any concern over relative cohort size. While relative income may be a function of relative cohort size, it is not necessarily a function *only* of relative cohort size. Thus, studies that attempt to model variables like fertility directly as a function of relative cohort size, rather than relative income, may miss effects of other important variables.

Easterlin has stressed in all of his work on long swings that he saw relative cohort size effects operational (in the sense that they might be expected to produce relative income shifts) only in economies that are relatively closed to migration. Thus, in the United States prior to the mid-1920s he does not claim that relative cohort size shifts in the indigenous population would have led to relative income shifts: instead, migration flows would have acted to equilibrate the supply of and demand for labor.[16]

This is a consideration that's been largely overlooked in tests of the Easterlin hypothesis in the European context. To the extent that the EEC has caused a number of countries to be integrated as an economic unit and has encouraged flows of labor across international borders, relative income shifts would become increasingly dissociated from indigenous relative cohort size shifts. In addition, the relatively free use of "temporary" workers in European countries over the past two decades (and to some extent, perhaps, the flows of illegal immigrants into the United States, the international trade deficit there, or both) would have had a depressant effect on the earnings of young, unskilled workers—just at the time when their relative cohort size in the indigenous population was becoming more favorable.[17]

Another complicating factor during the period under analysis in this book is the Vietnam War. Because the military is composed largely of young men, any mobilization as extensive as the Vietnam War will have a dramatic effect on relative cohort size in the civilian labor force. In addition to this distortionary labor supply effect that must be taken into account in estimating the effects of relative cohort size on male relative income, there is also a demand effect as the war effort swells government expenditures.

For these reasons, it's highly doubtful that a relative cohort size measure could be expected adequately to proxy relative income over the past several decades in Europe or in the United States in studies of fertility and other demographic decisions.

Defining a Relative Income Variable: Wages, Earnings, or Income—and Whose?

A relative income variable is defined as the ratio of young adults' earning potential (the numerator) relative to parental income a few years earlier (the denominator). In defining earning potential of young adults, the attempt has been to focus on the ultimate aim of the full Easterlin model: to determine the demographic adjustments made by individuals in response to changes in relative income. Are individuals' decisions with regard to marriage, divorce, fertility, labor force participation, and investments in education influenced by the level of their own available resources relative to their material aspirations? The theory is that, in our gender-differentiated society, both males and females are affected by male relative income: when it is low, young men will be less willing to marry and have children, and they will attempt to take advantage of higher education as a way of reducing the gap between their potential labor market return and their aspirations, although their success will be tempered by the effect of their own enrollment rates on the college wage premium.

Young women, in turn, may see these young men as less attractive marriage prospects when male relative income is low, and thus opt for alternatives outside of marriage. But whether taking an active role (preferring and choosing a career over marriage) or a more passive role (finding themselves without a marriage partner, or with a partner whose earnings must be supplemented by their own labor market participation), they will invest in education at increased rates in anticipation of more intensive labor market participation than would otherwise have been the case.

There is thus a series of decisions to examine, and it is assumed in the analyses presented here that all decisions other than the young men's investment in higher education will be based on young men's "optimal" relative income—that is, the highest relative income they can achieve given parental income, market-determined wages for high school and college graduates, and college costs. This "optimal" relative income is estimated using the average for *all* unenrolled males in their first five years of work experience, regardless of education level. However, it is assumed that the most appropriate relative income figure when young men make their educational choices will be the average relative income of all unenrolled *high school graduates* in their first five years of work experience: their choice is between college enrollment and a career as a high school graduate.

It must be acknowledged that this assumption is problematic, however. A standard labor force participation equation contains controls for one's own wage and for the level of non-earned income, and in theory the equations for husband and wife should be symmetric, with the earned income of each partner treated as the non-earned income of the other. This formulation of the relative income model implicitly assumes a sequential rather than a simultaneous system, in which the male labor force participation (and educational) decision takes precedence over female participation: the woman is treated as a "secondary" worker. Although this is an unpalatable assumption, it does seem to reflect behavior on average during most, if not all, of the period under analysis here. One of the analyses described in chapter 7 does not rely on this assumption, however.[18] That study sets up a system in which the male and female participation decisions are assumed to be symmetric—each dependent in part on the choice of the other.

But should young adults' earning potential be measured using wages, earnings, or total income? Wages are calculated on an hourly basis, in order not to confound pay with hours or weeks worked, whereas earnings are the annual total remuneration for labor market participation during the year. And whereas wages and earnings are measures of "earned income," total income includes along with annual earnings, all "non-earned" income such as interest and dividends. Some would argue that the numerator of the male relative income figure should be the male wage rate, since any other figure will be affected not just by the market's willingness to pay, but also by young men's response to the wage rate: the extent of a young man's participation in the workforce.[19] However, it has been shown that not only wages are affected by relative cohort size: participation rates, employment rates, and hours and weeks worked are all adversely impacted by increases in relative cohort size,[20] so that the use of wages alone as opposed to earnings will severely understate the effects of relative cohort size.

In the analyses in this book it's assumed that any variation in hours and weeks worked will be more a function of changes in relative cohort size than of changes in work preferences of young men. The numerator of the male relative income measure is approximated using the real average annual earnings of all males no longer enrolled in school who are in their first five years of potential work experience.[21] Males in their first five years of potential work experience are used, rather than males within a specific age category, in order to incorporate the effects of changing education levels that are assumed to result from young males' attempts to improve their earnings relative to those of their parents. All males are used, rather than only males working full time, in order to incorporate the effects of cohort size on workers' hours and weeks worked. The average age of males in this group is about 21.1 in the early years, rising to 22.5 throughout the remainder of the period.

But the measure as described thus far does not adequately take into account the effects of changing relative cohort size on labor force participation rates and unemployment. Government surveys report earnings only for those who are actually working: what about those who are unable to find work, or those who, discouraged, have dropped out of the labor market altogether? One way of taking these marginal workers into account is by including in the earnings measure an indicator of the probability that an individual will have any earnings at all. For this probability the "activity rate" is an appropriate measure: the proportion of those no longer in school who are actually working. Thus the average earnings might be, say, $25,000, but if an individual has only an 85 percent chance of getting a job, his "expected earnings" are on average only $25,000 \times 0.85 = $21,250$. It is assumed that young adults' decisions will be influenced by changes in this measure of "expected" or "potential" male earnings.

Earnings Relative to What?

Material aspirations—the standard of living in one's parents' home when growing up: how is this concept best measured? The analyses presented here use the average real annual income of all families with at least one child under 18 and with a head (of either sex) aged 45–54. These families are assumed to be representative of families of the young men and women who are the focus of this study. The use of family income allows for changing trends in terms of average number of labor market participants per family.[22] In any given year young adults' material aspirations are assumed to be a function of this parental income five years earlier, when they were teens in their parents' homes.

Some have argued that this family income figure should be expressed in per capita terms, since family income of a given amount will provide a very different standard of living for a family of six than for a family of three. This implies, then, that some control for number of children, or number of persons, should be included in any test of the relative income concept. Presumably the effect of this variable would be positive; that is, relative income would increase as number of siblings increases, with a given level of parental family income (since this would reduce the per capita income in the denominator). But there could be another effect of this variable: it has been hypothesized that number of children might be significant because of intergenerational correlation in family size preferences. Some researchers suggest that this hypothesis is not substantiated by the data,[23] but to the extent that it applies, the correlation could be either positive or negative, so it could either enhance or counterbalance the effect of family size on per capita income. In analyses reported in a later chapter, it was found that a control for family size is not significant in a fertility equation,[24] and the analyses in appendices to chapter 4 demonstrate that adding family size controls has very little effect on the historic pattern of male relative income.

Measures of Male Relative Economic Status Used in This Book

Although the "best" measure of male relative economic status is considered to be "expected male relative income" as defined in this chapter, a few other measures appear in various parts of this book: In order to produce results that are comparable with those of more traditional labor market analyses, chapter 6 (like the papers it's based on) contains measures of "male relative wages"—that is, focusing just on unenrolled white civilian males working full time, full year, the average hourly wage of those in their first five years of work experience relative to the average hourly wage of those with 25–34 years of work experience. These are not "expected" wages in that they are not moving averages, nor are they multiplied by activity rates. As a compromise measure between the demands of the relative cohort size hypothesis and the need for some compatibility with standard labor economics analyses, chapter 5 (and the papers it's based on) makes use of "expected male relative earnings"—that is, expected annual earnings of unenrolled men with 1–5 years of experience relative to the contemporaneous expected annual earnings of unenrolled men with 25–34 years of experience. Chapter 8 (and the papers it's based on) uses two measures, one for young men and one for young women. Both use in the denominator the *unlagged* moving average of annual income in families with children, with head aged 45–54. This figure is not lagged because it's assumed that the young people (who are aged 17–18 and deciding whether to enroll in college) are still living in their parents' homes and are thus making a contemporaneous comparison. The numerator for women is a moving average of expected annual earnings of *all* unenrolled men in their first five years of work experience, assuming that young women assess what the earning potential of all young men will be after they have completed their chosen levels of education. For young men this numerator is restricted to the earnings of *high school graduates only*, assuming that they are assessing the earning potential they would enjoy in the absence of any college education.

Summary

The following measures have been selected as best representing the concepts in *Birth and Fortune* with regard to relative cohort size. Only the second of these (the lagged general fertility rate) was used in econometric analyses of cohort size effects on wages reported in chapters 5 and 6, however, because it is an "exogenous" measure. That is, current labor market conditions might have an effect on current age ratios by inducing inter- and intranational migration, with workers moving to areas with higher wages and lower unemployment. This is a confounding influence in attempts to measure the effect of age ratios on wages, so it's preferable to use a measure like the GFR that was determined twenty-some years earlier and thus cannot be construed to be affected by current labor market conditions.

1. Males aged 20–22 (to correspond with the average age of young men no longer enrolled in school, in their first five years of work experience) relative to males aged 45–49 (to correspond with the median and average age of fathers as calculated above). This is intended to be a precise measure incorporating the two age groups where labor market substitutability is expected to be lowest. A broader measure (for example, Easterlin's 15–29 relative to 30–64) would dilute any effects of imperfect substitutability. We know, for example, that workers nearing retirement are often fairly good substitutes for younger workers. But by the same token, what is the labor market relationship between 20–24 year olds and those 25–29, or 30–34: are they substitutes or complements, on average? A narrower, more precise measure of relative cohort size avoids such problems.

2. The average of the general fertility rate that occurred twenty, twenty-one, and twenty-two years prior to the date under analysis (i.e., a three-year moving average centered on a period twenty-one years earlier). For econometric analyses, this measure is a useful proxy for the 20–22/45–49 age ratio. It provides a method of forecasting conditions at labor market entry twenty-some years in advance, and can be thought of as an exogenous measure, as explained above.

It is important to bear in mind, however, that further work is required to determine the potentially differential effects of absolute and relative cohort size. These two effects are difficult to disentangle, since trends in the two types of measure have been so similar during the period under analysis. Particularly in terms of aggregate demand effects of cohort size, it may be that producer and investor expectations are sensitive to changes in absolute numbers of young adults. If so, additional research is urgently required given the current divergence of these measures: would it be better in some cases to use lagged numbers of births, rather than lagged fertility rates?

The measure of male relative income used in the studies here, for testing effects on fertility, marriage and divorce, educational decisions, and female labor force participation, is composed of a numerator—the young adults' own potential earnings—and a denominator—the proxy for their material aspirations. As numerator, the studies reported in chapters 7, 9, and 11 use the real average annual earnings of all males no longer enrolled in school who are in their first five years of potential work experience, multiplied by their probability of working. The denominator uses the average real annual income of all families with at least one child under 18 and with a head (of either sex) aged 45–54. The next chapter illustrates trends in this measure over the past thirty-five years for various subgroups of young men.

PART 2

First-Order Effects of Changing Relative Cohort Size

4

Patterns of Male Relative Income over the Years

The boom generation now faced the prospect that it had been almost as damaged by its passage into the world of work as the generation of 1930 was by the Depression.

Landon Jones, *Great Expectations: America and the Baby Boom Generation* (1980)

How has the earning potential of young men in the United States fared relative to their fathers' earnings and their parents' total income? The short answer is, Not very well at all! The trends in expected male relative income for white and African American young men are illustrated in figure 4.1.[1] This graph depicts what will be referred to as "expected male relative income": expected annual earnings (a five-year moving average of annual earnings multiplied by the young men's probability of actually working) of all unenrolled males in their first five years of work experience relative to a five-year moving average of the annual income, five years earlier, of all families with children and with a head aged 45–54. The measure is termed "expected" in the sense that actual average earnings have been multiplied by the young men's probability of working—of finding a job at all. This probability has been strongly affected by relative cohort size, as well.

Although the magnitude of the change in relative income differs, there have been strong underlying similarities among groups over the past three decades: a virtually continuous fall from 1970 to 1985,

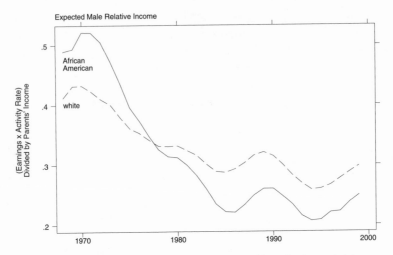

Figure 4.1. Expected male relative income, by race. (See table 4.1 for data underlying these graphs and Macunovich 2002 for corresponding graphs by education level.) Source: author's tabulations of data from the March Current Population Survey public-use tapes.

with a rally between 1985 and 1989, followed by another dip from 1990 through 1994 and then another rally.

Consider the case of a young African American college graduate in his first five years of work experience. Under Easterlin's hypothesis, he would evaluate his current earnings in terms of a standard of living set in his parents' home five years earlier. Thus, for example, in 1970 he would have compared his 1970 earning potential with the total income in his parents' home in 1965 or his father's earnings in 1965 (with 25–34 years of work experience), or both.

In 1970 the first of these comparisons produced a ratio of 1.13: on average his annual earnings would have been 13 percent greater than his parents' entire family income just five years earlier! (Appendix B presents these data.) But this ratio declined by nearly 50 percent between 1970 and 1985, to only 0.6. If his father was a college graduate, as well, and his comparison was with his father's earnings, he wouldn't have felt any better: that ratio dropped from nearly 1.0 in 1972 to only 0.5 in 1984 (not shown).

Lest this college graduate feel sorry for himself, though, he should compare his situation to that of young African Americans with only a high school diploma: their relative earning potential fell from nearly 0.6 in 1970 to less than 0.2 in 1985: a drop of nearly 70 percent. Or to young African Americans without a high school degree: theirs declined by a phenomenal 82 percent during that period, from a 1970 "high" of only 0.33. On average, young African American men experienced a drop of nearly 60 percent in their relative earning potential between 1970 and 1985.

The experience of young white college graduates wasn't as dramatic, although they still lost a lot of ground: they started out able to reproduce about 70 percent of their parents' living standard, and by 1985 this had declined to about 50 percent. The relative income of the average young white male slipped from a level of over 43 percent in 1970 to only 29 percent in 1985.

A common feature of all of these ratios is the contrast between African American and white, with the former nearly always exhibiting higher highs in 1970 and lower lows in 1985 and 1994. No one was spared: this pattern is exhibited within all education groups and can be shown to have occurred within all income quintiles as well.

The underlying pattern that's so clear in figure 4.1 emerges regardless of the method used to define relative economic status. We find it whether we compare the annual earnings of young men to the income of older families, or to the average annual earnings of men their fathers' age—or compare the hourly wages in the older and younger groups. And it is not an artifact of the five-year lag between numerator and denominator, as some have suggested. The pattern is also impervious to a change from expected averages (those multiplied by activity rates) to simple observed ones, and it remains even after controlling in various ways for changing average family size.[2] On average, regardless of the measure used, young people experienced a decline of 30–40 percent in their own earning potential relative to various measures of their "material aspirations"—and the declines for African Americans were 50 percent larger than those for white Americans.

It's unfortunate that the data only permit calculations of male relative income going back to the late 1960s—but in a separate analysis a coauthor and I prepared estimates based on aggregate data going back into the 1950s.[3] These data suggest that male relative income—calculated in that analysis as the ratio of the earnings of all young men aged 20–24 relative to those of men aged 46–50—was as high as 1.10 in the mid-1950s but then dropped, in a pattern very

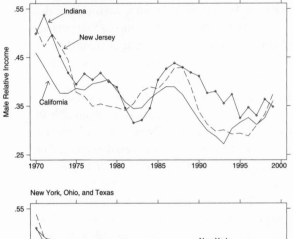

Figure 4.2. Expected male relative income (defined and derived as in chapter 3) for males of all races and education levels, showing variation for selected states. There are strong similarities, but also significant differences in the patterns, which can be exploited in statistical analyses.

similar to that shown in figure 4.1, to about 0.75 by the mid-1980s, with the same "humped" pattern of recovery thereafter.

Yet, despite the strong overall similarity among the trends in all groups, there have been important variations—for example, in the strength of the rebound in relative income in the late 1980s: the characteristic "hump." These variations appear at the state and regional levels, as well as among all racial and education groups, as illustrated in figure 4.2, and provide a statistical basis for carrying out fairly disaggregated tests of the relative income hypothesis, as will be demonstrated in chapters 9 (marriage and divorce) and 11 (fertility). Figure 4.2 uses data from California, New York, New Jersey, Texas, Indiana, and Ohio to illustrate the regional variations that have occurred in trends despite the fact that levels of male relative income have been fairly similar across states, as have the percentage declines between 1970 and 1985.

The following chapters show that the historic pattern exhibited in all these measures of relative economic status, which appears to reflect the rate of change in cohort size as displayed in figure 3.5, is in turn mirrored in many types of behavioral data, such as marriage and fertility rates, suggesting a strong linkage between male relative income and those types of behavioral decisions.

5

First-Order Effects of Relative Cohort Size

Long-term Trends in Unemployment, Relative Income, and Returns to College

[T]hese differences in returns to skill can largely be explained by differences in supply shifts.

Peter Gottschalk and Mary Joyce, "Cross-National Differences in the Rise in Earnings Inequality" (1998)

To what extent are the patterns of male relative income (RY) presented in the previous chapter a function of changing relative cohort size (RCS)?[1] The relationship between relative cohort size and relative income is a central element in the relative cohort size hypothesis. Male relative income is hypothesized to be the mechanism that transmits relative cohort size effects to demographic factors such as marriage, divorce, fertility, and female labor force participation rates. Thus, if the RCS:RY relationship doesn't hold, then obviously the hypothesized relationship between RCS and all of those demographic factors doesn't hold, either. As a result, my first focus in this book is on testing that RCS:RY relationship. Because the concept of male relative income deals with the relationship between the wages of fathers and sons, this chapter uses aggregate data to look at the effects of changing relative cohort size on the earning potential of younger men, relative to that of older men; chapter 6 places those effects in the context of relative cohort size effects on the entire wage structure, using detailed microlevel data for all age groups.

Econometric analyses of the wage structure in the United States always tend to focus on the period since the early 1960s, because it wasn't until then that the detailed microdata necessary for conducting such analyses became available. It is tantalizing to speculate about the extent of any relative cohort size effects prior to that time, but virtually impossible to construct precise measures encompassing the 1950s. Easterlin demonstrated graphically an apparently close (inverse) relationship between relative cohort size and male relative income during this period that suggests a considerable decline in relative income between the 1950s and the mid-1960s, when the analyses described here take up the story. Similarly, independent estimates a coauthor and I prepared using aggregate wage data suggest a drop of some 15 percent prior to the period covered by the analyses reported in this chapter.[2]

Relative Cohort Size and Inequality

But why should relative cohort size affect male relative income? Because, as stated in earlier chapters, researchers have found (perhaps not surprisingly) that younger workers are not good substitutes for more experienced, older workers, so when their ranks swell relative to those of older workers, their wages will tend to be depressed, in relative terms—a simple supply and demand story, with younger and older workers as complements in the labor market.

Labor economists began to examine this effect of changing relative cohort size in the late 1970s. The most widely cited of these studies, by Finis Welch in 1979, estimated that the entry-level wage relative to that of peak earners was depressed as much as 13 percent by the increase in relative cohort size just between 1967 and 1975. Both that study and another well-known one identified a further aspect of such cohort size effects: large relative cohort size will tend to depress the relative wages of young college graduates more than those of workers with less than a college education, since substitutability between older and younger workers declines with increasing levels of education.[3] That is, it is even more difficult to replace an experienced with an inexperienced college graduate than it is to replace an experienced with an inexperienced high school graduate.

These early results, based on data only through the mid-1970s, suggested that despite the depressing effect of relative cohort size on early wages, wage growth for large cohorts would improve rapidly with increasing levels of experience, allowing them to "catch up" to more normal cohorts as they aged. In addition, these early studies suggested that the advent of smaller cohorts in the 1980s promised a recovery even in entry-level wages. "Our projections for 1990 entrants foresee career earnings equal to those of the 'most favored' entrants of the mid-1950s and early 1960s."[4]

This was a common refrain among analysts during the period: they thought that prospects for the 1980s and 1990s looked rosy—not only for the smaller cohorts entering the labor market in the 1980s, but even for the baby boomers as they aged. A later set of analyses agreed that the 1980s looked bright for the small cohorts born in the 1960s, but predicted that the negative effects of large cohort size would follow baby boomers throughout their careers.[5] One of those studies pointed out that a specification error in earlier work appeared to have led to an erroneous conclusion regarding later career wage growth for the baby boomers.

Several studies in the late 1980s, however, again seemed to indicate that baby boomers would catch up as they aged, so that overall career wage effects of cohort size would be small.[6] But even more important, by this time sufficient data were available for the 1980s to make it apparent that none of the rosy predictions based on cohort size had materialized. The assumption had been that since the size of new cohorts entering the labor market began to fall sharply in the 1980s, the wage effects of cohort size should begin to be positive in that decade—but since wages continued to stagnate, and inequality to grow, something much bigger than cohort size was assumed to be at work, obliterating any positive effects of declining cohort size.

Thus the late 1980s brought in an era in which cohort size effects began to be dismissed as relatively unimportant. One regional analysis of inequality that controlled for "the share of the state's workforce aged 18 to 24 . . . to measure the effect of the changing demographic composition of the labor force," found the effects of this variable "small and insignificant."[7] And another is typical of this literature in dismissing cohort size effects: "That the inequality trends continue despite the baby boomers' entry into middle age and the decline in the labor force growth rate due to the baby-bust generation does not comport well with the demographic hypothesis."[8]

But are we in danger of throwing out the baby with the bath water? What if those models of age structure effects were mis-specified and created unrealistic expectations for the 1980s based on these mis-estimates? The results presented in this analysis are put forward in support of that hypothesis. They suggest that we should take into consideration potential aggregate *demand* as well as supply effects of cohort size and allow for asymmetries in aggregate supply effects. When we do, we find a very different picture of the relative importance of cohort size effects over the past thirty-five years.

Reexamining the Theory of Relative Cohort Size Effects

A majority of the studies over the past twenty years that have attempted to measure cohort size effects—and virtually all of the most widely cited of these studies—have had two features in common. First, they assumed that cohort size effects would be symmetrical about the peak of the baby boom. That is, members of the baby boom born prior to the peak in 1957–1959 were assumed to have experienced the same effects of cohort size as individuals born after the peak, *ceteris paribus*, as long as their measures of relative cohort size were the same. It was this assumption of symmetry that led researchers to expect labor market conditions for baby boomers—to the extent that those conditions were a function of cohort size— would begin to improve immediately after 1980, because relative cohort size measures would begin to decline for labor market entrants at that time.

Second, they examined these (assumed symmetrical) cohort size effects on the relative wages of older and younger workers only within education groups, and using labor force counts as measures of cohort size. That is, for example, among college graduates they counted the number of labor force participants with one year of experience relative to the total number of college graduates in the entire labor force. But this approach tends to underestimate the full effects of relative cohort size. Why? Because the amount of education an individual receives, and his chances of finding a job—or being able to work full time if he wishes—are affected by relative cohort size, in the same way that relative wages are affected. Completed education is affected by cohort size because cohort size adversely impacts the return to education (since the relative wages of young college grads are depressed more than those of young high school grads).

Young men in a relatively large cohort see that they won't gain much by going to college (remember the reports of baby boomer college grads resorting to driving taxis?), so fewer choose to make that investment. Thus if we look only at the effect of relative cohort size on the wages of inexperienced relative to experienced *college grads,* we miss the fact that many who in a smaller cohort *would* have been earning college wages are instead earning only high school grad wages—or are perhaps even unemployed, or involuntarily working less than forty hours per week. That comparison (of inexperienced to experienced college grads) doesn't show us the full effect that relative cohort size has had on individuals.

This problem of underestimation has been recognized by a few researchers,[9] but in general, studies have all followed the lead of Welch's 1979 analysis, which examined only these very specific effects within education groups. Most of the succeeding studies used variables formulated under Welch's methodology, often even using his data.

The basic premise underlying the results presented here is that one must estimate the *full* effects of relative cohort size—including those on wages, on educational attainment, and on hours and weeks worked—and that relative cohort *size* alone will not be sufficient to predict these effects. It is hypothesized that a cohort's *position* relative to peaks and troughs is also important—that the effects of cohort size are not symmetric about the peak of the baby boom.[10] It is hypothesized that those who tended to fare worst as a result of large cohort size were those born on the "trailing edge" of the boom (1959 and after): these young people entered a labor market already congested with previous baby boom entrants, and so took longer to establish themselves in a career trajectory.

Demand Effects of the Baby Boomers

In addition, as explained in a later chapter, researchers have begun to identify strong effects of the age structure of the population on a number of variables at the macro level, including real interest rates, inflation, income, and unemployment;[11] on housing investment;[12] and on consumption, money demand, and housing investment.[13] Analyses have found a higher level of consumption relative to income among those in the younger age groups, and thus higher levels of consumption relative to income in the aggregate when the population contains a larger proportion of young adults. Growth in consumption spurs investment (as long as capital is available) and leads to overall higher growth rates in the economy. These same effects are found in the analysis described in chapter 13.

This suggests another reason for asymmetry in the effect of cohort size: those on the "leading edge" of the boom will benefit from the positive effects of an expanding economy, while those on the trailing edge will enter the market following the economic dislocations caused by a change from high to low rates of growth in personal consumption expenditures, related to their own smaller cohort size. Since young and unskilled workers tend to be the hardest hit by cyclic effects ("last hired, first fired"), this differential aggregate demand effect could be significant on the relative earnings and income of younger and less skilled workers. This will depress the relative wages of cohorts on the trailing edge even more than those of same-sized cohorts on the leading edge—and the effect will be worse for unskilled workers, especially those without a college education.

Effects of the Military on Relative Wages

In addition to cohort size effects, one must take into consideration the effects of the military on young men's labor market outcomes. One researcher, for example, has pointed to dramatic changes in the size and composition of the military as having a potential effect on youth labor markets.[14] He estimated that "over half the rise in the civilian labor force for young men during the 1970s can be traced not to the baby boom but to the military 'bust.'" His figures show that while nearly 30 percent of youth aged 18–24 were in the military in the 1950s, that figure dropped to 15 percent before the Vietnam War, and then increased to 20 percent before declining below 8 percent.

In the results presented here, it's assumed that the proportion of the active military aged 20–24 will have two effects on the relative income and earnings of young males. On the one hand, there will be an aggregate supply effect resulting from the removal of young males from the civilian labor market, which is expected to have a positive effect on the relative wages of young civilian males. On the other hand, there will be an aggregate demand effect created whenever the level of military expenditures changes. The effect of this second factor on young males' relative wages depends on the extent to which there are distributional effects of such changes in aggregate demand. That is, do military expenditures in the civilian economy create a greater demand for experienced or for inexperienced workers? If one group is favored over another, its relative wages will tend to rise.

Because changes in the size of the active military are normally accomplished by hiring more young men, we can use changes in the proportion of the military aged 20–24 as a proxy for changes in the level of military expenditures.[15] Historically, the proportion of the active military represented by those aged 20–24 increased dramatically during the Korean and Vietnam Wars—tripling during the Korean War in the 1950s, when nearly one-third of young men were in the military, and doubling during the Vietnam War, when about one-fifth of young men were in the military.

Effect of International Trade

Finally, the per capita levels of real durable exports and imports were included in the studies reported in this and the next chapter, under the assumption that there may be distributional effects of imports and exports in the economy. Again, "distributional" in this sense refers to the fact that different types of product may require (in the case of exports) or replace (in the case of imports) different types of workers. If these effects are not spread evenly across all types of workers, then the wages of some workers may be affected more than those of other workers. Some of the stronger advocates of this hypothesis suggest that at least until the end of the 1980s the long-run trend of the skill premium—the ratio of wages of college graduates relative to the wages of those with less than a college education—has been largely a function of net durable goods imports.[16]

Although several analysts have questioned this relationship between globalization and the skill premium, the question is left open with regard to the overall effect when comparing the earnings of younger and older men. The combination of skill and experience effects could be much larger than the skill effect alone. The assumption in this study, therefore, is that imports may disproportionately affect the labor market outcomes of unskilled young males, since the types of goods imported are more likely to compete with products requiring less-skilled workers. Exports may also have distributional effects, particularly to the extent that they are composed of high tech goods and services provided by college educated workers, where young workers are disproportionately represented.

We will see that trade effects appear to have operated strongly, along with cohort effects, on the college wage premium over the last three decades, but that the effects of trade appear to have been much less—although still measurably significant—on male relative income.

Male Relative Wage versus Male Relative Income

A minor complication is introduced into the analysis by the fact that the primary interest in this book is to explain male relative income, whereas standard labor market analyses focus on male relative wages or male relative earnings. The three concepts are summarized in table 5.1, and additional data available online (Macunovich 2002) demonstrate the strong similarities in their patterns over time.

Because male relative income is supposed to describe the earning potential of young men relative to their aspirations, it's necessary to look at *annual* figures that incorporate not only hourly wages, but also hours and weeks worked and unemployment. That earning potential must be compared with the standard of living the young men enjoyed in their parents' homes, which is assumed to be directly related to total annual income from all sources in those homes *in the recent past,* when the young men were still living with their parents. That annual income will reflect, in addition to older men's earnings, changing levels of female labor force participation as well as any non-labor income in the parental household, such as dividends and interest on savings. But standard labor market analyses focus just on the hourly wage structure in the economy: the average hourly wages of young versus old and skilled versus unskilled workers, at the same point in time—or their annual earnings at the same point in time.

Researchers focus on contemporaneous hourly wages because standard theories are most applicable there: differential effects of

Table 5.1 Defining Various Measures of Male Relative Economic Status

	Numerator	Denominator	Denominator Lagged?
Male relative income	expected* average annual earnings of young men	average annual income of middle-aged families	yes
Male relative wage	average hourly wage of young men	average hourly wage of prime-age men	no
Male relative earnings	expected* average annual earnings of young men	annual earnings of prime-age men	no

*Where "expected" earnings are the earnings multiplied by the activity rate (the number employed divided by the total non-enrolled population in a particular group): the probability that a young man will find employment in order to enjoy those average earnings.

changing demand for and supply of labor in year t will be reflected in the wage structure in year t: the pattern of wages paid to workers with different levels of skill and experience. These changes in the wage structure are the basic reason for changes in measures of male relative income: if changes in the overall wage structure can be explained using cohort size effects then, indirectly, most of the changes in male relative income will be explained as well.

Probably the best "compromise" between the standard labor market analyses of contemporaneous hourly wages and the concept of male relative income presented in chapters 2–4 is that of male relative earnings: this measure includes, along with hourly wages, the additional elements of hours and weeks worked and probability of being employed—but the comparison is between younger and older men. This chapter focuses on the analysis of male relative earnings, examining the implications for male relative income and leaving the more standard type of labor market analysis for the next chapter.

Effects of Relative Cohort Size at the Aggregate Level

The models I have developed, based on just three elements—relative cohort size and position; the level and rate of change in young men's share of the total military; and the level of durable goods imports and exports—perform very well in explaining the historic patterns of male relative earnings (the return to experience), the college wage premium (the return to skill: the ratio of college graduates' wages to those of high school graduates), and unemployment rates.[17] They explain over 97 percent of the longer-term variation in male relative earnings over the 1964–1996 period, 82 percent of the longer-term variation in the general male unemployment rate over the 1953–1996 period, and over 97 percent (85 percent) of the total variation in men's (women's) return to a college education over the 1964–1996 period. (Estimation periods differ among the models due to problems of data availability.) These results are displayed in figure 5.1 (for the unemployment rate and returns to college education) and figure 5.2 (for male relative earnings and income), which present the actual trends in each of the variables, together with the "fitted" values—those obtained using econometric models. It is immediately apparent that the models fit the actual values extremely well.

Male and Female Returns to a College Education

The top and middle panels of figure 5.1 present the college wage premium: the percentage by which the hourly wage earned by an individual with a college education exceeds that of someone who completed high school only. There have been dramatic changes in this measure over the past thirty-five years, with the premium first de-

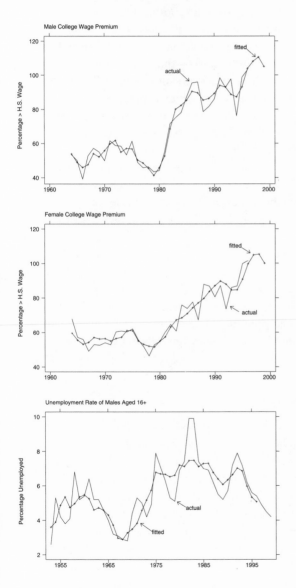

Figure 5.1. Actual and fitted values for male and female returns to college education and the male unemployment rate, using the general fertility rate twenty-one years earlier as the measure of relative cohort size. The fitted values demonstrate the ability of models presented in Macunovich 2002 to explain historic trends in these variables.

clining from about 60 percent to 45 percent between 1965 and 1980, and then more than doubling in size, to over 100 percent. That is, college graduates now earn on average twice what high school graduates do.

The model explains these patterns in the data very well: it accounts for over 97 percent of the variation in the male college wage premium and over 85 percent of the variation in the female college wage premium over the last three decades. Both cohort size and cohort position exert a negative effect. That is, large cohorts appear to receive a lower wage premium than small cohorts, and this negative effect is stronger for leading-edge cohorts—those born before 1959.

For young men, the military exerts a positive effect: this could be because strong military recruitment while a cohort is in college raises the "opportunity cost" of education.[18] Any increase in potential wages or benefits offered by the military raises the opportunity cost of college and might tip the balance for young men who are not overly committed to the idea of a college education. In general, those with a weak commitment to college will be those with lower academic standing; as these more marginal students opt out of college, the overall quality of the remaining pool of college graduates increases.

Net per capita durable imports exert a positive effect (since they tend to substitute more for high school graduates than for college graduates, and thus bring down the wages of high school graduates more than those of college graduates), and exports exert a negative effect on the college wage premium. These effects of international trade are highly significant for young men, but only marginally so for young women.

The General Unemployment Rate

The bottom panel of figure 5.1 illustrates the historic pattern of male unemployment in the United States as it nearly tripled between 1955 and 1985 and then began its remarkable decline to the current level of about 4 percent. Commentators are fond of pointing out that this is a level not seen in thirty years—no surprise to anyone who believes in relative cohort size effects. It is apparent in figure 5.1 that the model, which incorporates the three elements set out in the previous section (international trade and relative cohort size in the population and in the military), explains the longer-term trends in unemployment over the last fifty years. Peaks and troughs around that longer-term trend, not reproduced by the model, correspond to short-term business cycles. The values that the model generated explain over 50 percent of the total variation and over 80 percent of the long-term variation (i.e., the variation in a five-year moving average) of the male unemployment rate over the last forty-five years.

Relative cohort size was found to raise male unemployment, but as hypothesized this effect was less for leading-edge cohorts than for those on the trailing edge. In addition, the size of the military has a significant negative effect on male unemployment because of reductions in the supply of civilian workers. Notably, the effect of international trade was not significant in the model. This is probably because imports are often used in the production process, so the level of imports tends to increase when economic activity increases. Thus the increases in unemployment that isolationists have attributed to international trade have in fact been the result of changes in relative cohort size. A simulation presented later in this chapter illustrates the magnitude of the effect of relative cohort size on unemployment, and results not presented here demonstrate that the effects of relative cohort size on young people aged 16–19 are even stronger and more significant than those on the labor force generally.

Results for Male Relative Earnings

As hypothesized, an augmented relative cohort size model fits the data on expected male relative earnings very well, explaining 98 percent of the longer-term variation in male relative earnings. This can be seen in the close match between actual values and the model results as demonstrated in the panel on the left in figure 5.2. The model fits the data so well that based only on data through 1988, it is able to "predict" what actually happened to male relative earnings in the ensuing nine years, as presented in figure 5.2. This is particularly notable at the "turning points," when relative earnings declined around 1990 and then recovered again around 1995: these were accurately predicted by the model.

These model results indicate that male relative earnings will indeed be lower when relative cohort size is large, but that as hypothesized this effect is somewhat less on the leading edge of the baby boom than on the trailing edge. This is consistent with the hypothesis that the strong economy generated by the entry of the baby boom

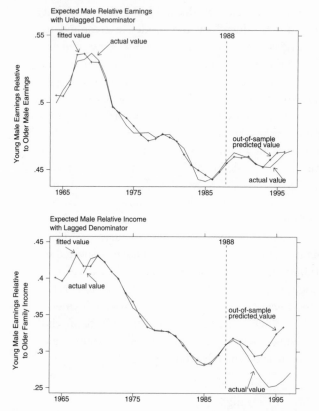

Figure 5.2. Actual, fitted, and projected values for expected male relative earnings and expected male relative income (for definitions, see table 5.1) using the model results available in Macunovich 2002. The model was fitted using data from 1964–1988 and then used to predict values from 1988 onward. Also see Macunovich 2002 regarding changes in CPS data post-1988 that probably account for discrepancies between actual and projected male relative income in the bottom panel.

into the young adult years actually buffered early baby boom cohorts from the full effects of their large cohort size.

The model suggests that military build-ups have a beneficial effect on male relative earnings, as hypothesized. Large international trade deficits are estimated to depress relative earnings, because of a negative effect of per capita durable goods imports. However, the strong positive effects of exports on relative earnings are estimated to far outweigh the negative effect of imports.

The bottom panel of figure 5.2 presents actual and fitted values for male relative income: the model explains over 99 percent of the variation through 1988, but "predictions" after 1992 appear to overshoot actual values during the later period. A good deal of this discrepancy is likely due to discontinuities in the income data provided by the Bureau of Labor Statistics. In 1989 and again in 1993/94, the Bureau introduced changes in their methods of collecting and reporting data that tended to reduce estimates of young men's earnings while increasing estimates of total income in older families.[19] Independent estimates of male relative earnings (using a lagged denominator) based on aggregate wage data from 1952–1996 suggest that the "predicted" values on the right in figure 5.2 are in fact the correct ones.[20] They show the ratio of the earnings of men aged 20–24 relative to those of men aged 46–50 falling by about 35 percent between the 1950s and the early 1980s, and then rising more than 25 percent by 1996, in a hump-shaped pattern like that shown in figure 5.2.

Simulations: What Might Have Been—and What Might Come to Be

In order to see the strength of the effect of relative cohort size and position, I prepared simulations for each of the four measures examined in this chapter—expected male relative income, the unemployment rate, and male and female college wage premia—in which both the military and trade variables are held constant at their 1980 levels. These simulations demonstrate the "pure" effects of relative cohort size: what would have happened to each of these measures over the past thirty-five years if nothing had changed except relative cohort size. Figure 5.3 demonstrates that the effects of changing relative cohort size correspond in general terms to those hypothesized by researchers back in the 1970s. The solid lines on the graphs in figure 5.3 show the paths of the variables as they would have been if nothing other than relative cohort size had changed. The lighter lines on the graphs show what actually happened, given the added effects of factors other than relative cohort size.

The bottom panel of figure 5.3 shows that the depressing effects of increasing relative cohort size began operating on male relative income at least as early as 1965. But a comparison of simulated and actual values shows that the Vietnam War countered this strong negative effect in the late 1960s: those young men lucky enough to remain in the civilian labor force during that period fared very well.

The strong downward pressure of relative cohort size ended not in 1980, as assumed generally by researchers, but rather in the later 1980s, because of dislocations in the economy caused by slowing and then negative growth in cohort size: the demand effects of relative cohort size. The respite in the late 1980s was short-lived, however. Another decline occurred in the early 1990s, also caused by cohort

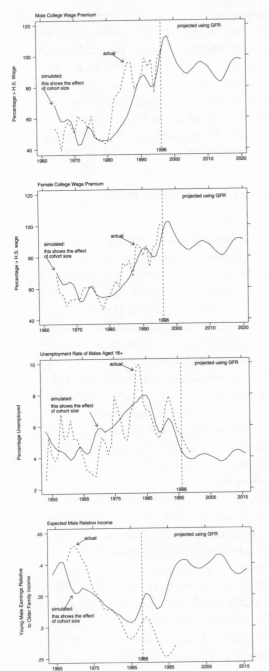

Figure 5.3. Simulations depicting the underlying patterns of returns to college, male unemployment, and male relative income due to changing relative cohort size. In each case, the simulation depicts the pattern that would occur if all variables other than relative cohort size remained fixed at their 1980 levels.

size effects. Relatively sharp fluctuations in relative cohort size occurred during this period because of a "mini baby boom" that occurred during the Vietnam War, when deferments were granted to men with children. They can be seen clearly in the cohort size measures presented in chapter 3 (see figure 3.5), which appear to be directly related to the "hump" in male relative income in the late 1980s and early 1990s. Relative cohort size effects have tended to boost male relative income since about 1993, however. During the next decade, in the absence of other effects, relative cohort size should take relative income back up to levels not seen since the 1960s.

The third panel of figure 5.3 presents a simulation for the unemployment rate: the pattern that would have occurred if only relative cohort size had changed during the study period. Emerging very clearly in the solid, simulated curve is the strong effect of relative cohort size effects alone on the unemployment pattern, which rose steeply (doubled, in fact) through the 1970s and then began to decline in the late 1980s. Even in earlier analyses, when I prepared this simulation using data only through 1993, the model accurately predicted the steeply declining unemployment rates experienced during the remainder of the 1990s, as declining relative cohort size took us back to levels not seen since the early 1960s.

The two upper panels of figure 5.3 show the patterns that the male and female college wage premia would have followed over the last three decades if all factors other than relative cohort size had remained constant at their 1980 levels. Cohort measures have had a dramatic effect on this variable throughout the period. They exerted sufficient force to reduce the college wage premium for both men and women by over 30 percent during the 1960s and 1970s and to raise it from a 1980s low of about 50 percent to over 100 percent in the late 1990s.

Summary

The analyses presented in this chapter demonstrate that a model based on just three measures—relative cohort size, relative military size, and international trade—can explain a substantial proportion of the longer-term variations over the last thirty or more years in the earnings of young men relative to those of older men, the unemployment rate of males aged 16+, and the college wage premium enjoyed by both men and women.

Even more important, these analyses have established that relative cohort size and position—as measured by a simple variable like the general fertility rate observed twenty years earlier—are the dominant factors in determining the variations in these economic variables. This finding would have generated little controversy twenty years ago: researchers at that time were deeply involved in measuring and explaining these effects. But in the intervening years, as more data became available for the early 1980s, researchers commonly dismissed or downplayed cohort size effects: these effects were assumed to have been important only through the 1970s.

The results presented here constitute strong evidence that cohort size effects have in fact been the most important factor in determining the labor market outcomes of young men and women and are showing signs of exerting strong positive forces over the next few decades. The pattern of cohort size effects on male relative income and on the college wage premium for men and women, as identified in analyses described here, exhibit a pronounced U shape just as researchers predicted twenty years ago, but the upswing of that U begins not in 1980, when it was expected, but in the later 1980s. The work presented here suggests that this difference in expected and actual turning points was due to the fact that cohort size effects are not symmetric about the peak of the baby boom. When this asymmetry is taken into account, it is possible to explain the strange pattern of ups and downs observed in these economic variables over the past decade.

The great beauty of a model whose dominant factor is the lagged general fertility rate is the opportunity it provides for looking forward and making some prognostications about the future paths of these economic variables. Simulations prepared using a model estimated on data only through 1988 accurately predicted the upswing in male relative earnings experienced since that time, as well as the sharp decline in unemployment rates. The indication from these models is that—holding other factors constant—we can expect a continuation of these beneficial trends over the next decade. These results suggest that much of the stagnation and growing inequality observed in the labor market over the past twenty-five years did not represent a secular trend doomed to continue in the future, but rather one more manifestation of the post-WWII baby boom.

Effects of Relative Cohort Size on Inequality
and the Overall Structure of Wages

> The income of low-wage workers finally is rising and wage inequality has
> slightly declined. This surprising turn of events is forcing economists and
> policymakers to reopen the debate about why income distribution in Amer-
> ica, which once prided itself on being a middle-class society, has evolved
> over the last twenty years into the most unequal in the industrialized
> world. . . . [E]vents of the past eighteen months have raised new doubts
> about the conventional wisdom. Workers on the bottom half of the wage
> ladder, including those with minimal skills, have seen real gains for the first
> time in a generation. If a lack of education and skills held them back before,
> what's causing their wages to rise now?
> — Merrill Goozner, "Gains by Low-Wage Workers Raise Eyebrows" (1998)

The previous chapter looked at the RCS:RY (relative cohort
size:relative income) relationship among just the youngest workers, using summary measures of relative income and earnings at the
aggregate level. It examined the average wage of all entry-level workers relative to that of all prime-age workers, given the size of the entry-level cohort relative to the size of the prime-age cohort for whom
it is assumed to be least "substitutable." This is the element of relative cohort size most relevant to the "second-order effects" that will
be discussed in subsequent chapters: behavioral changes in things
like marriage, divorce, fertility, juvenile crime rates, and the labor
force participation of younger women.

It was assumed in the analysis in chapter 5 that if the RCS:RY relationship didn't show up at the aggregate (national) level, then even

if it exists at more disaggregated levels it must not be very important. But there's a downside to the more intuitive aggregate analysis in chapter 5: social scientists are often not satisfied with findings based on such aggregated data—especially when the data consist of annual observations just since 1960. For various technical reasons relationships that appear at this aggregate level might be "spurious" rather than real or causal. Findings are much more believable if they can also be demonstrated to exist among subgroups and individuals in more disaggregated data, where there is a great deal more variation in behavior. Thus a more stringent test of the RCS:RY relationship demonstrated in chapter 5 would be based on such disaggregated "microlevel" data.

In addition, the findings reported in chapter 5 have much wider implications. They raise questions about potential cohort size effects that might account for wage differences throughout the labor force, among workers at all levels of experience. Do cohort size effects follow workers throughout their career: do large cohorts never escape their fate? Or can that longer-term fate be affected by what else is happening in the age structure of the population? In other words, for example, is it better to be a large prime-age cohort when entry-level cohorts are small, or when they're large? And, given the huge variations in the size of entry-level cohorts that we've experienced over the past thirty-five years, is it possible that cohort size might account for the disturbing changes in income inequality that have also occurred?

It's ironic that if these cohort size effects do reverberate throughout the labor force, affecting workers at all levels of experience, then individuals actually influence their own fate in the labor market through their fertility decisions early in life: the child you have at age 25 becomes the new entry-level cohort when you're 45. If there are positive effects of the size of entry-level cohorts, an attempt to improve one's economic status when young by reducing or postponing fertility might backfire later in life.

Past Trends in Income Inequality

Although a search of the economics literature over the past fifteen years would turn up little in terms of "male relative income," it would produce volumes on the more general issue of "rising income inequality." Between 1968 and 1994, income inequality in the United States increased 22.4 percent—more than wiping out the 7.4 percent improvement that had occurred in the 1950s and 1960s.[1] Analysts tend to trace a large proportion of this change in family and household income inequality to increasing inequality in male earnings.[2] While the average wage in the bottom quintile[3] increased 20 to 30 percent relative to the top quintile in each of the three decades prior to 1970, it grew only 5 percent in relative terms in the 1970s and actually declined 8 percent in the 1980s. It is true that the rich have been getting richer and the poor, poorer.

This change is apparent in table 6.1, which shows that those in the eleventh to twentieth percentiles experienced a real wage gain of 31.5 percent between 1940 and 1950, far outstripping the gain of those in the eighty-first to ninetieth percentiles, who saw only a 9.1 percent increase. But that situation had more than reversed itself by the 1980–1990 period, when the lower wage earners *lost* 16.9 percent of their earnings while the wealthiest experienced a 1.1 percent gain. As a result, the United States enjoys the unenviable distinction of having the largest standard deviation[4] of earnings in any developed country: in the late 1980s this was 0.774, as compared with a non-U.S. weighted average standard deviation of 0.480.[5]

There is little consensus among analysts regarding the cause of this dramatic deterioration in the relative (and absolute) position of lower-paid workers over the past twenty-five years. Early researchers identified the labor market entry of the post-WWII baby boom as an important factor: a dramatic increase in the supply of younger, less experienced workers that depressed their wages and generally reduced their employment prospects. In recent years researchers have focused on other factors such as sectoral shifts ("deindustrialization" and the growth of the service sector), technological change such as computerization, and globalization of the economy reflected in immigration and the trade deficit. They point out that what had

Table 6.1 Real Wage Growth Rate, by Wage Percentile, 1940–1990

Percentile	1940–1950	1950–1960	1960–1970	1970–1980	1980–1990
11–20	.315	.278	.192	−.015	−.169
21–40	.277	.292	.207	.015	−.116
41–60	.197	.301	.232	.073	−.072
61–80	.127	.302	.252	.096	−.024
81–90	.091	.300	.284	.089	.011
1–100	.194	.297	.241	.050	−.078

Source: Juhn and Murphy 1995, 27.

been an "increased return to experience" (i.e., the wages of older, more experienced workers rising relative to those of younger, less experienced workers) became in the 1980s an "increased return to skill" (a sharp rise in the wages of college graduates relative to those with less than a college education).

The purpose of the analysis reported in this chapter was to determine whether the age structure of the population—as measured by relative cohort size—has had a significant effect on the primary dimensions of inequality in the United States over the last thirty-five years: on the return to experience, the return to skill, hours and weeks worked, and on the general structure of wages and level of inequality. That analysis is reported with full technical detail elsewhere.[6] Here we'll just look at the implications of its findings.

Comparing the Experiences of Lucky, Big Bob, and Little Larry

The data available to researchers indicate that there are significant differences among cohorts not just in their entry-level work experience, but throughout their working lifetimes. My analyses using those data have led me to believe that these lifelong differences have been largely the result of variations in cohort size and position, and that they depend not just on the size of one's own cohort, but also on the pattern of births (that is, changes in cohort size) throughout one's lifetime. In order to highlight the very different lifetime experiences apparent in the data, I'll personify the characteristic patterns exhibited in three cohorts using the stories of Lucky, Big Bob, and Little Larry.

"Lucky" is perhaps a misnomer for members of the first of these cohorts—born between 1935 and 1940—since they were born during the Depression and then spent their childhood in the throes of World War II. But they certainly lucked out in the labor market. Fertility rates were very low when Lucky was born, so his cohort was small relative to his parents', and he thus entered the labor market when starting wages were soaring relative to the average wage. Some estimates put his relative income at an extraordinary 1.0 or higher: that is, his starting salary in his early twenties matched his parents' total annual income just a few years earlier, when he was still living at home (and his parents were in their 40s or 50s).

Lucky benefited not just from an optimal relative cohort size: he was followed in the labor market by ever-larger cohorts—the product of the 1950s baby boom. His cohort position was optimal. These larger cohorts in his wake generated an increasing demand for goods and services that contributed to growth in an economy already buoyed up by returning soldiers forming households. Thus Lucky enjoyed a rapid rate of increase in his already generous starting wage. Then, to top it off, in his prime years he found himself once again benefiting from small relative cohort size—but this time small relative to the size of entry-level cohorts, rather than relative to the size of his parents' cohort. As the wages of younger workers fell, his continued to rise. He decided to cash in on his favorable career and switch from his full-time job to a part-time one as he moved closer to retirement. And here again he benefited since entry-level cohorts were now very small, thus generating little competition for the less-demanding jobs that now attracted him.

Big Bob was born in 1955—went through school with Lucky's son, in fact. Schools were having trouble accommodating the growing numbers of students during that period, so most of his education occurred in overcrowded classrooms and porta-cabins, and often on half-day schedules. Predictably, then, he found himself nearly crowded out when he tried to enter the labor market. But he figured college wouldn't help him much, since his older friends who'd gone to college were having a tough time finding jobs. He was forced into part-time work, even as his father's wage was rising—so his relative income, only about 0.4, was very low in comparison with Lucky's: he earned only 40 percent of his parents' income. He decided he'd have to put off any hopes of starting his own family, and for a time he even continued living with his parents, to make ends meet. But he at least benefited from the fact that for a time the size of entry-level cohorts following him was still growing and generating new demand for goods and services in the economy, so he was eventually able to settle into a full-time job.

Then, just as Big Bob was beginning to feel more confident about his career, the bottom seemed to fall out of the market. The economy stumbled as the size of entry-level cohorts began to decline and the demand for goods and services no longer grew at expected rates: producers cut back on production as inventories grew. They began downsizing and Big Bob was laid off. His fortunes finally turned when he entered his 40s, however: the size of entry-level cohorts began to grow and the economy recovered its old dynamism.

Little Larry entered the world in 1970. He was part of a much smaller cohort than Big Bob's, relative to that of his parents, but that didn't seem to help when he tried to strike out on his own twenty years later. The economy was still stumbling along as entry-level cohort size continued to decline and demand failed to increase at historic rates. Nearly 20 percent of his older friends were unemployed, so he figured he wouldn't lose much by taking time out for college. Things still looked pretty gloomy when he graduated, so he had to take a job at lower pay than he'd hoped for and work as a "temp." His relative income was just 0.25: that is, he was earning only 25 percent of his parents' income. He decided to share a large apartment with several friends. But then his fortunes began to improve dramatically after 1995 as the size of entry-level cohorts began to increase once more, and producers cashed in on the spurt in demand.

Where will Little Larry's fortunes take him over the next two decades? My analyses suggest that at any given point in his lifetime the trajectory will be strongly affected by the pattern of births that occurred twenty-some years earlier. The point of these tales has been to emphasize that one's own cohort size and position are important not only at the point of labor market entry, but also later in life, and that the size of the cohorts following one into the labor market play a significant role, as well. It is too simplistic to expect one's lifetime wage profile to reflect only one's own cohort size and position. Both Lucky and Little Larry were members of smaller birth cohorts, but their lifetime experiences diverge because Lucky was followed by a surge in births while Little Larry was followed (initially) by a continued decline.

In order to control for this dynamic effect of changing cohort size, I used an augmented version of the model described in chapter 5 in the analysis underlying the results presented in this chapter. That is, while the augmented model is based on the same three factors used in chapter 5—relative cohort size and position (the GFR twenty-one years before an individual's labor market entry, and its rate of change); the level and rate of change in young men's share of the total military; and the level of durable goods imports and exports—it controls not just for each cohort's own size and position, but in any given year it also controls for the size of the *current entry-level cohort*. I used this augmented model to try to explain movements over the last thirty-five years not just in the wages of the youngest workers, but in the entire wage structure: wages at all levels of education and experience.

The data I analyzed with this augmented model focus specifically on the hourly wages of unenrolled white male, full-time, full-year workers, rather than on the relative income of all entry-level workers—a change aimed at making its results comparable with those of standard labor models. But related analyses I have conducted show that the results I found using the more restricted data set are very similar to those found for the total labor force, including non-white workers and those working less than full year, full time.

A Pictorial Summary of Model Results

The model's results can be examined in many different ways. It's possible to look at the absolute wages of various groups as well as their levels relative to each other—measures such as male relative wages and the college wage premium that were discussed in chapter 5. In addition, one can examine hours and weeks worked, together with what is termed "within cell variance": the degree of variation that's observed among the wages of workers with the same level of experience and skill. Researchers have found that this within-cell variance accounts for the lion's share of the growth in inequality since 1980. In all of these dimensions, relative cohort size appears to account for most of the changes we've observed in the wage structure over the past thirty-five years.

The detailed results of the analysis are presented in the full study.[7] As in the simple model in chapter 5, the results demonstrate a strong and highly significant negative effect of own RCS (birth cohort size), which is stronger for those born on the trailing edge (Little Larry) than on the leading edge (Big Bob) of the baby boom. In addition, there is a strong positive effect of the size of the current entry-level cohort each year (because of its members' demand for goods and services as they set up their own households), which varies for an individual worker depending on his own level of experience as suggested in the tale of Lucky, Big Bob, and Little Larry. A large entry-level cohort competes with me for jobs when I'm a younger, inexperienced worker or an older worker approaching retirement, but complements me (effectively making me more productive) when I'm in my prime years. In addition, any demographically induced economic slowdown will hurt me more if I'm a more "expendable" worker with little experience.

The model described here—the model from chapter 5, aug-

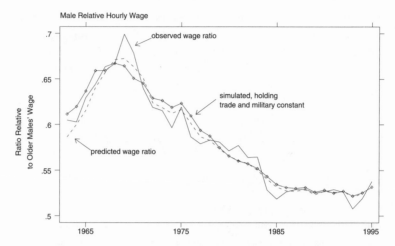

Figure 6.1. Observed, simulated, and predicted wages of young white males working full time relative to males with 26–35 years of work experience. The high degree of correspondence between the observed and the simulated values suggests that the model explains the time trend of the data extremely well, although it uses just individuals' own cohort size and the size of the current entry-level cohort at each stage in those individuals' careers.

mented to control for current as well as birth cohort size—was fitted on data describing workers at all levels of education and experience: nearly 150,000 observations of individuals and their wages over a thirty-five year period.[8] It's not possible to present here the many graphs I've prepared for all of these education and experience groups: instead I've just presented graphs showing the model's "fit" for the youngest age group, which are very representative of the model results as a whole.[9]

Figures 6.1 and 6.2 address the two basic concepts from chapter 5: male relative earnings and the college wage premium. These two measures trace the patterns of what statisticians term "between-cell" variance: variations among individuals' wages that can be explained by differences in experience and education.

Figure 6.1 presents the results for male relative hourly wages: the wages of younger relative to prime-age workers. Included in the figure are three different sets of values: those actually observed in the data; fitted, or "predicted," values produced by the full model (including controls for own and current cohort size, the military, and trade); and what are termed "simulated" values, produced by the model when all variables other than own and current cohort size measures are held constant. This model explains the time trend of the data extremely well, although it uses just individuals' own cohort size and the size of the current entry-level cohort at each stage in those individuals' careers (i.e., there is a high degree of correspondence between the observed and the "simulated" values).

Figure 6.2 presents the same type of information for the college wage premium. This graph shows that the military and trade variables add more explanatory power (i.e., the "fitted" curve matches the observed data better than the "simulated," in which military and trade are held constant). The difference between the simulated and actual values of the college premium show that trade and the military depressed the college wage premium in the 1960s (because the actual value is lower than the simulated) and boosted it in the 1980s. But even here, changing relative cohort size explains most of the marked decline and then rise in the return to a college education over the last thirty years that's been the focus of so much concern among analysts (because the actual and simulated values still follow very similar patterns over time).

Figure 6.3 addresses "within-cell" variance—differences among

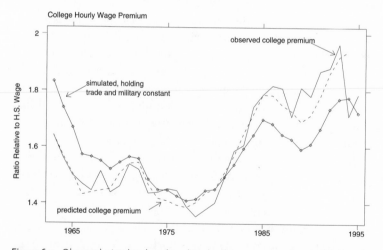

Figure 6.2. Observed, simulated, and predicted college wage premium (ratio of average hourly wage of college grads relative to that of high school grads) for young white males working full time. The difference between the simulated and actual values of the college premium show that trade and the military depressed the college wage premium in the 1960s (because the actual value is lower than the simulated) and boosted it in the 1980s. But even here, changing relative cohort size explains most of the marked decline and then rise in the return to a college education over the last thirty years.

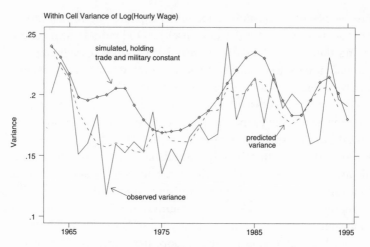

Figure 6.3. Observed, simulated, and predicted variance of logged hourly wages within year-state-education-experience cells for white males working full time. Similarities between the simulated and predicted values indicate that the longer-term trends in variance were the result of changing age structure in the population.

wages earned by individuals with the same levels of education and experience that have proven very difficult to explain. The observed values in figure 6.3 show the substantial increase in within-cell variance observed in the labor force since about 1975: corresponding graphs in Macunovich 2002 demonstrate that this was a common trend across experience levels.[10] This variance has been one of the major factors underlying the growing inequality in U.S. society in recent decades. Similarities between the simulated and predicted values in figure 6.3 indicate that the longer-term trends in variance were the result of changing age structure in the population.

But why—or how—would changing age structure increase within-cell wage variance? As indicated in chapter 5, between-cell variance is thought to be the result of "imperfect substitutability" between different categories of worker. Recent work by other researchers suggests that increased within-cell variance may be accounted for by variation in (1) the proportion working full time; (2) hours worked per week; and (3) weeks worked per year.[11] When there is a supply glut, employers can choose among workers and will tend to favor those within any given category who demonstrate higher levels of ability and motivation—qualities not necessarily captured by simple measures like years of experience and education. My

analyses, reported elsewhere, demonstrate that changing relative cohort size can explain a significant proportion of the variation over
time in measures of work intensity, such as hours and weeks worked
and the proportion working full time, at all levels of experience.[12]

The model appears to explain well the long-term trends in
wages—both relative and absolute—at all levels of education and experience: the strong increases of the 1960s and early 1970s as well as
the marked declines experienced by younger and less skilled workers
since 1973, with stable and sometimes even increasing wages among
other groups.

Summary

The results presented in this chapter support and extend those in
chapter 5, and in the two chapters together I have tried to demonstrate the "first-order" effects mentioned in the overview. Cohort size
effects—on wages, unemployment, and hours and weeks worked—
have occurred not just among younger workers, but throughout the
labor force, providing a plausible explanation for a significant portion of the disturbing rise in income inequality observed in our society since 1980.

Younger workers were hurt relative to older workers, and the
"return" to investing in a college education dipped and then soared
as the baby boom began entering the labor force. Marginal workers
(those with less education, experience, ability, or training) were initially carried on a rising tide of growing aggregate demand for goods
and services as the baby boomers set up households, but those marginal workers were then the "first fired" when the wave ebbed and the
economy stumbled. Those with less skill, motivation, or ability were
often forced into part-time work, creating differences between their
wages and those of other workers with similar levels of education
and experience. But this was a cyclical effect related to the life cycle
of the baby boom, rather than a gloomy indicator of what was to
come in the twenty-first century. This argument is perhaps more easily accepted now after the economy's recovery in the mid-1990s, but
in the early 1990s it was very difficult to convince many analysts of
its merits.[13]

The analyses I have described in this chapter indicate that these
effects are significant not just in aggregate data at the national level,
where we have relatively few years of observation, but also using

observations on the wages of hundreds of thousands of individuals over a thirty-five-year period. Changing relative cohort size has been a major factor increasing all types of inequality in our society over the past few decades. My findings accord with recent work by other researchers using international data. Their results suggest that cohort size also accounts for a significant proportion of changes in inequality in countries around the world, at all stages of development.[14]

Not least among the sources of inequality here in the United States has been the growing gap between the wages of entry-level and prime-age workers that accounts for declining male relative income. Thus the first link has been forged in the chain of effects leading from cohort size to many of the societal changes that have perplexed us in the post-WWII period. The next chapters in part 2 will carry on the analysis, looking at connections between male relative income and many of those societal changes. In this chapter and in chapter 5, the "prime mover" in explanatory models—the most significant independent variable—has been relative cohort size, approximated using the general fertility rate twenty-one years earlier. In part 2 the focus shifts to the indirect, or "secondary" effects of relative cohort size. There, relative income becomes the primary independent variable.

PART 3

Second-Order Effects of Changing Relative Cohort Size

Women's Roles

Labor Force Participation and the Emergence of the "Career Woman"

[C]hanges in market work opportunities as manifested in wage changes are not enough to account for the profound inter-cohort changes that have taken place in the market work of women.

John Pencavel, "The Market Work Behavior and Wages of Women, 1975–94" (1999)

Many of the dramatic changes our society experienced during the second half of the twentieth century revolved around the changing role of women, as marriages were postponed or forgone, fertility rates declined, labor force participation increased, and divorce rates skyrocketed.[1] The bulk of this change occurred between 1965 and 1985, those crucial years when the baby boomers achieved the age of majority. To what extent were these changes related to changes in relative cohort size and the resultant changes in male relative income?

Major Upheavals: A Response to the Birth Quake?

A young woman in the early 1960s had only a 20 percent chance of having attended college—even for just one year—and only 44 percent of young women aged 22–24 were either enrolled in school or in the labor force. By the mid-1980s, however, those figures had approximately doubled. What were the young women of the 1960s— my own cohort!—doing, if not attending school or participating in the labor force? In the mid-1960s close to 80 percent of young

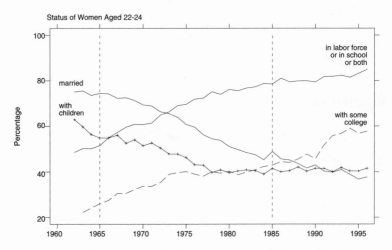

Figure 7.1. Trends for women aged 22–24. Source: Author's tabulations of data from March Current Population Surveys.

women aged 22–24 and not in school were married, and 65 percent had at least one child. Those percentages both fell to about 40 percent by the end of the 1980s—among my daughter's cohort—as shown in figure 7.1.

And of course there has been the widely publicized "emergence of the career woman" during the same period. Among young women aged 22–24 in the labor force and no longer in school, the proportions of women in "high status" occupations in administration, medicine, law, engineering, math, and science tripled; the proportions in skilled blue collar "traditionally male" occupations like transport equipment operating, protection services, and precision production work quadrupled; and the proportions in sales, service, and management-related occupations more than doubled.

The occupations women moved out of in order to take up these new careers were teaching and nursing, clerical and manual work—sectors which accounted for over 70 percent of women's jobs in the 1960s, but by 1990 had dropped to about 50 percent. However, the above moves sound somewhat less impressive when one notes, as illustrated in figure 7.2, that the tripling and quadrupling mentioned above result simply from the fact that the percentages started out so low: less than 2 percent in each of the top three panels of figure 7.2. Currently fewer than 9 percent of these young women are in the "high status" category (the first two panels in figure 7.2), and fewer

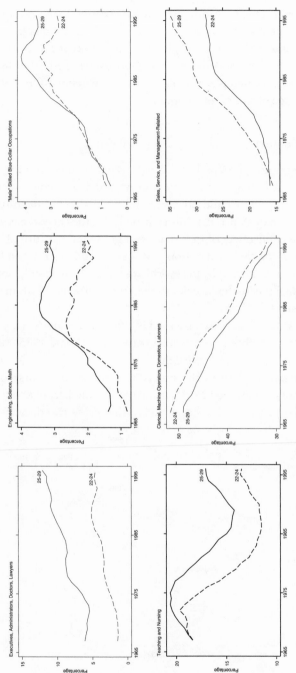

Figure 7.2. Percentages of women aged 22–24 and 25–29 in the labor force and no longer in school, by occupational grouping. Source: Author's tabulations of data from March Current Population Surveys.

than 3 percent are in "traditionally male" occupations. The lion's share of the moves has been into sales, service, and management-related occupations (for example, auditors, personnel workers, training, purchasers, and business agents). However, these moves tend to be the ones that play the biggest part in what might be called "the emergence of the 'career woman.'"

Historical Context

These changes are perhaps best characterized by the stunning increase in the labor force participation of married women—especially those with young children. Figure 7.3 highlights the magnitude of the change that occurred, within a broader historical context. Apparent there is the effect of industrialization around the turn of the twentieth century; the acceleration that occurred during the first few decades, perhaps spurred by the World War I and the women's movement; and then the further acceleration in the 1940s and 1950s in the wake of Rosie the Riveter.

But the rates of increase observed in the early periods were only about a quarter of those experienced between 1965 and 1985. Married women's labor force participation increased more in that twenty-year period than in the preceding seventy-five years combined. That of women aged 25–34 more than doubled, from about 30 percent to 70 percent. What happened during those two decades to

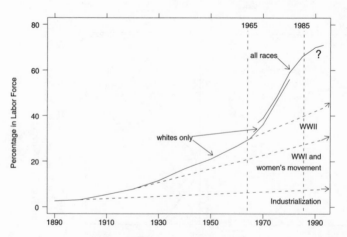

Figure 7.3. Labor force participation rates of married women aged 25–34, 1890–1993. Sources: Goldin 1990, table 2.2, for years 1890–1980; SSA 1994 for years 1968–1993.

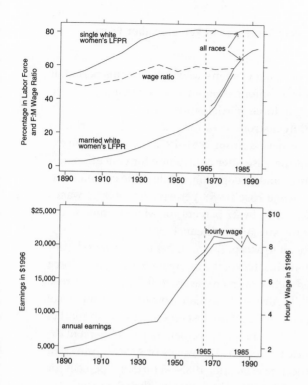

Figure 7.4. *Top:* Labor force participation rates for married and single women aged 25–34, and the female:male wage ratio based on all urban full-time workers. Sources: Goldin 1990, table 5.1 for wage ratio; Goldin 1990, table 2.2, for LFPR for years 1890–1980; SSA 1994 for LFPR for years 1968–1993. *Bottom:* Real annual earnings of white urban women working year-round, full time ($1996), and real hourly wage of all unen-rolled women aged 20–24 ($1996). Sources: Goldin 1990, table 5.1, for earnings; author's tabulations of data from March Current Population Surveys for wages.

bring about a change that so drastically altered the character of the "traditional family"?

It's often thought that pronounced changes in the demand for fe-male labor during this period raised women's wages and "pulled" women into the labor market as the opportunity cost of their time spent at home increased. But figure 7.4 shows that in the crucial pe-riod 1965–1985, this dramatic change among young married women was not accompanied by any corresponding change among single women, or in the level of women's wages.

One might suspect that the change was due primarily to declin-ing fertility—that the increase occurred largely among childless married women. But this was not the case. Statistics show that the rates of increase among young mothers were significantly greater than those observed among childless married women: the participa-tion rate of married women with children under 6 increased from 28 percent to 55 percent between 1968 and 1985, while that of childless married women only increased from 71 percent to 87 percent.

Do Wage Changes Explain Increases in Female Labor Force Participation?

Because of the image of rising women's wages during this period, it has been popular—at least among economists—to attribute the rise in young women's labor force participation to increases in their wages. There is certainly a strong case for this hypothesis prior to about 1972. In that early period (from 1961–1972), white women experienced a 19 percent increase after controlling for education, potential work experience, and occupation, while African American women's real average wage rose by 58 percent. Entry-level wages rose even more dramatically: by 27 percent for white women and a staggering 79 percent for African Americans!

But it is more difficult to accept this argument in the period from 1972 to 1985, when more than half of the recent increase in labor force participation occurred: white women's average full-time wage rose by only 1 percent, while African American women's full-time wage *dropped* by 3 percent; and among those just entering the labor market there was a 5 percent *decline* for white women and an 11 percent *decline* for African American women. The wages of African American women continued to decline even after 1985—a further 3 percent for all women and 4 percent for those just entering the labor market— while those of white women experienced no increase until after 1993. Some researchers have argued that the labor force increases after 1972 were the result of momentum created by wage increases prior to that date: that women entered in anticipation of further increases.[2] It's difficult to imagine, however, that women would continue flooding into the market for more than two decades in the expectation of continued wage increases that had clearly ceased to exist.

If increasing wages were indeed the impetus for women's increasing labor participation, to what do we attribute the fact that married women who were aged 25–34 during 1940–1960, *while this dramatic increase in earnings was actually happening,* seemed nearly oblivious of the change? Between 1940 and 1960 the labor force participation of older women shot up dramatically—perhaps in response to the wage change—while that of younger women maintained the slower historic pattern of increase, as indicated by the trend lines superimposed on figure 7.5. This situation was then reversed between 1960 and 1980: while the younger married women's labor force participation more than doubled, the older women's

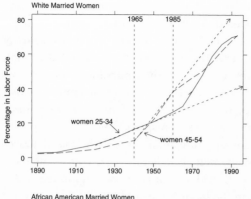

White Married Women

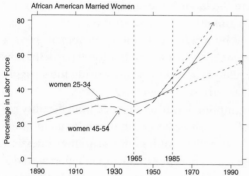

African American Married Women

Figure 7.5. Comparing trends in labor force participation rates of younger and older white *(top)* and African American *(bottom)* married women. The light dotted lines highlight the disparity between trends in the two groups in the 1940–1960 period and again in the 1960–1980 period. Sources: Goldin 1990, table 2.2, for 1890–1980; SSA 1994 for 1968–1993.

settled back into the slower rates observed prior to 1940. This was in fact a cohort phenomenon, because the unresponsive 25–34-year-olds in the 1940–1960 period were also the unresponsive 45–54-year-olds twenty years later. They were mothers of the baby boomers, who seem to have been immune to whatever inducements pulled surrounding cohorts into the market at such high rates.

Thus although the wage argument seems plausible as an explanation for the increased female labor force participation in the period prior to 1965 or 1970, something else is needed for the 1965–1985 period to explain the wholesale movement of young married women into the labor force and the emergence of the "career woman" in the absence of financial inducements.

A Matter of Changing Attitudes?

There have, of course, been many other explanations put forward to explain these phenomena—most notably women's increasing level of education and "changing attitudes" about women's roles.[3] Some researchers have suggested that women felt compelled to provide a second income in order for the family to afford the increasing array of consumer goods, and that this motive in turn provided women with a "socially acceptable excuse" for their pursuit of a career outside the home: they were simply providing for their family's needs.[4]

It is often suggested, too, that the strong feminist movement of the late 1960s and 1970s was largely responsible for changing attitudes, together with a general disillusionment with the role of housewife, as expressed so well by Betty Friedan in 1963. This would have acted on two fronts: first, in waking young women up to the wider opportunities available in the labor force; and second, in mounting an attack on gender discrimination in the labor force and the "glass ceiling." But why then? Why would the feminist movement have a disproportionately large effect on women's labor force participation in the 1960s and 1970s, relative to its effect, say, during the struggle for women's suffrage at the turn of the century?

Another popular assumption has been that declining fertility reduced the importance of women's role in the home, making labor force participation more attractive—although researchers question the direction of causality: isn't it possible that women's increased desire to work outside the home led them to reduce their fertility?[5] A more compelling argument might be that women's entry was facilitated by their new control over timing and spacing of fertility that came with the introduction of the Pill. That leaves open the question of increased participation among mothers of young children, although some researchers suggest that the ability to control the spacing of children may have played a role here.[6] But although the Pill made fertility control easier, we know that women have been capable of controlling their fertility—when they choose to—since at least the 1930s, when U.S. fertility rates were about as low as they are now (and many European rates were even lower), and even as early as the nineteenth century.[7] And at least one set of researchers has suggested that the change in attitudes about women's role underlying all of these arguments was the result, rather than the cause, of changing behavior among young women—a response to cognitive dissonance.[8]

Effects of Male Relative Income on Changes in Married Women's Labor Force Participation

The argument pursued here is that birth cohort size played an important role in shaping the socioeconomic choices of young women during this period. It seems more than coincidence that such massive changes should have occurred from 1965 to 1985, precisely the time when baby boomers (born 1946–1964) were entering into their 20s and 30s. Chapter 3 illustrated the dramatic change in population age structure that occurred during this period. Chapters 4–6 documented the concomitant economic changes: the boomers' wages fell, and unemployment rose, as they flooded the labor markets. But even more important than that absolute decline in earning potential was the extent to which their earnings fell relative to that of their parents.

That decline in male relative income would have triggered the compensatory behavior among young adults described in chapters 1 and 2. They made a series of adjustments in order to improve their own personal disposable income relative to their material aspirations. Fewer young men and women chose to marry, as we'll see in chapter 9, and chapter 11 will demonstrate that fewer felt able to support children. Lower marriage rates appear to increase the average labor force participation rate of young women simply because that rate is traditionally higher among single than among married women. The same holds true for lower fertility rates. Those two factors alone would have produced sharp increases in the average labor force participation rate of all young women. Note that in these cases the behavioral change is not in terms of labor force participation—rates specific to a given marital status or presence of children need not change—but rather in terms of marriage and fertility, causing compositional changes that create the impression of altered labor force orientation.

The truly significant behavioral change was the increased labor force participation of married women with children. Young women who married during this period would have felt a strong need to supplement their families' incomes in order to bring per capita disposable income up to a level commensurate with their material aspirations. This certainly would explain the disproportionate increases in labor force participation during this period among married women, particularly among married women with young children.

This hypothesis, that the observed increases in female labor force participation were largely the result of increases in the female wage prior to 1972 and reductions in male relative income thereafter, is strongly supported in two of my own studies.[9] Both of these analyses, which use two different methodologies to test the hypothesis, are able to explain a large proportion of the increase observed in the labor force participation of young women between 1952 and 1995. The latter analysis estimated that the combined changes in the female wage and male relative income accounted for about 77 percent of the increase in female labor force participation in the 1964–1978 period and about 74 percent of the increase between 1978 and 1984.

The Emergence of the "Career Woman"

One of the most interesting manifestations of relative cohort size between 1965 and 1985 has been its effect on young women's occupational choices. Though it's generally thought that the most important factor leading to the emergence of the "career woman" in the United States was sharply rising wages, women's wages have barely risen, in real terms, since the early 1970s. The "observed" average real wage among young women aged 20–24 and no longer in school has indeed risen, but these increases are virtually eliminated in the period since 1970 after controlling for changing levels of hours and weeks worked, education, experience, occupation, and race.[10] That is, the average real wage for a *given job* increased about 20 percent between 1961 and 1972, but between 1972 and 1985 it rose by only 1 percent. This means that most of the observed increase in the average woman's wage has occurred as a result of her own behavioral changes—her choices regarding education and intensity of labor force participation—rather than causality working in the other direction.

While it's true that the removal of gender-specific occupational barriers might have given women access to higher-paying jobs during this period, figure 7.2 demonstrated that only a very small proportion of young women actually moved into formerly restricted occupations. My own work analyzes women's labor force participation and occupational choices in a number of ways and concludes that one of the most important factors influencing change during the 1965–1985 period, especially after 1972, was once again changing relative cohort size.

Understanding this requires that one think of women as choosing between two different categories of lifetime wage profile. The first is relatively flat, either because the woman is in an occupation with little prospect for advancement or because she chooses to work part time or on an otherwise flexible schedule, perhaps with interruptions to raise children. I'll refer to that flat earnings progression as the "dead-end" wage profile. It's a bit difficult to characterize the jobs associated with this dead-end profile. Some occupations, such as teaching and nursing, make greater allowance for flexible schedules, so even though the occupation itself may not be "dead-end," women can more easily choose a "mommy track" in these occupations, which ends up producing little real wage growth. And using a full-time/part-time distinction doesn't fully capture it either, since women might well work full time in dead-end occupations.

The second category of lifetime wages I refer to as the "career" profile. Career jobs offer relatively steep wage increases at higher levels of experience and are normally associated with full-time employment, with no major interruptions over time. They can and do occur in occupations like teaching and nursing, but are often thought of in association with more "male" occupations like managerial and executive positions.

As indicated in figure 7.6, prior to the emergence of the baby boom into the labor market, when there was an excess demand for labor in the economy, employers were forced to pay a premium in order to attract workers into dead-end jobs. This would have been the case for jobs in dead-end occupations as well as for part-time and temp jobs in other occupations. Thus, for example, in the early 1960s (holding all other factors such as education and experience constant), prior to the entry of the baby boom into the labor market, young women just starting out could earn a higher hourly wage, on average, in part-time than in full-time work: white women 10 percent more, and African American women 30 percent more! As the baby boom began entering the market in the 1960s this premium gradually disappeared, eventually becoming a 10 to 25 percent *penalty*. The growing labor surplus created by the boomers meant that workers preferred a dead-end job to no job, and the increased supply of workers for these jobs pushed down their relative wages.

What type of worker is most likely to respond to a premium and be attracted into a dead-end job? Women, who anticipate some discontinuity in lifetime labor force participation and therefore weight immediate earnings relative to future earnings more heavily than do workers who anticipate no future discontinuity. Hence, prior to the

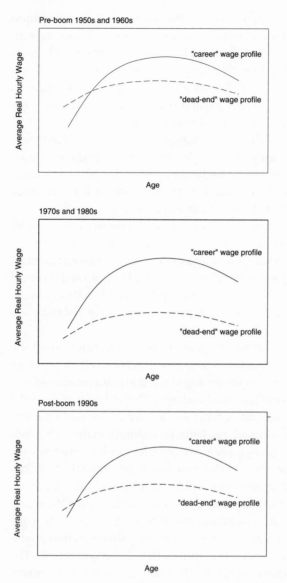

Figure 7.6. Stylized representations of the baby boom's effect on the premium paid to young women in "dead-end" jobs.

emergence of the baby boom, women were attracted by the wage premium into more dead-end jobs. Then, as the baby boom entered the labor market, women were given increased motivation for job commitment because of declining male relative income. At the same time, however, their own wage premium disappeared. They no longer saw any benefit to these dead-end jobs and began looking

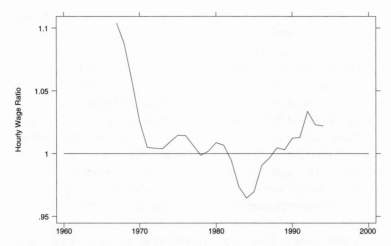

Figure 7.7. Ratio of part-time to full-time starting hourly wage (paid to those in their first year of work experience) for women with sixteen years of education, after controlling for occupational changes. Source: author's analyses reported in Macunovich 2002.

more toward career jobs, switching out of clerical, teaching, and nursing jobs and into professional and management jobs.

Again, I must emphasize that not all jobs in, say, teaching and nursing are dead-end, but there tends to be a higher proportion of women who choose a dead-end wage profile, that is, working part time or discontinuously, within these occupations than in many others. To give an indication of this dead-end versus career wage effect, figure 7.7 shows how dramatically women's starting wages in part-time jobs fell, relative to their starting wages in full-time jobs, throughout the 1965–1985 period.[11] In the early 1960s college graduates netted nearly 10 percent more for an hour of part-time work than for an hour of full-time work. But that ratio dropped throughout the period from the mid-1960s to the mid-1980s, to a point where these women earned less in part-time than in full-time work. Women with only a high school education lost a part-time premium of nearly 15 percent during the same period.

Prior to 1965, when the part-time hourly wage exceeded the full-time wage—by 12 percent for white women, and 34 percent for African American women—the balance was tipped in favor of part-time employment, and large proportions of women opted for this type of work. In excess of 20 percent of women in sales, technical work, domestic work, protection services, other services, farming, and transport equipment operation worked part time in the early 1960s, whereas considerably less than 10 percent of men in these occupations worked part time.

The proportion of women working part time and in the more "female" occupations dropped rapidly through the 1970s, however, as the premium paid to part-time work vanished in the face of excess labor supply caused by the entry of the baby boom into the labor market. Those women who could moved out of part-time work as young men with no other option moved in. Even in the face of declining relative part-time wages for men, men's proportions working part time in corresponding occupations *increased* during the same period, as they began to accept part-time work rather than find themselves out of a job altogether.

Another way of looking at women's tendency to work part time is to examine the flow of women who are in the labor force, back and forth between full-time and part-time status. For the most part, there has been a striking decline after 1970 in the percentage moving into part-time work, becoming eventually an absolute decline in the percentage working part time, as figure 7.8 shows for young women aged 25 and 30. These data were calculated by looking at the behavior of individual birth cohorts of women as they aged from 24 to 25 and from 29 to 30—subtracting the percentage working part time at the older age from the percentage at the younger age.

As can be seen in the occupational trends for young women presented back in figure 7.2, however, the movement into executive, administrative, skilled blue collar, engineering, and science occupations appears to have stalled in the mid- to late-1980s and has even begun to reverse itself. Similarly, the decline in the proportion of young women working part time appears to have ended after the mid-1980s—and in many occupations that proportion has even *increased* since the mid-1980s. This change can be seen most clearly in figure 7.8, where the downward trend away from part-time work that began after 1965 among 25-year-olds reversed itself after 1985. At the same time, the proportions of young women entering teaching and nursing have increased markedly. Why?

Figure 7.7 demonstrated the turnaround that occurred in the ratio of part-time to full-time starting wages after the mid-1980s. That ratio has improved dramatically, and part-time jobs are once again paying a premium. The timing of this increase suggests that it—

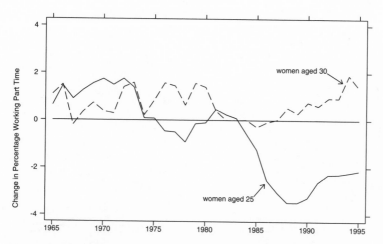

Figure 7.8. Annual change in percentage of young women in the labor force who work part time. These data were calculated by looking at the behavior of individual birth cohorts of women as they aged from 24 to 25 and 29 to 30—subtracting the percentage working part time at the younger age from the percentage at the older age. They show that the downward trend away from part-time work that began after 1965 among 25-year-olds reversed itself after 1985, and the percentage of 30-year-olds working part time began to increase at the same time.

together with rising male relative income—played a role in this new set of occupational shifts and the move back into part-time work. This was more than a coincidence since, as my own work shows, the contemporaneous increase in the part-time wage ratio was, like the rise in male relative income, due in large part to favorable shifts in relative cohort size.

One final demonstration of women's changing career orientation, and their underlying concern with family, looks at women within "own wage quintiles"—that is, analyses of women in the workforce categorized by their own hourly wage level, with those earning the most on an hourly basis in the top 20 percent, or fifth quintile, and those earning the least in the first quintile. These analyses demonstrate that women who can "afford" to, who are married and have children, are beginning to choose to work part time rather than full time. Figure 7.9 illustrates this point, comparing women in the top earnings quintile with those in the bottom two—the bottom 40 percent of earners on an hourly basis.[12]

Figure 7.9 looks at women aged 36–40 who are married with

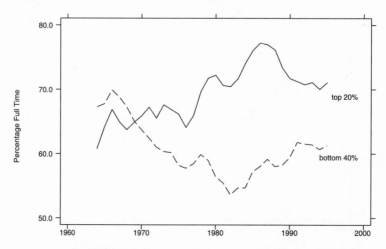

Figure 7.9. Percent of those in the labor force who are working full time, among married women aged 36–40 with children, by hourly wage quintile (three-year moving average). This graph demonstrates that married women with children who can "afford" to—those whose hourly wages put them in the top 20 percent of women in their age group—have been moving from full-time to part-time work since about 1985. This trend does not appear, however, among women in the bottom 40 percent of the hourly wage distribution, where the percentage working full time has been increasing since the early 1980s. Source: author's tabulations of data from March Current Populations Surveys.

children and in the labor force. In these figures it's apparent that these women have been moving away from full-time work if they are in the top earnings quintile, while those at the bottom of the earnings profile have been increasing their full-time participation. Additional data not shown here demonstrate that this difference applies across educational groupings, as well, in terms of labor force participation generally. College graduates' movement into the labor force ended in the mid-1980s and has even declined marginally since then, while there is little apparent trend among high school dropouts—or even an increase in recent years.

Thus, it appears that—the misgivings of many pundits notwithstanding—women still value family and will use additional earnings to "buy back" time with family.

Summary

The labor force participation of young married women (aged 25–34) rose dramatically between 1965 and 1985, a period when, contrary to popular belief, women's real wages remained stagnant—after controlling for changing levels of education and experience. Conversely, during a period of virtually skyrocketing real wages between 1945 and 1965, their participation rate did not increase any faster than the long-term historic trend. Complicating the puzzle even more, this behavior was diametrically opposed to that of older married women (45–54), whose participation rate quite logically jumped when wages jumped and then dawdled when wages stagnated. In addition, the 1965–1985 period marked the emergence of the "career woman," strongly committed to the labor force in full-time work, moving into occupations previously considered more appropriate for men and out of "female" occupations like nursing and teaching. Is there an explanation for this behavior, given that the traditional economic model appears to fail the test?

In this chapter I've tried to demonstrate that these striking changes in young women's behavior coincided with equally dramatic movements in two economic variables: male relative income and the ratio of women's part-time to full-time hourly wages. Both of these variables plummeted between 1965 and 1985, and I have argued that the first of these played a significant role in young women's increased labor force participation, while the second influenced their occupational choices and preferences regarding part-time work. Bolstering this argument is the fact that the trends in all of these variables then reversed themselves—virtually simultaneously—after the mid-1980s. Male relative income and women's wage ratio began to increase, and at the same time young women began moving out of the "male" occupations and full-time work and back into teaching, nursing, and part-time work.

Furthermore, I have argued that since the movements in male relative income and women's wage ratio were a function largely of changing relative cohort size, as the baby boom was absorbed into the labor market, the dramatic changes in young women's labor force behavior must also have been functions—at least in part—of changing relative cohort size. This argument is not intended to suggest, however, that other factors have not been important as well—factors that have been operating since at least the turn of the last century, such as changing levels of education for women concomitant with rising real family incomes. It is intended rather to demonstrate that there has also been a significant cyclical component in the trend, an aftershock from the birth quake.

The following chapters will attempt to demonstrate that changes in patterns of school enrollment, marriage, and family formation—traditionally thought to have been additional causal factors affecting women's labor force participation—also appear to have been functions, at least in part, of changing relative cohort size.

Boom and Bust Cycles in College Enrollment Rates

> For the first time in American history, the relative earnings of college
> graduates declined. . . . It is not surprising, given the erosion of incentives,
> that the later cohorts of the baby boom began to back away from higher
> education.
>
> Landon Jones, *Great Expectations: America*
> *and the Baby Boom Generation* (1980)

The previous chapters have demonstrated significant effects of
relative cohort size on the labor market outcomes (unemployment, hours and weeks worked, and wages—both absolute and relative) of young men and women and have suggested that women's behavioral choices in terms of labor force participation and occupation
were strongly influenced by these outcomes. To what extent have college enrollment decisions been influenced as well? Here again, as
with women's labor force participation, many have suggested that a
general change in attitudes toward women's roles, growing largely
out of the women's movement, led to young women's increasing college enrollment. The analysis presented here is not meant to suggest
that this was not a powerful motivator, but rather to explore the possible role of economic factors underlying those societal changes.[1]

It is theorized that enrollments are a function of the economic
"return" earned by a college education—the expected additional lifetime earnings of a college graduate minus the costs of attending college, including the "opportunity cost," an individual's forgone wages
while in school. In addition, education probably serves to some

extent as a "consumption good": something individuals enjoy for its own sake, independent of any economic return.[2] In that sense, it's expected that the demand for a college education will increase as real family income rises. This has probably been true historically, especially for young women, in periods like the 1950s when very few female college graduates spent any appreciable time in the labor market. (Although some have speculated that women enjoyed an economic return that was independent of their own labor force participation: the increased likelihood of marrying a more affluent college graduate, rather than a high school graduate.)

To the extent that these theories hold true, we would expect to see a long-term increasing trend in enrollments as average family incomes improve, with fluctuations in response to changes in the economic return to college—the "college wage premium." This would be the case for both young men and women, with the "consumption" aspect of the rising trend perhaps somewhat stronger historically for young women. In addition, women's enrollment rates might be sensitive to those of young men to the extent that the "MRS degree" is valued.

Recall that one of the "relative wages" strongly affected by relative cohort size, as demonstrated in chapters 5 and 6, has been the college wage premium for both men and women. Additionally, although the MRS degree might look less attractive to young women when young men's relative earnings are low, the economic return from their own labor market participation would carry more weight for young women aimed at the labor market rather than the nursery. Thus it is expected that relative cohort size should exert a significant effect on college enrollments.

Historic Trends

Somewhat surprisingly, perhaps, the absolute number of 18–24-year-olds enrolled in higher education in the United States changed relatively little in the period between 1969 and 1989, despite the fact that this period marked the entry of the baby boomers into that age group. This is shown in figure 8.1, where it can be seen that the only significant change in numbers enrolled in this group occurred among women aged 20–24, who accounted for an increase of about 1.7 million during this period. And yet during this same period, the

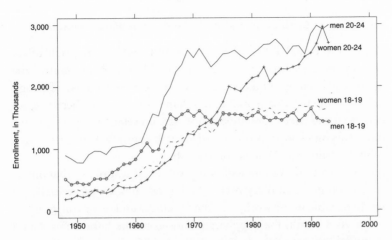

Figure 8.1. U.S. college enrollments, in thousands, for men and women aged 18–19 and 20–24. Source: U.S. Bureau of the Census, Current Population Reports, series P20, "School Enrollment—Social and Economic Characteristics of Students," annually.

total number of young people aged 18–24 experienced tremendous fluctuations: from 23 million up to 31 million and then down to 26 million, as the baby boom passed through this age group. Why didn't the baby boom have a greater impact on higher education—as it did on elementary and secondary schools, which were forced to expand into porta-cabins and to implement half-day schedules?[3]

Two influential studies in the 1980s, both based on relative cohort size effects, postulated that a "leveling" effect occurred as the baby boom passed through—a sort of demographic "cut and fill" operation in which smaller cohorts enrolled at high rates and larger cohorts enrolled at low rates, thus filling in demographic troughs and diminishing demographic peaks.[4] Although these two models were both correct about the decline in (male) enrollment rates in the 1970s, they differed in their prognostications for the period after 1980. The first of these models (which I'll refer to as ACE) forecast an increase in enrollment rates, while the other (WW) foresaw a decline. So far the ACE model has had the best track record, as enrollment rates have skyrocketed since 1980—but even the ACE model underpredicted enrollment rates in the late 1990s. Was the ACE model's predictive power in the 1980s just a fluke?

The Effect of Birth Cohort Size on the College Wage Premium

Both of these models hypothesized that birth cohort size would affect enrollment rates through its effect on the college wage premium—the additional earnings of a college graduate relative to those of a high school graduate. Chapters 5 and 6 demonstrated that there was indeed a strong effect of relative cohort size on relative wages, and this effect was much more pronounced for college graduates than for high school graduates. That is, on-the-job experience does not confer much benefit on workers with low levels of education, so that on average, younger and older high school graduates are more easily interchangeable in the workplace than younger and older college graduates. As a result, the supply glut caused by the baby boom had a more deleterious effect on the wages of college graduates. If we accept that a primary motivation for attending college is this college wage premium, then the motivation is lower in larger birth cohorts and, all else equal, a lower proportion of larger cohorts will choose to attend college. This is the "leveling" effect mentioned above.

The Relative Income Effect of Birth Cohort Size

This negative effect of birth cohort size on enrollment rates would be even stronger, were it not for the changes in male relative income that accompany changes in cohort size, as demonstrated in chapters 4–6. A young man approaching high school graduation can either join the labor force with only a high school diploma or invest in further education. In the first case the relative income he achieves will be that of a high school graduate relative to his family's current income. If he is in a large cohort facing reduced earning potential, he can improve on his earning potential relative to his family's income by achieving a higher level of education relative to his parents'. In this regard he experiences some increased motivation to continue in school if he is in a large cohort and anticipates that his earnings as a high school graduate will fall short of his aspirations.

On the other hand, as discussed in the previous section, large cohorts face a declining college wage premium—the difference between a college wage and a high school wage—and this effect of cohort size will *reduce* their motivation for further education. Thus the net effect of cohort size on their enrollment probability will be a combination of these two forces, positive and negative.

For young women, declining male relative income would tend to have a positive impact on college enrollment rates. In a gender-differentiated society like the United States in the post-WWII period, in which young people have traditionally looked first to male earnings for household support, declining male relative income signals delayed/forgone marriage and childbearing—or, in the event of marriage, an increased possibility of forming two-earner households. Thus there will be an increase at the margin, over and above any longer-term trend in young women's educational attainment and labor force participation, in the proportion of young women who anticipate an increased likelihood of, and increased intensity of, future labor force participation.

That is, given the low level of young males' earning potential relative to these women's material aspirations, they might choose to forgo marriage entirely, or else to participate themselves in the labor market to supplement their partners' earnings. In either case their labor force participation will be increased, and economic models suggest that in this situation young women would be more likely to invest—and to invest more intensively—in higher education. This is not to say that declining male relative income has been the *sole* factor affecting female labor force participation and enrollment rates, but rather that it has been an additional factor overlaid on any longer-term trends.

Perfect Foresight Leading to Evasive Tactics?

WW added yet another twist to the cohort size hypothesis: they felt that young people would anticipate the college wage premium effect of cohort size and would strategize in order to distance themselves as much as possible from large cohorts in timing their own entry into the labor market. Thus, individuals born in the early years, on the leading edge of the baby boom (1946–1955), would have tried to achieve their college education as early and quickly as possible, in order to reach the job market before larger cohorts; while cohorts born on the trailing edge of the boom (1959–64) would have been more likely to delay or prolong their college attendance. This would have the effect, they hypothesized, of increasing enrollment rates in the first group of 18–24 year olds and decreasing the rates of the latter: another instance of asymmetric cohort size effects.

By contrast, the ACE model did not assume that individuals

strategize on the basis of an awareness of their position relative to the peak of a baby boom, and thus did not assume any asymmetry in cohort size effects. Rather, ACE assumed that young people simply respond to "labor market signals" as embodied in the relative wage rates of cohorts immediately preceding them—for example, among older siblings and acquaintances and as reported in the media.

Variables Used in the WW and ACE Models

These two models were very similar, containing a cohort size variable together with a control for the effects of average family income (recognizing the "consumption" aspect of education) and the military.[5] Their cohort size measures differed, however. While ACE controlled for the size of younger relative to older cohorts using the lagged general fertility rate as in chapters 5 and 6, WW simply controlled for the growth rate in absolute cohort size—a position variable that doesn't actually reflect the labor market demand/supply effects described earlier—the question of substitutability between younger and older workers.

In testing these two cohort size models (ACE and WW) using postwar data through 1980, WW found that their own model appeared to "fit" better; thus they confidently predicted that as the size of cohorts leaving high school diminished in the 1980s, enrollment rates would decline, as well. But the data through 1980 contained a significant complication due to the Vietnam War: Did young men in the late 1960s and early 1970s enroll at such high rates because they were trying to beat out later, larger cohorts, or did they do so in order to avoid the draft? Analysts call this an "identification problem," something difficult to resolve until more years of data can be added that are free from one or the other of these two effects.

We now have those additional years of data, and they show that the ACE model clearly dominates the WW model, as indicated in figure 8.2: small cohorts have tended to enroll at higher rates than larger cohorts, but cohorts on the leading edge of a boom don't seem to enroll at higher rates than cohorts on the trailing edge, all other things equal (including cohort size).[6] Note in considering figure 8.2 that WW modeled total enrollments in an age group while ACE modeled just college enrollments.

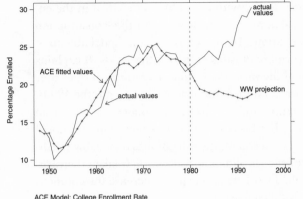

Figure 8.2. Forecasting 1981–1993 enrollment rates for men aged 20–24, using the WW model (which assumes asymmetric cohort size effects and uses a rate of change in absolute cohort size as a measure of that effect) and the ACE model (which assumes symmetry in the cohort size effect and uses the general fertility rate as a measure of that effect).

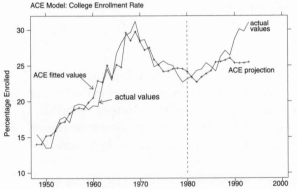

Effects of International Trade

It's obvious in figure 8.2, however, that even the ACE model appears to underpredict college enrollment rates in the 1990s. Recent literature on the domestic wage effects of international trade suggests what might be going wrong here. There is a growing consensus that imports have a stronger effect on the wages of unskilled than skilled workers: the labor embodied in these imported goods is more unskilled than skilled, so imports tend to replace domestic unskilled workers. Exports, on the other hand, tend to demand skilled labor. Thus as both imports and exports rise, there is increasing incentive for young workers to move into more skilled occupations, which require more education: rising levels of international trade tend to produce rising college enrollment rates.

Including in the ACE model a control for per capita international trade makes it directly comparable with the models in chapters 5 and 6—containing controls for relative cohort size, the military, and international trade (with an additional control in the enrollment model for real family income to allow for the "consumption good" element in education). Doing so produces a model able to fit the actual data on enrollment rates even into the 1990s. It explains well over 90 percent of the variation in college enrollment rates over the past fifty years, for both men and women,[7] even into the 1990s, and demonstrates that, in addition to strong cohort size effects on enrollment rates, there has been a significant effect of international trade in recent decades. Increasing globalization is increasing the incentive for higher college enrollments, as imports weaken the earning power of less-skilled workers and exports increase the competitive position of more-skilled workers.

Summary

Since at least the early 1970s, researchers have hypothesized that birth cohort size operates on college enrollment rates in the United States. Several studies have demonstrated the effects of cohort size on the college wage premium. Others have demonstrated the effects of cohort size on enrollment rates, but with opposing hypotheses regarding future trends.

This chapter has described very briefly an exercise that updated the most successful of these models, referred to here as the ACE model, which was developed in 1976. That updating allowed for the effects of international trade, and the results of the revised model indicate that a combination of relative income effects and college wage premium effects—all emanating from cohort size—has been operating on both male and female enrollment rates. Both young men and young women tend to enroll at higher rates when male relative income is low and when the wage premium is high. The combination of these two effects produced greatly reduced enrollment rates among young men in larger cohorts and higher enrollment rates as cohort size declined through the 1990s.

For young women, these effects seem to have strengthened an already marked increase in enrollment rates as real family incomes rose and parents became more willing to invest in their daughters' education. Thus a significant proportion of the increase in young women's educational level—which is often cited as the "cause" of rising female labor force participation and occupational shifts—

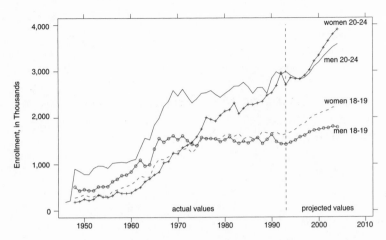

Figure 8.3. Actual college enrollments and projected demand, in thousands, among men and women aged 18–19 and 20–24.

appears to be yet another repercussion of the baby boom. Projections using the revised ACE model suggest that young women's enrollment rates will continue to increase during the next decade, with young women accounting for well over 50 percent of all college students in future, as suggested in figure 8.3.

9

Effects of Changing Male Relative Income

on Marriage and Divorce

> Our findings suggest that only the male partner's economic resources affect
> the transition to marriage, with positive economic situations accelerating
> marriage and deterring separation. Our results imply that despite trends
> toward egalitarian gender-role attitudes and increasing income provision
> among women, cohabiting men's economic circumstances carry far more
> weight than women's in marriage formation.
>
> Smock and Manning, "Cohabiting Partners'
> Economic Circumstances and Marriage" (1997)

> Only a statistician could even *imagine* that we're through with marriage. The
> truth is that Americans are nuts about the institution.
>
> Peter Godwin, "Happily Ever After: Americans Will Always
> Love Marriage and Polls about Other People's Lives" (1999)

Are Americans really "nuts" about marriage?[1] Have we simply
been living through a temporary aberration caused by the birth
quake, or does the much-heralded decline in marriage rates signal
the inevitable demise of the institution? Will husbands and wives be
replaced by a "posslq"?[2] You'd be hard-pressed to answer that question using official statistics on age-specific marriage and divorce
rates: the government stopped publishing such statistics back in
1988/89. Ironically, as it turns out, that's just about the time when
things began to get interesting. Marriage trends that had followed a
seemingly inexorable downward trend since 1970 have begun to turn
around, as indicated in figure 9.1.

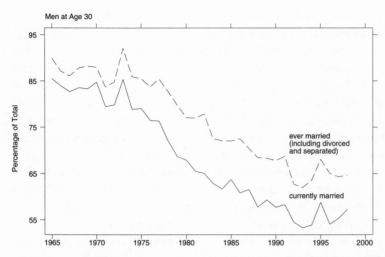

Figure 9.1. Percentage of men who have been married by age 30, 1965–1998. Official statistics stop in 1989, so they don't show the "turnaround" that appears to have occurred in the 1990s. Source: author's tabulations of data from March Current Population Surveys.

The previous chapters documented dramatic changes in male relative income and female wages and related these to changing relative cohort size. The relative income hypothesis suggests that these declines in ex ante income relative to aspirations should have brought about demographic adjustments aimed at improving the ex post incomes of young adults. There should have been a movement away from marriage, as growing proportions of young men perceived an inability to support a family at a level commensurate with their own material aspirations and as young women responded to the independence afforded them by increased labor force participation. And divorce rates should have risen due to the stresses caused by difficulties in "making ends meet." The obvious question, then, is whether the turnaround illustrated in figure 9.1 is related to the turnaround in male relative income that began after 1985.

The timing seems right, since these effects should show up most clearly at younger ages, where relative cohort size effects in the labor market are felt most strongly. A turnaround in the economic fortunes of 20-somethings after 1985 would be expected to show up by 1995, in the proportions of men who have chosen to marry by age 30.

You might well question the data presented in figure 9.1: what are they, if not official statistics? They are my own tabulations using another set of data provided by the Bureau of Labor Statistics and the Census Bureau—the March Current Population Survey (CPS) for the years 1962–1998. The CPS doesn't provide marriage *rates*, but does indicate individuals' current marital status, along with a great deal of other demographic information, in a representative sample of the population. Using these data it's possible to calculate not just the proportion currently married or divorced, but also the change in those rates for a given birth cohort from year to year: effectively, cohort marriage and divorce rates.

The cohort marriage rate is calculated as the increase in the proportion ever married from one year to the next, divided by the proportion never married in the previous year.[3] The cohort divorce rate is similarly calculated as the change in the proportion divorced from one year to the next, divided by the proportion who were married or separated in the previous year. This is true of all statistics presented here. It should be noted that the divorce rate is more error-prone than the marriage rate, however, since individuals can move out of the divorced state as well as in, through remarriage. Divorce rates calculated in this way may well be underestimates, especially at younger ages, but both the derived marriage and divorce rates accord well with official statistics up to 1990.

Thus, whereas the official statistics present a fairly bleak picture with no suggestion of a turnaround in marriage rates, the derived rates indicate that there have been tantalizing changes since 1989. Figure 9.2 illustrates some marriage rates estimated in this way, among young men and women by length of time out of school. The annual rates by single year of age derived using the procedure described above have been averaged into three-year age groups in order to minimize "noise" in the data. In addition, data are presented for young men at slightly older ages than for young women, reflecting the traditional age difference between marital partners.

Because of the virtual embargo on age-specific marriage and divorce rates imposed by federal budgetary restrictions since 1990, the data presented here and in Macunovich 2002 contribute significantly to knowledge about recent changes in marital behavior. They confirm the suspicions of many of us who've felt barraged by marriage announcements in recent years: marriage rates are up, particularly among those in their later 20s, and there is a slight trend back toward marriage at earlier ages.

The long-term decline in marriage rates at younger ages that

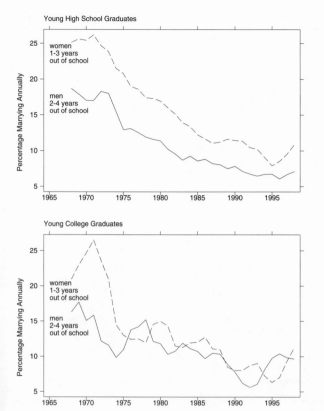

Figure 9.2. Annual marriage rates among young men and women between 1968/70 and 1998, showing the dramatic decline after 1970 and the tendency toward stabilization and even turnaround after 1985. Patterns here appear to mimic those displayed in the graphs of male relative income in chapter 4. Source: author's tabulations of data from March Current Population Surveys.

proceeded unabated for over fifteen years from the early 1970s appears to have been arrested since the late 1980s, and the break after 1985 appears to be more pronounced among males than among females. In addition, among all of the young women and among male college graduates there has been a marked upward trend in marriage rates at younger ages in the latter part of the 1990s.[4]

That the post-1985 stabilization was most pronounced among young men suggests that causes of the trend acted more directly on them than on young women: this would be the case with changes in male relative income. That is, 20–22-year-old males responding to increases in relative income may select partners their own age, or in any one of a number of other cohorts. Thus the effect of any change in their relative income on women's marriage rates will be diluted to the extent that males choose partners in various age groups.

If space permitted it would be possible to demonstrate that, as

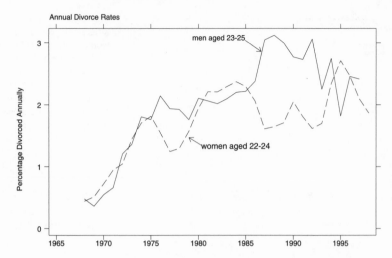

Figure 9.3. Estimated annual divorce rates between 1968 and 1998 among young men and women who were previously married or separated, showing the dramatic increase after 1970 followed by an apparent stabilization and turnaround after 1985. The patterns here suggest a strong response to changes in male relative income—especially the decline, increase, and renewed decline in the period after 1985. Source: author's tabulations of data from March Current Population Surveys.

with male relative income in chapter 4, the time trends in marriage rates exhibited in figure 9.2 emerge in all conceivable breakdowns of the data on young men and women, for example, by race, region of the country, educational attainment, and part-time/full-time employment status. Just as all young groups experienced staggering declines in male relative income, ranging from one-half to two-thirds, with a hump-shaped recovery after 1985, the proportions of young men entering marriage plunged, as well, by 60–80 percent—with a similar tendency toward resurgence, decline, and resurgence between 1985 and 1995.

Figure 9.3 demonstrates that divorce rates among younger men and women have tended to increase when marriage rates decline and vice versa. This suggests that the same factor(s) might be relevant in explaining both sets of trends. Divorce rates seem to have topped out since about 1985 and have even begun to decline, as male relative income has stabilized and begun to improve.

Cohort or Period Effect?

Andrew Cherlin, a respected researcher in the study of marriage and divorce in the United States, has acknowledged the possibility of cohort effects in the trends observed in the post-WWII period, but like many other social scientists he comes down fairly firmly on the side of period effects: "something in the air."[5] His reasoning relies on the fact that many age-specific rates appear to have moved in parallel when major transitions were occurring.

A comparison of trends by age group, however, in percentage ever married suggests that the only reason rates appeared to move in parallel is because the decline at younger ages was so long lasting that downward trends among the first baby boomers as they aged were matched by those of later baby boomers in their early 20s. This is demonstrated in figure 9.4, in which the age groups presented are five years apart—25, 30, 35, 40, and 45. The decline in percentage ever married at each age really began in earnest only after the baby

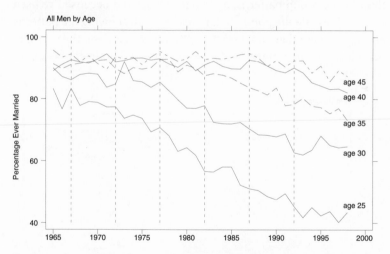

Figure 9.4. A comparison of time trends in percentage ever married across age groups and time. The vertical lines define five-year periods following the initiation of decline in the percentage married among 25-year-old men. There was a slight drop in that age group after 1967 (that is, among cohorts born 1942–1946), and then the prolonged decline among the baby boom cohorts set in after 1972. The vertical lines indicate that the declines in successively older age groups began only once those same baby boom cohorts had begun entering the age group. Thus, although the trends appear to be parallel, they did not all begin at the same time: this suggests a strong cohort effect, rather than a period effect.

boom cohorts (post-1947) had begun entering successively older age groups. As demarcated by the vertical lines, there was an initial drop in percentage married at age 25 among cohorts born 1943–1947 (in 1967–1972), but the real decline occurred among the cohorts born after 1947, from 1972 onward. The decline among 30-year-olds began approximately five years later. This is the case for each successively older age group, suggesting that the decline was a cohort rather than a period effect.

Another point that emerges from figure 9.4 is that this apparent decline was largely a case of *delayed marriage,* rather than marriages forgone altogether. By the time the boomers reach age 45, their percentage ever married is not much lower than that of their parents. And although I haven't included it here, this is even more the case by age 50: 93.2 percent of 50-year-olds in 1998 were ever married, while twenty-five years earlier that figure was 93.6 percent, and the highest it's been in the last forty years is 96.1 percent, in 1986. But, you might say, very few boomers have yet reached age 50. For this reason it's useful to examine tendencies as they emerge among cohorts rather than in age-group patterns, as in figure 9.5. (And because I've used men to illustrate the points so far, this time I'm showing the patterns among women: there are very few differences between the sexes, in overall marriage patterns!) The figure depicts the life course of co-

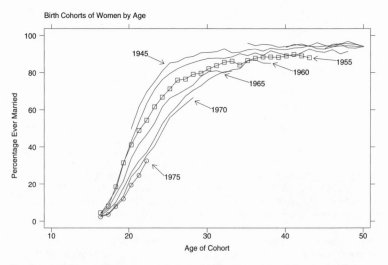

Figure 9.5. Cohort marriage patterns by age, showing the strong tendency toward convergence at older ages. Marriage isn't dead—it's just been delayed!

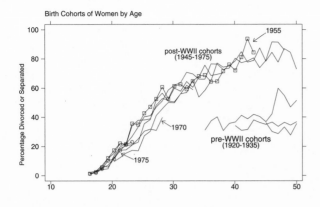

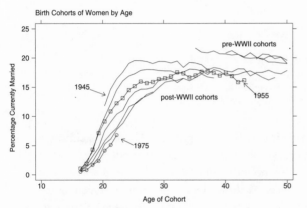

Figure 9.6. Cohort patterns of divorce among those previously married or separated *(top)* and their effect on percentages in intact marriages, showing the sharp dichotomy between pre– and post–World War II birth cohorts, as well as the lack of any trend across baby boom cohorts and the tendency toward lower divorce rates among post-boom cohorts.

horts of women, in terms of the percentage ever married at each age. It shows a wide dispersion at younger ages—up to about 30—as successive baby boom cohorts moved further away from traditional family formation in their 20s, but with a very strong tendency toward convergence after that age. Perhaps Americans really *are* nuts about marriage!

Despite the apparent tendency toward convergence in percentages *ever* married, however, a different trend emerges in percentages *currently* married (i.e., not divorced or separated), as shown in figure 9.6. There, a sharp dichotomy is apparent between pre- and post-WWII birth cohorts: there is a tendency toward convergence, but in two separate groups. For the baby boomers, higher divorce rates appear to leave permanent scars.

It's notable in figure 9.6 that there is no apparent trend in divorce rates at each age among the baby boomers themselves. All cohorts

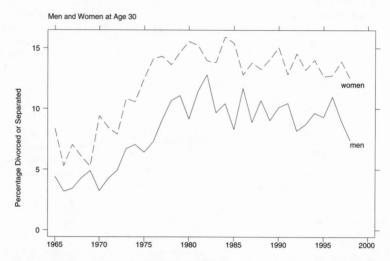

Figure 9.7. Patterns of divorce at age 30 among men and women who were previously married or separated, showing that the upward trend ended with the baby boomers: rates have been fairly level since the 1945 birth cohort turned 30 in 1975, and now there is evidence of a downward trend in post-boom cohorts.

seem to exhibit a very similar lifecycle pattern. There was simply a break from the pattern established among pre-War cohorts.

There is, however, some indication of a decline in divorce rates among post-boom cohorts, as shown by the position of the curve for the 1975 birth cohort. This is borne out by the pattern of the percentage divorced at age 30, among both men and women, as shown in figure 9.7. Divorce rates ceased their increase with the 1945 birth cohort in 1975, and the trend among these 30-year-olds appears to have been downward since the mid-1990s. Once again this is consistent with the hypothesis that divorce rates were responding to improvements in male relative income that began after 1985 for those in their 20s.

Thus if we wish to explain marriage trends we need to explain the forces that caused baby boomers to delay marriage at earlier ages: this appears to be the source of the overall trends that have emerged over the past thirty years. Why did such a large proportion of young people in the baby boom cohorts put off marriage—and why did so many of their marriages fail?

College Enrollment as a Deterrent to Marriage

Studies have confirmed that current enrollment in school has a marked effect on marriage rates. One influential study found that current enrollment was in fact one of the strongest deterrents: "[Y]oung men's earnings and the time spent in schooling to increase them were found to be important influences on marriage timing. Additional schooling had little effect net of the time it absorbed."[6] That is, the researchers found that being in school had a significant deterrent effect on the probability of marriage, but that additional schooling on its own, after controlling for the time taken to acquire it, had no significant impact on marriage probabilities.

That one study has tended to reinforce, in the minds of most researchers, Cherlin's dismissal of cohort effects. It "provide[d] no support for Easterlin's hypothesis that marriage will occur earlier when young men judge their economic prospects favorably with respect to their parents' income."[7] But this study, based on an analysis of Wisconsin males who graduated high school in 1957, bears closer examination. The database was unusual in its depth of coverage: it contained Social Security earnings records for the young males, together with income tax reports for their parents and follow-up information through 1975. Researchers conducted a year-by-year analysis, measuring the probability of marriage among these young males in the years 1958–1965. The results show a strong positive effect of the young males' own income on their propensity to marry, but little or no effect of their parents' income. The researchers concluded that the relative income concept is not only erroneous, but "obfuscates important effects of young men's current earnings."

This finding is extremely significant in that it appears to ignore the potential connection between relative income and enrollment rates. If enrollment rates as well as marriage rates are a function of relative income, then the analysis produced only a partial estimate of the effect of relative income on marriage, ignoring the secondary effect operating through enrollment rates. As described in the previous chapter, the relative income model suggests that young males, in making a decision regarding higher education, will compare their potential earnings *as high school graduates* to those of their fathers and will assess the potential returns to education relative to the size of the "gap" between these two. In this context, the males in the Wisconsin 1957 sample who enrolled in college would have been composed largely of those who had judged their potential high school earnings to be deficient relative to their aspirations. In this sense, then, the sample of wage earners was actually truncated, and truncated in a way that would have removed just those young males whose parental earnings were "high" and thus indirectly caused postponement of marriage.

Thus marriage postponement that may have resulted from relative income effects showed up as simple college enrollment in the Wisconsin sample—which did, indeed, have a strong negative effect on propensity to marry. It seems possible that a re-estimation of the Wisconsin model with college enrollment as a function of relative income would have shown support for the relative income hypothesis, and hence for cohort size effects on male marriage rates.

Changing Values

Probably the most common theme running through various analyses of delayed and declining marriage (and fertility) rates is that of "changing values": attitudinal changes that have, in the words of one group of researchers, "undermined the social and economic forces that maintained the institution."[8] Some feel that these changes were essentially independent of economic forces, instead arising from the continuing growth of individualism that began with the Enlightenment.[9] But others maintain that such change is not autonomous: it derives from—or at least is intensified by—a host of factors, including the growing financial independence of women; the decline of religious values; improved contraceptive methods, which made sex outside of marriage less risky; and lower fertility, which reduced some of the "function" of marriage.[10] Also stressed, however, is the increasing social acceptance of such factors: not only are the associated behaviors more attractive, they are also less "costly" in terms of potential social sanction. This leads one to envision a snowball effect in which one set of attitudinal changes brings about behavioral change, which then reinforces the original attitudinal shift. My own position is that declining male relative income was a significant factor in accelerating the snowball.

The Marriage Squeeze Hypothesis: Too Many Women?

There is another theory, in addition to the relative income hypothesis, that links cohort size and marriage rates: the "marriage squeeze" hypothesis.[11] Because women tend to look for marriage partners among males approximately two years older than themselves, periods of mismatch between any given cohort and the cohort two years older—such as those that occurred during the baby boom—will affect marriage rates, due to imbalances between the demand for and the supply of mates. This suggests that cohorts born during the first half of a baby boom will exhibit declining marriage rates for females, while cohorts born during the latter half of such a boom will exhibit increasing marriage rates for females, because of this tendency for women to marry older men. In other words, young women will be "squeezed out" of the marriage market when there is a relative shortage of unmarried men about two years older than themselves—and this type of shortage would occur on the leading edge of any baby boom.

It is not entirely clear, however, how this variable is expected to affect *male* marriage rates: arguments of symmetry would imply that the marriage rates of young men should move inversely to those of young women in the same birth cohort, since a period of abundant mates for women will coincide with a period of scarcity for young men, and vice versa. But here again, symmetry may not hold. The "too many women" hypothesis suggests that young men will not feel compelled to marry when there is an abundance of potential mates: they need not commit themselves to any one woman.[12] In this case male and female marriage rates would be expected to move together, declining (increasing) in periods of increasing (declining) relative cohort size.

Testing the Various Theories on Marriage and Divorce

How can competing explanations of marriage and divorce trends be tested? To what extent, if any, are marriage and divorce rates a function of relative cohort size (whether through male relative income or through the "marriage squeeze") or of absolute incomes, both male and female?[13] To what extent are economic variables important? Of these potential factors, the relative income hypothesis is the most difficult to test because of the need to compare the earnings of young adults with the income of their parents, a task hampered by the lack of appropriate data.

I have made two attempts to get around this data limitation, one using aggregate national-level data and the other using more disaggregated regional data.[14] In both cases the March Current Population Survey data have been invaluable. These data on hundreds of thousands of individuals over a forty-year period can be aggregated up to any level—whether a neighborhood, county, city, state, region, or nation—and used to "simulate" parent-child groupings by comparing the average earnings of young men in an area with the average income of older families in the same area. Using this approximation makes it possible to test for a relationship at the national level between economic variables (young men's earnings, women's wages, and older families' income), as well as the "marriage squeeze" variable, and annual observations of age-specific marriage rates provided by *Vital Statistics* for the years through 1990 in a simple time-series analysis.

In addition, by using CPS data on proportions married and divorced, the analysis can be extended down to the regional level for a much larger and richer time series of data cross-sections.[15] The overall trends across regions are similar, as was demonstrated in figure 4.2, but there are significant regional differences as well, which permit testing to determine whether the apparent relationship between male relative income and marriage/divorce patterns is statistically significant. Specifically, I have identified subgroups of young adults by year, race, region, educational attainment, and years out of school[16] and tested to see if there is a relationship between proportions married and divorced in each subgroup and the following economic and non-economic variables:[17]

1. the average annual earnings of young men in each subgroup by year, race, region, educational attainment, and years out of school;

2. the average starting hourly wage of young women (that is, the average wage in the first full year of work experience) in each subgroup by year, race, region, and educational attainment;[18]

3. the average income of families with children with head of either sex aged 45–54, by year, race, and region;

4. the "marriage squeeze" variable; and

5. a simple time trend.

In both sets of analyses I have found a strong and highly significant effect of male relative income on marriage, as hypothesized. That is, young men's absolute earnings exert a strong positive effect on marriage for both young men and women, as hypothesized by other researchers, but an additional and much stronger effect—of the opposite sign—is exerted by older families' income. Young men's earnings were not found to be significant for divorce, but once again the effect of parental income was estimated to be very large and significant (positive). This finding in my analyses is consistent with recent survey data. In 1999 the *New York Times* and CBS News conducted a survey in which "1,038 young people aged 13–17 were asked to compare their lives with their parents' experience when growing up". There was a definite effect of parental income, with the more affluent teenagers "whatever their race or gender, substantially more likely than those from more modest homes to report that their lives were harder and subject to more stress." The comparative percentages were 50(38) reporting their lives as harder, 28(41) easier and 21(18) about the same among those with household incomes of $75,000+(<$30,000).[19]

In disaggregated analyses I have found that for both men and women, *a 10 percent change in older families' income results in a 5 percent change in both divorce and marriage rates among younger adults.* The effect on divorce for men and women six to ten years out of school is even stronger: a 10 percent change in parental income would produce an *11 to 12 percent increase* in divorce.[20] These disaggregated results support my additional finding that at the national level a relative income model explains 99 percent of variation over time in marriage rates among young men 20–24 years old and even explains 75 percent of the year-to-year change at that level.

I have found in the disaggregated analysis that consistently, in regions, periods, and racial subgroups in which older families' incomes are high, marriage rates tend to be lower and divorce rates tend to be higher among young adults—even after controlling for other factors such as education and race—suggesting that these young people's material aspirations are indeed a function of older families' income. And, consistent with the hypothesis, this effect of older families' income tends to be strongest among the youngest adults (those less than seven years out of school), gradually weakening with age.

The female wage appears to play a less consistent role in these disaggregated analyses. It has a less certain effect than that of the relative income variables: negative and significant in most cases on young women's propensity to divorce, and positive and significant in most cases on their propensity to marry.[21] But its effect on male marriage and divorce propensities is significant in only one case, for young men's divorce propensity in the first five years out of school. There it exerts a significant *negative* effect.

Interestingly, however, these estimated positive effects of women's earnings on their own propensity to marry contradict a popular belief that women's increasing financial independence has been the cause of declining marriage rates. One researcher, however, has argued strenuously that women's financial independence is not the cause, but that the real culprit has been declining male earnings and employment prospects.[22] These results support her contention, but add to young men's own characteristics the very significant negative effect of parental income on their children's marital propensities.

There remains, however, even after controlling for these variables, a very significant time trend: negative in all cases for men's and women's propensity to marry. This might be the result of a reinforcing "snowball" effect mentioned earlier, but it might also reflect changes in societal attitudes not captured by the economic variables. The models also estimate a significant negative time trend with respect to the propensity of younger men and women to divorce (that is, men and women less than ten years out of school). This could be a feedback effect of declining marriage rates: a self-selection process weeds out those who might have had a higher propensity to divorce.

The estimated effect of the "marriage squeeze" variable in the disaggregated analysis is paradoxical, however. It is highly significant, but its estimated effect on marriage rates is negative, rather than positive: an abundance of marital partners for women appears to decrease women's chances of marrying, rather than increase them. This result contradicts the expectations of the marriage squeeze hypothesis and seems somewhat nonsensical until one realizes that it simply means marriage rates continued to decline even for baby boom cohorts born after the peak. If the variable isn't measuring a marriage squeeze effect, it might be acting as a proxy for some type of "snowball" or "cascade" effect of relative cohort size on marriage propensities, as younger cohorts respond to the negative marital experiences of cohorts preceding them. This hypothesis is supported by the fact that the marriage squeeze variable loses its significance in analyses at the national level, after controlling either for a time trend or for male relative income. Many researchers have begun to suggest that a negative time trend of this type could well be attributable to the rising acceptability and incidence of cohabitation, a natural outcome of a "snowball" effect in terms of changing social attitudes and mores. Young adults still value many of the benefits associated with marriage, it would appear, but given the economic uncertainties associated with low male relative income, they haven't been prepared to make as firm a commitment as in the past. One researcher has concluded, "The increase in the proportion of unmarried young people should not be interpreted as an increase in "singlehood" as traditionally regarded: young people are setting up housekeeping with partners of the opposite sex at almost as early an age as they did before marriage rates declined. . . . The picture that is emerging is that cohabitation is very much a family status, but one in which levels of certainty about the relationship are lower than in marriage."[23]

Summary

Statistics presented in this chapter suggest that the media's marriage obituaries may have been premature, if not altogether off track. Those obituaries were encouraged by the virtual embargo on official age-specific marriage and divorce statistics that has existed since the late 1980s because of federal budgetary restrictions. Since 1990 we have seen only "crude" marriage and divorce rates (rates per 1,000 total population) from official sources, which are severely distorted by changing age composition in the population. Because the baby boom during the 1990s was moving out of marriageable ages and into divorce-prone ones, it seemed like marriage rates were continuing their inexorable decline, and divorce rates their worrying increases.

Age-specific rates presented in this chapter demonstrate that trends appear to have turned around among young adults: they're beginning to marry at earlier ages and at higher rates, and their divorce rates—which in any case hadn't increased in this group since about 1975—are on the decline. And the time trends in this behavior are remarkably similar to time trends in male relative income, suggesting that young adults were significantly affected by declines in this measure and scrambling to maintain their desired living standards by delaying family formation.

Statistical analyses confirm this relationship that seemed so apparent visually. As suspected by many researchers, declining male absolute earnings did play a role in the marriage decline—but this was a contingent role. The prime mover was parental income: young people were significantly affected by the rising standard of living in their parents' homes and felt compelled to establish a standard in their own households at commensurate levels. This tendency was so strong that for every 10 percent increase in the income of older families, marriage rates declined by 5 percent among younger adults— and divorce rates increased by about 5 percent. But since 1985 young people's earnings relative to those of their parents have begun to rise for the first time since the 1960s, and marriage rates appear to be following. It seems that marriage rates declined not so much because marriage was becoming unpopular as an institution, but rather because it began to seem increasingly out of reach for young adults.

But, as in so many other cases, male relative income was probably not the only factor operational during this period. A significant negative time trend in the statistical analyses suggests either there are other—presumably non-economic—factors at work here, or else declining marriage rates have created over time a "cascade" or "snowball" effect, with younger baby boom cohorts responding not only to their own relative economic circumstances but also to the lifestyle example set by older baby boomers. If this latter is the case, however, it demonstrates even more the power of male relative income: it implies that recent economic changes have been influential even in the face of strong antimarital cultural biases that have developed against marriage as a result of baby boomer experience.

One last significant finding of the analyses reported in this chapter is that young women's increasing financial independence has in fact played a positive rather than the often expected negative role in its effect on marriage rates, after accounting for the effects of male relative income. Rising women's wages appear to have encouraged marriage and discouraged divorce among young working women, but their effect was swamped by the strong discouragement of declining male relative income (and, presumably, other non-economic factors).

The Disappearance of the Marriage Wage Premium

> If it were possible for each married couple to limit by a wish the number
> of their children, there is certainly reason to fear that the indolence of the
> human race would be very greatly increased.
>
> Reverend Thomas R. Malthus, *An Essay of the Principle of Population* (1817)

One element in the observed stagnation in men's wages over the past few decades has been a decline in the "marriage wage premium": the higher average wage paid to married men as compared with men who remain single. Researchers have come to accept that married men earn more, on average, than unmarried men, even after controlling for differences such as age, experience, education, and hours and weeks worked,[1] and for occupational characteristics.[2] The marriage wage premium has been estimated to be as high as 50 percent for older married men in the 1970s,[3] though it seems to have declined sharply between 1967 and 1988.[4] Might changes in relative cohort size have played a part in that decline, thus contributing to the observed stagnation in average male wages?

Many explanations have been suggested for the marriage wage premium, including:

1. Selection bias
   a) Men with higher earnings are more likely to marry, because they anticipate greater returns to specialized gender roles within marriage; because women tend to select partners with higher earnings or with characteristics correlated with earning potential; or both.

   b) Men with higher *earning potential* (and therefore with *faster earnings growth*) are more likely to marry, for the same reasons.

2. Employer discrimination/favoritism

   a) Employers perceive a greater need among married men, because such men have dependents to support.

   b) Employers favor married men because such men conform with accepted social norms.

   c) Employers assume that married men will be more stable and responsible (a phenomenon known as "statistical discrimination").

3. Higher productivity

   a) Role specialization within marriage frees married men from household duties, allowing them to devote more energies toward market work.

   b) Married men can draw on their wives' support, financial and otherwise, to accumulate more labor market-oriented human capital, either through specialized training or through additional time in the market.

   c) An employer gets "two workers for the price of one" with married men:

      (1) Wives perform functions valued by employers, such as hosting dinner parties and other social functions.

      (2) Wives actually assume some of their husbands' work responsibilities (e.g., typing and proofing manuscripts or assisting with background research).

   d) Married men are healthier and more efficient workers because of the emotional, psychological, and other support their wives provide.

   e) Wives (especially better-educated ones) help their husbands make better career decisions.

   f) Marriage, with its additional responsibilities, motivates men to increase their earning capacity by working harder or for longer hours.

Another reason that hasn't been made explicit in this controversy, but which is related to (3*f*), is the hypothesis that the presence and number of dependent children provides a strong motivation for increased productivity in marriage. Thomas Malthus made this argument (see the passage quoted at the start of this chapter), and the influential work of economist Ester Boserup, who found that increased use of technology and innovation in agrarian societies was motivated by increased population pressure, provides supporting evidence.[5]

Obviously, if (1) above is the real reason for the observed marriage wage premium, then it is simply a statistical artifact caused by a grouping of high-wage males into the married category: marriage in no way *causes* the higher wages. And this would be related, to some extent, to (2c): marriage simply acts as a "signal" that employers use in attempting to identify more productive workers. Some discrimination might be involved, but it would be based on observed historic differences between the average married and unmarried worker.

But if (2) and especially (3) are the predominant reasons for the marriage wage premium, then changes in three factors that have been influenced by relative cohort size—declining marriage rates, decreased fertility, and increasing female labor force participation—would have played a major role in reducing both the incidence and the size of the marriage wage premium. A simple reduction in marriage rates—a combination of older age at marriage and a reduced propensity to marry at any age—would lower the incidence of the marriage wage premium. An increase in the proportion of childless marriages, and a decline in the number of children in other marriages, would reduce men's (and women's) motivation to maximize earnings. And an increase in the labor force participation of married women would tend to reduce the size of the average marriage wage premium by removing at least some of the productivity gains hypothesized in (3). All three of these changes would lower the observed average male wage.

Several researchers in recent years have attempted to identify the source of the premium, with varying levels of success. One popular argument in favor of at least *some* real productivity effects of marriage has been the observed reduction in the marriage wage premium among separated, divorced, and widowed men, and the fact that the premium tends to decline as a man approaches divorce or separation.[6] These effects would not be expected to occur if the premium were due solely to selection bias. In addition, four groups of researchers performed careful analyses that allowed them to separate the effects of (1) from those of (2) and (3), and all found a significant proportion of the marriage premium that was not due to selection bias (and was therefore due to real productivity, employer responses to marital status, or both).[7] All four used longitudinal data

(data containing multiple observations on the same individuals, following them over a period of time), observing the same individuals both before and after marriage in order to separate these effects.

But, if there is wage premium that isn't due to selection bias, is it attributable to (2), employer discrimination, or to (3), real productivity increases? One way to approach this question is to examine the effects of wives' labor force participation on the marriage wage premium, on the assumption that the more a wife works outside the home, the less she is able to support her husband's specialization in market work. Some researchers simply demonstrate that married men with stay-at-home wives earn a much higher premium than married men with working wives and use this to argue in favor of real productivity effects.[8] But these particular researchers failed to control for the possibility of *reverse causation* (what analysts term "endogeneity bias"). That is, married women might seek employment outside the home *because of* their husbands' low wages: the women's employed status might not have been a factor at all in the level of their husbands' marriage wage premium.[9]

Another researcher questioned the productivity hypothesis and attempted to test it by including controls for the number of years of wives' labor force participation (<2 years, 2–4, 4–6, 6–8, and 8+ years), along with number of years married, in a wage equation for all white males (married and unmarried).[10] Using this test he found a *positive* effect of wives' labor force participation on their husbands' wages. This is a highly unusual result, especially since he included no control for the endogeneity of such labor force activity (which would on its own produce a *negative* relationship between wives' labor supply and their husbands' wages). His result appears to be an artifact of his model formulation, however: it forced the female labor supply variables to act as proxies for number of years married (since, for example, only men who had been married for eight or more years could have had a wife who had worked for eight or more years). And if there is a productivity effect, number of years married would be expected to increase a man's marriage wage premium, given other researchers' findings that marriage steepens the earnings profile.[11]

Another of this same researcher's tests of the productivity hypothesis was also questionable. He assumed that a true productivity effect should be reflected in the wages of self-employed as well as traditionally employed married men, but he found no such effect for the self-employed. However, one would not expect to see a premium among these men if, for example, self-employment among married men represents a self-selection by men who wish to work at home and combine home and work responsibilities. It is not clear that self-employment represents a valid test of the productivity hypothesis.

Two recent studies have provided the most comprehensive and convincing analyses indicating strong productivity effects of marriage that are diminished when a man's wife enters paid employment.[12] Researchers in both studies controlled carefully for the potential endogeneity of marital status and wife's work status using longitudinal data that observed the same individuals both before and after marriage. In addition, one researcher made use of *two* such longitudinal data sets—one group (the National Longitudinal Survey [NLS] of men aged 14–24 in 1966) observed in 1976, 1978, and 1980 and the other (the National Longitudinal Survey of Young Men [NLSY] aged 14–21 in 1979) observed in 1989, 1991, and 1993—in order to examine the decline in the observed marriage wage premium between those two periods.[13]

The latter study found that "the decline in the productivity effects of marriage results from less specialization taking place in marriages, rather than any decrease in the return to specialization. Moreover, some of this researcher's results[14] suggest that the returns to specialization actually increased slightly over the 1980s, as a wife's labor market activity had an increasingly negative impact on her husband's marriage wage premium." In other words, the premium for men with stay-at-home wives actually increased over the period, but because the proportion of married men with stay-at-home wives declined so dramatically, the productivity-related marriage wage premium was virtually eliminated. This study estimated that the productivity-related wage premium for men with stay-at-home wives increased from 11 percent to 13 percent between 1976–1980 and 1989–1993, while the penalty for wives' labor force participation (controlling for endogeneity) increased from 1 percent to 3 percent for each ten hours of weekly work during the same period.

Unfortunately, neither of these researchers attempted to identify or control for the number of children in a married man's family, but because of the strong inverse correlation between the presence of young children and the incidence and extent of female labor force participation, it seems likely that at least part of the reason for the observed marriage wage premium might be the presence of children.

Another contributing factor in the loss of the productivity-related premium, besides increasing wives' labor force participation, appears likely to have been the sectoral shift toward low-wage service jobs among young men. One researcher hypothesized that marital status differentials would be larger in occupations that are more stressful, involve more peripheral tasks, have potentially steeper earnings profiles, and have more complex and potentially substitutable central tasks, because wives' opportunities for providing many types of support would be maximized for husbands in such occupations.[15] Her hypotheses are supported by other independent estimates that the marriage wage premium for managers and professionals was three times greater than that for blue collar workers.[16] Similarly, one of my own thesis students reproduced a well-known analysis, but broke the results down by income quintile, and was thereby able to determine that the declining trend in the wage premium was almost completely the result of a trend among workers in the lowest income quintiles.[17] She attributed this phenomenon to the "de-skilling" of low-wage jobs, which removed much of the benefit to specialization in the traditional household division of labor.

Summary

In combination with the findings in previous chapters, these results provide evidence that increasing relative cohort size was indeed a major factor in the loss of the marriage wage premium and stagnation in average male wages observed over the last twenty years. Increasing relative cohort size reduced male relative income, which in turn reduced marriage rates and fertility, and motivated much of the increase in young married women's labor force participation.

Reduced marriage rates then lowered the incidence of men who enjoyed a marriage wage premium. In addition, increased labor force participation of wives eliminated the bulk of the productivity gains associated with specialized roles in marriage, and reduced family size removed much of the motivation for men to increase their productive capacities. And finally, women's tendency, as they entered the labor force, to replace their own home production with purchased goods and services generated a marked increase in the proportion of jobs in low-wage retail and service sectors—and men holding such jobs tend to benefit little from any increased specialization in marriage.

Relative Cohort Size and Fertility

The Boom Turns into a Bust

> In the struggle for what is deemed a desirable mode of existence at the
> present day, marriage is being held less desirable, and its bonds less sacred,
> than they were forty years ago. Young women are gradually being imbued
> with the idea that marriage and motherhood are not to be their chief objects
> in life, or the sole methods of obtaining subsistence; that they should aim
> at being independent of possible or actual husbands, and should fit them-
> selves to earn their own living . . . [and] that housekeeping is a sort of do-
> mestic slavery.
>
> John S. Billings, *The Diminished Birth-Rate in the United States* (1893)

> The wondrous creature marries younger than ever, bears more babies
> and looks and acts far more feminine than the "emancipated" girl of the
> twenties or thirties.
>
> *Look Magazine* (1950s)

All this focus on the baby boom—the birth quake—and I haven't
yet addressed the *cause* of that phenomenal surge in fertility
rates, or how it moved from boom to bust.[1] There have of course been
many theories, but one notable shortcoming in the literature is the
inability of many of them to explain both boom and bust.[2]

As with marriage and divorce (chapter 9), one of the most pervasive themes underlying fertility theories is "changing values"—but
the focus tends to be on the long-term decline in fertility that has occurred over the past century, rather than on the 1950s' deviation
from that trend: the deviation highlighted so nicely by contrasting

the two quotes at the start of this chapter. Thus the discussion of non-economic factors usually focuses, for example, on the growth of individualism, declining religious values and marriage rates, increasing materialism in a consumer society (arguably an economic factor), improved contraceptives, environmental concerns, and the increasing desire for "quality" over "quantity" in children.[3] But many of these factors can be thought susceptible to changes in economic conditions, and it's usually by including economic fluctuations that the baby boom is explained as a component of the longer-term trend.[4] That is, fertility rose in response to postwar euphoria combined with a booming economy and incentives like the GI Bill. It's harder to explain the baby bust in those same terms, however, since fertility rates began to decline in the late 1950s, long before the economic slump of the 1970s.

My focus in this chapter is on two attempts by economists to develop a theory that encompasses both boom and bust. As I run through the two models, readers should bear in mind that any fluctuations these models explain might easily be superimposed on longer-term ideational trends: their relevance does not preclude the operation of non-economic factors like those discussed above. One of the two economic theories I'll focus on is known as the "price of time" model and the other, unsurprisingly given the focus of all the chapters thus far, is the "relative income" model. With both of these models, it's necessary to understand that economists analyze the decision to have a child in very much the same way as they do the decision to purchase durable goods, like cars or refrigerators.

Are Children "Inferior Goods"?

It's assumed that children are "normal goods," meaning that people wish to "purchase" more of them when their income rises, as opposed to "inferior goods," which individuals tend to purchase less as income rises. Wine, for example, tends to be a normal good, whereas beer is an inferior one. This assumption has been a problem for analysts because, as most laypersons are aware, fertility appears to *decline* in countries as the level of income rises. Does this mean that children are actually "inferior" goods? The relative income and price of time models have been put forward as explanations for this apparently counterintuitive result.

The price of time model is attributed to several members of

the "Chicago-Columbia School," which unlike the "Pennsylvania School" of Richard Easterlin, treats all preferences (such as the desired standard of living) as fixed and attempts to explain changes in behavior as functions only of changing prices and incomes. This model makes use of the fact that although individuals' income—their purchasing power—increases with rising earnings, the price of their time increases, as well—what is called the "opportunity cost" of time. That is, every hour not spent in labor market activities "costs" the wage that is forgone by not working. It's assumed that people need to invest time in order to derive utility from goods that they purchase: even a box of corn flakes can't give satisfaction unless we take the time to eat. And some goods are more "time intensive" than others—children being a prime example. Thus the hourly wage can be thought of as one factor in the "price" of children, and since children are more time intensive than many other goods, their price rises more rapidly than the price of many other goods, as the hourly wage increases. And it's generally thought that if the price of one good rises more rapidly than others, people will tend to "substitute" less costly for more costly items. This "price of time" effect is thought to counterbalance and even outweigh any tendency for individuals to "purchase" more children as their incomes rise.

The relative income model is based on a concept that can be seen in writings as far back as Thomas Malthus, that people's desired standard of living rises with successive generations during economic development: items once thought of as luxuries, like automobiles, become necessities to later generations. This desired standard of living might rise even more rapidly than average incomes, leading people to feel poorer over time, in relative terms, and thus less able to afford children. As explained earlier, Richard Easterlin's contribution to this model was his hypothesis that each generation's material aspirations are specifically a function of the standard of living experienced in their parents' homes, and that the earning potential of the younger relative to the older generation can be affected by their relative cohort size.

Explaining the Baby Boom

Easterlin pointed out that although in general the desired standard of living is expected to increase fairly continuously as economic development proceeds, there can be instances in which a period of economic hardship causes expectations to *decline.* He hypothesized that this was probably the case for the generation born and raised during the 1930s Depression. Raised during the Depression—and then World War II—their expectations were low. But their earnings fairly skyrocketed after the war, both in absolute and in relative terms, for at least two reasons. They were a relatively small cohort, because of the low fertility during the Depression, so their wages rose more rapidly than those of their parents, as explained in chapters 3–5. And they emerged in a booming market with fairly generous assistance to veterans for things like housing and education. Thus young couples in the 1950s entered enthusiastically into marriage and family formation, causing the postwar baby boom. The bust occurred when those baby boomers flooded the labor market twenty years later, depressing their own wages relative to those of their parents—and thus relative to their own expectations.[5]

It's assumed in the relative income model that the baby boomers' demographic adjustments, made as they scrambled to close the gap between income and aspirations, included increased female labor force participation and delayed/forgone marriage (as explained in chapters 7 and 9), as well as the decision to have fewer children in order to spread their income over fewer heads. This model replaces the common assumption that declining fertility and marriage rates resulted from changes in female labor force participation—or vice versa—with the assumption that all three behavioral shifts were at least in part responses to changes in relative income.

In addition to its application to the baby boom and bust, the relative income model sheds light on the occurrence of increased out-of-wedlock fertility among teens and young adults. When a pressured generation chooses to delay or forgo marriage, more young women will face the possibility of nonmarital pregnancy. This factor, together with delayed or reduced fertility within marriage—also a function of relative income—means that an increased proportion of all births will be outside of marriage. This would explain to a great extent the extremely high incidence of out-of-wedlock fertility that has occurred since the 1970s, as well as its marked decline in the 1990s.

The price of time model also has been used to explain the baby boom. Analysts hypothesized that since child care has traditionally been predominately a woman's responsibility, men's earnings should have almost exclusively an "income effect" on fertility—that is, a positive effect—while women's earnings should have a "price," or negative, effect. It's assumed that women's wages had little effect on fertility during the 1950s, probably because they didn't rise as rapidly as men's, and also because female labor force participation was so low.[6] Conversely, it's assumed that women's wages rose more rapidly than men's in the 1960s and 1970s, and in addition the strong increase in women's labor force participation dramatically increased the relative importance of women's wages, producing a net negative effect on fertility in those decades.[7]

However, some of my own work points out significant problems with assumptions used to estimate women's wages in the primary studies testing the price of time model. Women's wages didn't increase as assumed, after controlling for changing levels of education and experience.[8] In addition, both the relative income and price of time models failed to predict the actual course of fertility after the mid-1970s. The relative income model predicted that fertility should rise after about 1980, while the price of time model suggested that it should continue falling. As it turned out, fertility rates in the United States at that time simply stabilized and haven't changed greatly since.

Improving on These Models: The Importance of the Income Effect of the Female Wage

In my own work I've attempted to bring together these two models, testing for effects of both relative income and women's wages on young women's age-specific fertility rates, particularly the fertility rate of women aged 20–24, because as explained earlier the relative income theory is expected to be most relevant at younger ages.

The significant difference between Easterlin's original formulation of a relative income model of fertility and the model I have used is my strong emphasis on the female wage together with an allowance for its changing net effects. In theory, the female wage is expected to exert both a positive (income) and a negative (price of time) effect on fertility. In practice, however, proponents of the Chicago-Columbia model have expected that any positive effect would be greatly outweighed by its negative effect, ignoring the fact that theory dictates an increasingly dominant income (positive) effect with rising wages and hours worked. The positive effect is expected to increase because *total income* rises as hourly wages and hours worked rise and the total effect of a wage increase is greater as hours worked increases. At the same time, the utility derived from each additional hour of non-work activity rises as one works longer hours. An individual in these circumstances, who has more income to spend, will tend to "buy" time for non-work activities.

In addition to the standard theoretical explanation underlying an increasingly positive effect of the female wage on fertility over the last century, it is possible to imagine at least two others. The first has to do with a declining negative (price of time) effect of the wage. This negative effect is posited on the assumption that a woman is the primary provider of child care: every hour she spends in child care will "cost" her the forgone wage. However, to the extent that alternative (purchased) methods of child care are both available and socially acceptable, this negative price effect will be diminished: a woman can work the extra hour and pay for a replacement for her time in the home. We have certainly observed the development of such conditions over the past thirty years.[9]

Second, the positive (income) effect of the female wage will tend to be higher, all other things equal, the higher a woman's material aspirations. Why? Because her perceived value of her non-labor income (income from sources other than her own wages) will be diminished relative to those higher material aspirations, so her participation in the labor force will thus be higher, all other factors equal. In addition, to the extent that marriage is delayed or forgone in a period of low male relative income, fewer women will have husbands' wages as a source of non-labor income. In that event, even the absolute value of women's non-labor income will decline, on average—resulting, again, in higher female labor force participation rates, all other things equal. Women's greater number of hours in the labor force in both cases will tend to increase the income effect of a wage increase, since income equals the hourly wage times number of hours worked.

The idea of a changing net effect of the female wage is supported by the literature on female labor force participation, where successive studies find increasingly smaller positive, and even insignificant or negative, net effects of the female wage on female labor force participation. And yet this factor has been omitted in both price of time and relative income models of fertility. In addition, the majority of relative income studies have omitted any control for the female wage, while the majority of price of time models have omitted any control for material aspirations.

Selection of Age Groups

It seems natural to expect that the relative income effect would be strongest for those who have only recently emerged from their parents' households—or perhaps are still living there. This is not to say that the general concept of relative income excludes older individuals—only that any influence of parental income on older individuals would be greatly muted by the effects of other factors. Thus, to the extent that the feeling of economic well-being in the post-1950s extended to older individuals, their fertility would be expected to respond accordingly, creating strong period effects. But until researchers identify a better way of quantifying these older individuals' aspirations, it will be difficult to apply the relative income framework to them. Perhaps the best attempts made in this direction are the many studies that define a relative income measure using a group's current expected income relative to the historic trend in that same group's income.[10] But in terms of the relative income hypothesis, the focus has been on individuals up to the age of 30, or at most 34. My use of the 20–24 age group is an attempt to concentrate on the group for whom the measure would be most applicable, and it has the added benefit of including the ages of peak fertility for young women.

In addition, probably the most crucial factor in determining completed family size, as well as in period measures of fertility, is the timing of the first birth. The earlier this occurs, the higher will be completed family size, on average; and if one cohort brings its early fertility forward to overlap with delayed births in an earlier cohort, then period rates will rise even in the absence of any change in completed cohort fertility.

Although both of my published articles on fertility have focused just on the 20–24 age group, I have recently extended that work to include all women in the entire period from one to fifteen years out of school, in disaggregated regional analyses (like those described in chapter 9 for patterns of marriage and divorce).[11] One to fifteen years out of school includes high school graduates up to about age 33 and college graduates up to about age 37.

Historic Fertility Trends: Similarities with Male Relative Income

Two of my analyses have tested the combined model using published statistics on age-specific fertility that are available at the national level.[12] Unfortunately, although these fertility data are available through the entire post-WWII period, the data needed to construct appropriate measures of male relative income and the female hourly wage (the March Current Population Survey [CPS] described in earlier chapters) are, frustratingly, available only back through the mid-1960s. Thus it's not possible to test the model using data from the period when fertility was increasing during the baby boom, only during its decline.

Figure 11.1 shows the pattern of fertility during that period of decline for both white and African American women ages 15–17, 18–19, 20–24, and 25–29. For all eight groups, a characteristic pattern—like the one seen in male relative income—is apparent: declining in the 1970s, remaining low until about 1985, and with a hump-shaped recovery thereafter. The shape of the "hump" varies dramatically from one group to another, however, as it does in the pattern of male relative income across the groups. Figure 4.2 demonstrated this type of variation in relative income across regions within the United States, and if space permitted it would be possible to show similar variations across race and educational level.

In general the late 1980s recovery in male relative income was stronger for African American males (and for young men at lower levels of education), after a more pronounced decline through the 1970s (see the graphs in chapter 4). In addition, the relative income of African American males was more than one-third *higher* than that of white males in the late 1960s and early 1970s. Young African American males would have felt themselves to be in a better position than white males relative to their own material aspirations during that period. This could have been an important factor in establishing the notable differences between African Americans and whites in terms of age at first birth and age at marriage. In addition, both men and women in the African American community enjoyed a pronounced economic recovery after 1985—at the same time that African American women's fertility rose more sharply than white women's. The pattern of women's wages is shown in figure 11.2.

An Update of Official Fertility Statistics Using the CPS

One disadvantage of reliance on official statistics is that there's always a considerable delay in finding out what's happening currently. In addition, the official statistics sometimes seem to raise more ques-

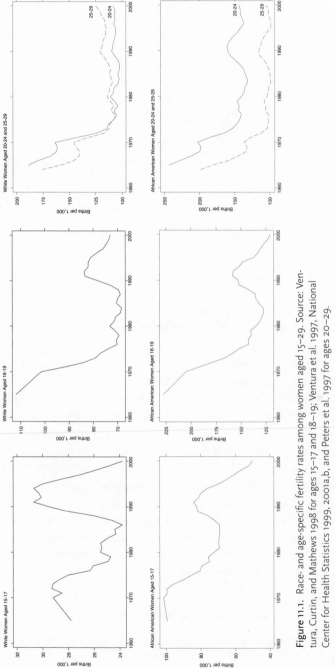

Figure 11.1. Race- and age-specific fertility rates among women aged 15–29. Source: Ventura, Curtin, and Mathews 1998 for ages 15–17 and 18–19; Ventura et al. 1997, National Center for Health Statistics 1999, 2001a,b, and Peters et al. 1997 for ages 20–29.

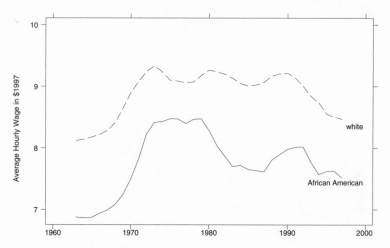

Figure 11.2. Average hourly wage, in 1994 dollars, of African American and white women in their first five years of work experience, holding education constant at the 1967 level. African American women experienced a sharp decline around 1980 but then, like African American males, enjoyed a pronounced recovery after 1985, at the same time that their fertility rose.

tions than they answer because they're usually not as disaggregated as researchers might like. Thus, as in earlier chapters, I have prepared some of my own "statistics" from the March Current Population Survey data using the methodology described in chapter 9. These statistics are less than perfect because they allow me to identify the probable occurrence only of *first births* to women in various demographic and economic groups: this obviously provides an undercount of actual fertility at older ages. But on the other hand these data allow me to examine patterns in subgroups that might be of particular interest. Some of these patterns are presented in Macunovich 2002 and indicate what seems to be a turnaround in fertility at all ages over 20 in recent years. This suggestion is borne out in the patterns among both high school and college graduates—where in many cases the post-1985 "hump" that seems to mimic the trend in male relative income also emerges.

Results from Testing the Combined Model

As in the cases of marriage and divorce in chapter 9, I have tested a relative income model of fertility both at the aggregate (national) level and at a more disaggregated (twenty-one-region) level. I will touch briefly on the aggregate results, but most of the following discussion relates to the disaggregated results, since it's at the more local level that one would expect the relative income effect to operate on fertility.

Results Using an Aggregate, National-Level Model

I have estimated two aggregate time series models of fertility: one analyzed the fertility of all women and the other considered white and African American women separately.[13] The data used in these studies were, with the exception of the fertility rate, drawn exclusively from the March Current Population Survey for the years 1964–1995. Individual data records were aggregated in order to identify labor force and population averages within various categories. The fertility rate used was the age-specific rate for women aged 20–24 in the United States as reported in *Vital Statistics*.

The model tested in these analyses contained controls for male relative income and the female wage, and in addition included an "interaction term" between these two variables that allowed the income effect of the female wage to vary depending on the level of male relative income. The analysis of racial fertility differences also contained a "cross-racial status" variable: white family income in the African American equation, and African American family income in the equation for whites.[14] And finally, the model included a time trend and the female unemployment rate, to control for unexpected shocks from changing economic conditions.

Given the strong similarities between historic trends in fertility and male relative income (as well as the female wage), it came as no surprise that the combined relative income/price of time model performs extremely well in explaining fertility over the last thirty-five years. Male relative income was found to exert a strong positive effect on young women's fertility. Individually, absolute male earnings were estimated to have a strong positive effect, but often this was the case only in the presence of a control for parental family income—which as expected had a strong negative effect.

Interestingly, the "cross-racial status" variable tested in the racially disaggregated model displayed a significant negative coefficient in the equation for African Americans, suggesting that upwardly mobile individuals in minority groups are particularly sensitive to changes in their own status relative to that of the dominant group. African American fertility appears to be nearly as sensitive to the ratio of own income relative to that of the dominant group as to own income relative to parental income. This is a stable element in the African American model, but, consistent with findings in other studies, this effect does not appear to hold for whites; if anything, there is an extremely weak positive effect there, probably due to correlations among fertility rates, incomes, and aggregate economic conditions.

In these aggregate analyses the combined model explained more than 98 percent of the variation in the level of fertility for 20–24-year-olds, over 70 percent of the changes in white fertility, and over 85 percent of the changes in African American fertility during this period. The aggregate model results also support the hypothesis of a changing income effect of the female wage as a function of changing levels of male relative income. As male relative income falls, the income effect of the female wage grows or, alternatively, as the female wage rises, the importance of male relative income declines. Thus around 1970, although young men's relative income was high, fertility declined in response to a strong negative price effect of sharply rising real female wages. After 1985 fertility rose in response to a brief increase in male relative income but also because of a strong income effect from the rising female wage.

Results Using Disaggregated Data

The results from my aggregate analyses using national statistics have been strongly supported by later findings using highly disaggregated data within twenty-one regions of the United States in the period since 1965.[15] This later study also made use of the March Current Population Survey data (1962–1998), but in this analysis instead of aggregating up to the national level, I examined patterns of fertility within sex-state-year-education-race-experience groupings. Specifically, as in chapter 9, I identified subgroups of young adults by year, race, region, educational attainment, and years out of school[16] and tested to see if there was a relationship between fertility in each subgroup and the following variables:

1. the average annual earnings of young men in each subgroup by year, race, region, educational attainment, and years out of school;
2. the average starting hourly wage of young women (that is, the average

    wage in the first full year of work experience) in each subgroup by
    year, race, region, and educational attainment;[17]
3. the average income of families with children with head of either sex
    aged 45–54, by year, race, and region; and
4. a simple time trend.

The assumption in all of these analyses is that the relative income comparison that's so difficult to quantify at the individual level using available data sources can be approximated using regional average parental income measures. Thus it is assumed that, all other factors constant, young adults in regions with high parental income will feel relatively poorer than young adults where parental income is lower.

Within each of these groupings, for women with fifteen or fewer years of potential work experience, I calculated the percentage in each group who had at least one child of her own, regardless of marital or family/household status. This is unfortunately a fairly crude measure of fertility—changes in the proportion of women with children will be an understatement of total fertility, since they reflect only the proportion with a first birth[18]—but it is the only one possible using this data set. Using these variables, the model estimated for fertility is similar to that used for marriage and divorce in chapter 9—except that the fertility analysis allowed for possible changing income and price effects of the female wage, since this was found to be a significant element in my two published analyses using aggregate data.

The results from estimating this more disaggregated model demonstrate a significant positive effect of young men's income on the fertility of women in their first five years out of school, and a significant negative effect of parental income, as hypothesized, with an estimated positive effect of the female wage. Even after controlling for age, education, race, and region, the estimated negative effect of "parental" family income is approximately 50 percent greater than the positive effect of male earnings, which in turn is double that of the female wage.

In addition, as hypothesized, the wage of women in periods or regions of high male relative income (in the fourth or fifth quintile among those in the same age-education group and year) exerts a significantly smaller net positive effect on fertility than does the wage of women in periods or regions of low male relative income. This is consistent with the idea of an increasing income effect of the female wage as male relative income falls. This effect is strong for women in their first five years out of school, so during those years the estimated (positive) effect of the female wage is nine times larger for women in first-quintile regions or periods than that of women in fifth-quintile regions or periods.[19] Overall for all women in their first fifteen years out of school the net (positive) effect of the female wage was estimated to be three times larger for women in the bottom relative income quintile than for women in the top quintile.

This finding of a positive effect of women's wages on fertility emerges at all ages, both with and without controls for changing income and price effects over time. Thus what has appeared to be a negative effect of women's wages on fertility in many other economic analyses might well have been a negative effect of parental income that pushed more women into the labor force and at the same time reduced their fertility, as young women attempted to achieve their material aspirations.

However, a more curious result emerges in this disaggregated analysis when the estimated effect of the female wage is allowed to vary over time, as well as across male relative income quintiles. The strong basic positive effect of the female wage on fertility is significantly strengthened, and a (negative) time trend becomes insignificant overall for women in the first fifteen years out of school—and even significantly positive for women less than ten years out. But it emerges that the basic positive effect of the female wage has been declining over time, and possibly has even turned negative in the last decade.

This result bears further examination in more refined analyses with the time trend. The inclusion of such a variable in an econometric model is a very clumsy technique: it is more an admission of what we don't know than of what we do. It could indicate that despite the increased availability and acceptance of paid child care over time (or perhaps because of its insufficient provision?), the emergence of women's strong career orientation during this period militated against childbearing. If so, it could be that allowance for nonlinearity in the time trend (which is after all what I argue for throughout this book!) will provide evidence of a turnaround when women began moving back toward the "mommy track" after about 1985 (as discussed in chapter 7).

Speculating on What Might Have Been

There has been just one significant female wage increase experienced by both African Americans and whites, occurring in the late 1960s and very early 1970s. This may have been an effect of the strong economy during the Vietnam War, together with the strong demand for goods and services created by the emerging baby boomers. What would have happened if women's wages had not experienced any increase during this period? Figure 11.3 shows the results of a simulation in which the average wage for all women is held at its 1968 (pre-increase) level throughout the analysis period.

The combined relative income/price of time model estimated using aggregate national data suggests that with female wages at this simulated lower level, the effects of changing male relative income would have produced *higher* than observed fertility in the late 1960s and early 1970s (because the female wage exerted a more negative price of time effect when male relative income was so high). But without the buffering effect of a higher female wage in the 1980s, the United States would have experienced lower than observed fertility levels, comparable to those experienced in European countries (on the order of 92 births per 1,000 women aged 20–24 in 1985, as op-

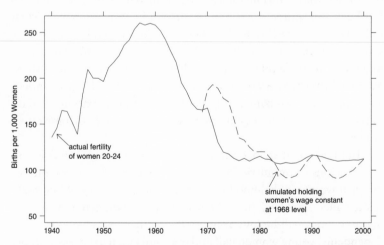

Figure 11.3. Actual and simulated fertility among women aged 20–24, holding the female wage constant at its 1968 level. Without the buffering effect of a higher female wage in the 1980s, the United States would have experienced fertility levels comparable to those experienced in European countries.

posed to our actual low of 108.3), before reversing again in the late 1980s.

Summary

Historic patterns of fertility among young adults—like those of marriage and divorce, school enrollment, and female labor force participation—suggest a clear response to changes in male relative income during the past thirty-five years. Both aggregate and regional analyses described in this chapter provide support for that hypothesis and demonstrate in addition a marked effect of women's own earning potential.

Young women respond to the opportunity cost of their own wage, and to their prospects for non-labor income, when making fertility decisions—but with two qualifications. First, they seem to assess their non-labor income in relative terms: relative to their material aspirations, as proxied by the recent income level in their parents' home. Second, their wage exerts a strong income effect as well as a price effect on fertility decisions, and the income effect appears to become stronger when prospects of other non-labor income decline relative to aspirations.

The primary source of non-labor income for young women in the United States has historically been husband's income, and this has been the source examined in this study. But, of course, when marriage levels are low, husband's income is a much less important source, as is reflected in the changing relative importance of the female wage as male relative income has declined over the past three decades. If married, a woman's non-labor income declines in tandem with male relative income, and her labor force participation will tend to rise, all other things equal, thus creating a stronger income effect of her own wage.

But male relative income can also be an important influence on the decisions of unmarried pregnant women and in general on unmarried women's likelihood of extramarital pregnancy. When male relative income is low, the incidence of single women marrying during pregnancy will be low. Young men will feel less able to support dependents, young women will find the young men to be less suitable mates, or both. In such a scenario, marriage and birth rates in general will decline, while at the same time the proportion of total births among unmarried women will rise.

The pattern of male relative income over the past three decades suggests that the relative income effect could be a significant factor in the rising proportion of extramarital births—for whites and for African Americans. In addition, male relative income could be one explanation for the significant differences between the races in terms of the timing of first births. Young African American males' relative income was significantly higher (about 30 percent) than that of white males in the late 1960s and early 1970s, which could have encouraged the development in the African American community of norms more accepting of early marriage and childbearing. This would have been even more likely based on the pattern of female relative income for highly educated young African American women, whose incomes relative to their parents' rose much more rapidly during this period than those of white women because of the more rapid rise in educational attainment in the African American community. Thus, relative income appears to provide many answers when trying to explain both historic trends and racial differences in early childbearing.

12

Relative Cohort Size Effects—Even in Developing Countries

The [world population] doubling time is currently about 35 years. . . . If growth continued at that rate for about 900 years, there would be some 60,000,000,000,000,000 people on the face of the earth. Sixty million billion people. This is about 100 persons for each square yard of the Earth's surface, land and sea. A British physicist, J. H. Fremlin, guessed that such a multitude might be housed in a continuous 2,000 story building covering our entire planet.

Paul Ehrlich, *The Population Bomb* (1968)

The West Germans today are on a course that yields fewer than 1.3 children per woman over the course of her lifetime. Recent demographic projections show that if that rate continues, it would reduce the West German population from 60 million today to 50 million by the year 2000, and down to 16 million by the end of the next century.

Ben Wattenberg, *The Birth Dearth* (1987)

The literature abounds with outlandish "projections" like those quoted above. Most of us don't really believe people breed so mindlessly, but is there a mechanism that checks wild swings in growth? Although most of my studies have kept me focused on U.S. data, a professional encounter with a fellow academic led me unexpectedly—fortuitously—to conduct a global analysis of the period since 1950.[1] The results honestly astounded me, since they suggested that the same relative cohort size effects I've been describing in previous chapters operate in the Third World, as well—operated, in fact, during our own "demographic transition" and that of other Western nations. If that is the case, then relative cohort size might be the mechanism through which populations avoid runaway growth or decline.

You might ask why I was surprised, given my obvious attachment to the relative cohort size concept. My training as an economist had led me to assume that the relative cohort size/relative income mechanism required formal—even sophisticated—markets to be operational. It required, I thought, a labor market that differentiates between workers with different levels of experience, producing traditional demand/supply effects in response to a glut of workers of one type relative to another. It's difficult to imagine such conditions holding in sub-Saharan Africa—or on the frontiers of the Wild West, for that matter. The RCS mechanism also required, I was led to believe, fairly closed international boundaries so that swings in relative wages wouldn't be damped out by international migration.

The evidence seems overwhelming, however, that small relative cohort size induces high fertility, or at least that large cohort size induces fertility reductions. Just as the post-WWII baby boom sowed the seeds of the baby bust that began twenty years later, the population growth produced by mortality decline in developing nations appears to lead inevitably to declining fertility, once the numbers of young adults begin to swell.

But that's the key: declining mortality rates don't inevitably lead to growth in the numbers of young adults. Traditionally mortality rates decline first among infants—those most susceptible to disease, especially the diarrhea caused by polluted water sources. The survival of those infants creates the burgeoning numbers of young children we see, often starving, in photos on the news. Those young children create the impression of runaway population growth, and it's certainly true that they do consume precious resources, but they must survive to adulthood—often through disease, famine, and war—in order for the effects of relative cohort size to register. Thus it is my contention that those who seem to imply that the death of those children would be a blessing are in fact arguing at cross-purposes to their own goal, which is the reduction of population growth in the Third World.

The Demographic Transition

"Demographic transition" is the period during which a country passes from high to low death and birth rates. Prior to this transition, there is little if any population growth, often despite fertility rates of seven births per woman or more, because of high mortality—especially infant mortality. This was the case in the currently developed countries prior to the nineteenth century and in many developing countries as recently as the middle of the twentieth century.[2]

Characteristically the transition to lower death rates precedes the transition to lower fertility, and the resulting imbalance between the two rates produces rapid population growth until fertility rates begin to decline. This was the case during our own transition in the West when our population increased several-fold, and it is now the situation in currently developing countries, which has led to the widely publicized fears about "population explosion." Exacerbating this effect, improvements in health that tend to accompany mortality decline often lead to temporary *increases* in the fertility rate, until couples' concerns about excessive family size provide motivation for the use of contraceptives.

Most of the population growth already experienced by the human species—and probably most of that which will *ever* be experienced—has occurred during such transitions. A well-known economist, Walter Rostow, has written about what he terms the "Great Population Spike," in reference to this explosive growth, emphasizing what an anomaly it has been in human history.[3]

Because most of the growth in world population over the past two centuries has occurred during such transition periods, an important aspect of demographic research has been the attempt to identify factors that determine the length of the gap between mortality decline and fertility decline. In general, the currently developed countries took fifty years or more to pass through the transition, while in a number of developing countries the transition has occurred within a single decade.

Although demographers and economists have demonstrated a strong correlation historically between fertility and infant mortality rates, suggesting that the motivation to control fertility arises from parents' concerns about excessive family size, decline in the latter has not been a good predictor of the initiation of decline in the former in currently developing countries. By the late 1980s many coun-

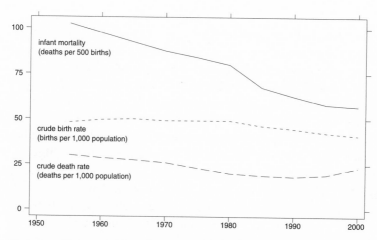

Figure 12.1. Vital rates in Mozambique, a country which has not yet begun the fertility transition, despite declines in infant mortality. Source: United Nations 1999.

tries—especially in sub-Saharan Africa—had not yet experienced any fertility decline despite decreasing infant mortality, as in the case of Mozambique (figure 12.1). We know that the reduction in infant mortality occurs as a result of the spread of modern medicine and hygiene, but what causes fertility rates finally to take the plunge?

The United Nations, at five-year intervals (1950–1995) for nearly two hundred nations, has provided estimates of some of the vital rates economists and demographers use in analyzing this question: crude birth and death rates, infant mortality, total fertility rates, and life expectancy. More important from the perspective of this analysis, the UN has also provided data on population age structure (the proportion of the total population aged under 5, 5–14, 15–24, and 60+). These data suggest that relative cohort size (approximated using the ratio of 15–24-year-olds to those aged 25–59)—probably acting through effects on male relative income—has played a crucial role in bringing about the fertility transition in developing countries during that period.

Relative Cohort Size Effects—in the Third World?

The RCS mechanism at work in the Third World is hypothesized to be similar to that observed in the United States and other industrialized nations. An excess supply of young relative to prime-age males depresses the relative wages of the young men, to the extent that they are poor substitutes for older, more experienced men. Alternatively, in less sophisticated economies, the relative decline in earning potential for younger workers may occur in the form of reduced size of land holdings passed from parent to child: parents are forced to split land among a larger number of surviving offspring. However it occurs, this decline need only be a *relative* one. That is, concurrent economic development might raise absolute wages at all age levels; but if the wages of younger workers progress more slowly than those of older workers, as they will for large cohorts, those younger workers will still tend to feel some level of relative deprivation.

The effects of this labor market crowding may be exacerbated by crowding in the family, given increasing child survival rates, and in schools to the extent that they are available. The earning potential of young men will be reduced relative to their material aspirations as shaped in their parental households. They will feel less able to support themselves at an (age-adjusted) standard commensurate with that experienced in their parents' homes. The resultant decline in relative income would lead young couples to wish to delay or forgo marriage, reduce fertility, or both in an attempt to maintain a higher level of per capita disposable income.

In this way, a society with little or no individual control of fertility will develop a strong motivation for such control. Large cohorts are known for their disruptive effects on social norms (as, for example, in the United States in the 1960s and 1970s and in Iran today). In this case, a large cohort's desire for fertility control may mark a turning point in the society's attitudes with regard to contraception, and with regard to the individual's—as opposed to society's—right to control fertility.

It is generally acknowledged that prior to a fertility transition, fertility tends to be controlled by "social sanctions" rather than by specific decisions of married couples. The development of deliberate individual control is a fundamental aspect of modernization. As large cohorts perceive a need to control fertility, cognitive dissonance could lead to the widespread acceptance of the concept of fertility regulation. Passing that milestone could have a cumulative "snowball" or "cascade" effect as declining average family size reinforces a society's acceptance of smaller numbers of children. This would explain the often-observed co-movement of fertility rates among older and younger women.

Undoubtedly institutional and cultural differences among countries must temper the relationship between relative cohort size and relative income across nations and regions. Strong unions, for example, which maintain high wages for current members at the expense of new labor market entrants (probably as a protective measure during periods of large relative cohort size), will tend to counteract positive effects of subsequent smaller relative cohort size.

Similarly, strong national policies encouraging wage cuts rather than layoffs during periods of excess labor supply might dilute relative cohort size effects, if wage cuts occur across all experience groups. Studies have found that while the United States tends to have "sticky wages" that promote high unemployment during such periods, many European countries trade higher unemployment for lower wages.

Japan, too, must experience more diluted effects of relative cohort size on relative income because of widespread adherence to rigid pay scales that are tipped strongly in favor of older, more experienced workers in order to entice employees into long-term commitment. Here again, young workers would rarely experience the benefits of smaller cohort size. The evidence in chapters 13 and 14 suggests that the present-day result of this policy in Japan is an economic slump.

The rigidity of a nation's boundaries with respect to immigration, and its policies toward "guest workers," as, for example, in Germany, Austria, and Oman, would also impinge on the relative cohort size/wage relationship. Tests for any relationship would be most appropriate at a regional rather than a national level when workers can cross international boundaries fairly freely. And conversely, it is possible that very large countries, such as China or the former USSR, might contain many subnational "markets" in which any relative cohort size effects would emerge most clearly—especially if the movements of their citizens are restricted by government.

At the other end of the causal network, it goes without saying that cultural and institutional differences must impinge on the relationship between relative income and factors such as marriage and childbearing. These cultural effects may show up only as differences in the overall *levels* of marriage and fertility, however, rather than in the response to changing economic circumstances.

The Evidence

The UN data suggest that relative cohort size—probably acting through effects on male relative income—has played a crucial role in bringing about the fertility transition in developing countries between 1950 and 1995. Countries appear not to begin reducing their fertility, despite reductions in infant mortality, until mortality rates fall among children and young adults, permitting the proportion of those aged 15–24 to rise relative to those aged 25 and over. This is apparent in country after country that has begun the fertility transition since 1950—more than one hundred in all. Several that have not, such as Gambia, Guinea-Bissau, and the Democratic Republic of the Congo, have not yet experienced any increase in the ratio of 15–24-year-olds to those aged 25 and over, despite marked and prolonged reductions in infant mortality in many cases.

The very pronounced relationship between relative cohort size and the total fertility rate is evident in both the aggregate and the country-specific data, even using data reported at five-year intervals. Figure 12.2 presents graphs for a selection of Third World nations around the globe, where a characteristic relationship begins to emerge. Total fertility rates are constant or even increasing until relative cohort size begins to increase: at that point, the total fertility rate begins to decline. Although the overall rate of decline might be affected by the trend in infant mortality, its point of initiation seems in all cases to depend on the trend in relative cohort size.

This relationship has been demonstrated around the globe, in country after country, both small and large, regardless of religious or political orientation. My analyses described more fully elsewhere show that it emerges even at the regional level, in all developing parts of the world.[4] It is important to note that the characteristic shape evident in these graphs is not a statistical artifact: the relative cohort size variable used here is calculated relative only to *prime-age adults*, not to the total population—thus RCS is not increasing as a result of the decline in the proportion of children in the population, since it is a ratio of 15–24-year-olds to those aged 25–59.

Scaled infant mortality rates are also presented in figure 12.2, and although not immediately obvious because of the scaling, the levels of infant mortality vary widely from country to country, at the point of initiation of fertility decline and throughout its full extent.

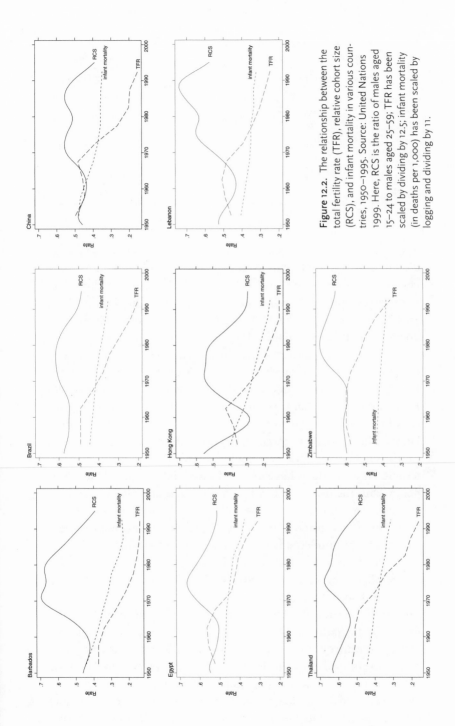

Figure 12.2. The relationship between the total fertility rate (TFR), relative cohort size (RCS), and infant mortality in various countries, 1950–1995. Source: United Nations 1999. Here, RCS is the ratio of males aged 15–24 to males aged 25–59; TFR has been scaled by dividing by 12.5; infant mortality (in deaths per 1,000) has been scaled by logging and dividing by 11.

Table 12.1 Infant Mortality Rates (Deaths per 1,000 Live Births) in Countries Presented in Figure 12.2.

	1950–1955	1990–1995	At Start of Fertility Transition
Barbados	132	9	87
Brazil	135	47	109
China	195	44	81
Egypt	200	67	175
Hong Kong	79	6	33
Lebanon	87	34	52
Thailand	132	32	84
Zimbabwe	120	70	101

Source: United Nations 1999.

For example, as indicated in table 12.1, the transition in Hong Kong did not begin until infant mortality was down to 33, while in Egypt it began at the very high level of 175. And although Thailand and Lebanon exhibit very similar infant mortality rates in 1990–1995 (32 and 34, respectively), the TFR in Lebanon (3.1) is over 50 percent greater than that in Thailand (1.9).

There are other aspects of the diversity among the nine countries in figure 12.2. Population size (in 1995) ranged from only 260,000 in Barbados to 1.2 billion in China. Hong Kong is only a city-state and Barbados only an island, as compared with the large geographic areas of the other seven countries. Lebanon has a large Muslim population, while Brazil has large proportions of Roman Catholics. And China is not a free-market economy—yet it still exhibits this characteristic pattern. Many have credited China's draconian "one child" policy with the dramatic fertility decline in that country. However, several recent studies have indicated that the decline began—at least in urban areas—prior to that policy,[5] and the data presented here suggest that the underlying motivation for such an urban fertility decline was the increase in relative cohort size.

Similar graphs have been prepared for the more than 130 countries that had not experienced a fertility transition prior to 1950.[6] Most of these countries have by now begun the transition and conform with the pattern discussed above, but the effect is not mechanistic: there are differences among countries, which undoubtedly result from cultural or institutional peculiarities not captured in these data. A few countries have experienced little if any fertility decline, but many, such as Gambia, appear to be on the threshold. Even more convincing (for statisticians, at least), econometric analyses pre-

sented in my two published articles demonstrate that this visual relationship is statistically significant—not just overall, but within separate groups of countries, as well.[7]

Experience during the Transitions of Currently
Developed Countries

I've assembled historical data for three currently industrialized
nations—Sweden, France, and England/Wales—around the time of
their own fertility transitions (fig. 12.3).[8] Although these data don't
include the TFR, unfortunately, they do provide information on age
composition, together with the crude birth rate

Although not as conclusive, perhaps, as the patterns exhibited in
most of the currently developing countries, the graphs in figure 12.3
do demonstrate a similar tendency for the fertility transition to begin just at the point when relative cohort size starts to increase. Only
decennial observations are available for England and Wales, so it's
possible that some of the increase there is missed, but there is a decided increase in RCS coincident with decline in fertility in France.
Sweden experienced a sharp jump in RCS after 1825 that seems to
have initiated a tendency for fertility to decline, but this was followed
by an equally sharp drop in RCS, with some recovery in fertility, so
that the real fertility transition occurred after 1870—when RCS increased once again. Additional data not presented here suggest that
improved survival rates among children and young adults were the
primary reasons RCS began to increase when it did in each of these
three countries.

Summary

In this chapter, I have attempted to demonstrate that changes in relative cohort size are important in determining the pattern of fertility
not just in developed countries but also, and perhaps even more important, in countries as they pass through the demographic transition. The increase in relative cohort size that occurs as a result of
declining mortality rates during the demographic transition acts
as the mechanism of transmission that determines *when* the fertility portion of the transition begins. The increasing proportion of
young adults generates a downward pressure on young men's relative wages that in turn causes young adults to accept a trade-off

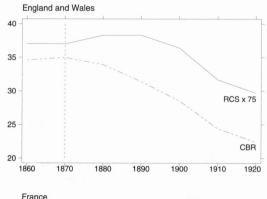

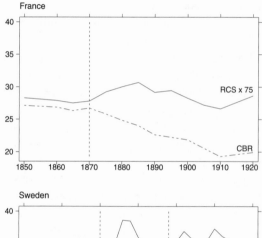

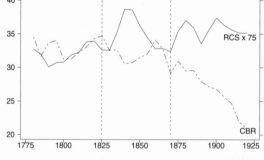

Figure 12.3. Relative cohort size and the crude birth rate during the fertility transition in England and Wales, France, and Sweden. Crude birth rate is births per 1,000 population. Relative cohort size is the population aged 15–24 relative to the population aged 25–59, but is scaled by multiplying by 75. Source: Keyfitz and Flieger 1968.

between family size and material well-being. This acceptance of a trade-off could mark a turning-point in a society's acceptance of contraception, setting in motion a "cascade" or "snowball" effect in which total fertility rates tumble as social norms regarding individual control of fertility and acceptable family sizes begin to change.

Thus relative cohort size can be thought of as the mechanism that prevents excessive rates of population change—reducing fertility when previous high rates, in combination with low mortality rates, have caused relative cohort size to increase, and increasing fertility when previous low rates have caused relatively small younger cohorts. The RCS mechanism appears to have been operating not just in currently developed post-transition economies, but also during both recent and historic fertility transitions, to the extent that social and economic institutions have permitted the transmission of relative cohort size effects to male relative income.

PART 4

Third-Order Effects of Relative Cohort Size

Aggregate Demand Effects of Changing Population Age Structure

We are passing, so to speak, over a divide which separates the great era of
growth and expansion of the nineteenth century from an era which no man,
unwilling to embark on pure conjecture, can yet characterize with clarity or
precision. . . . [Now we suffer from] secular stagnation—sick recoveries
which die in their infancy and depressions which feed on themselves and
leave a hard and seemingly immovable core of unemployment, . . . the main
problem of our times. . . . Overwhelmingly significant was the decline by
one-half of the increase in U.S. population in the 1930s as opposed to the
rate of increase in the 1920s and pre-1914.

Alvin Hansen, presidential address, fifty-first meeting
of the American Economic Association (1938)

The total demographic swing was an enormous 13.6 percentage points,
which would appear to account for the entire rise in the savings rate in East
Asia during these twenty years.

David Bloom and Jeffrey Williamson, "Demographic Transitions
and Economic Miracles in Emerging Asia" (1998)

An important component of my approach to the analysis of the
link between relative cohort size and male relative income, presented in chapters 5 and 6, is the hypothesis of an "aggregate demand
effect" of changing population age structure. The assumption has
been that, in addition to any supply effect of the baby boom (i.e., the
increased supply of labor when the boomers entered the labor market), there must also have been a demand effect—some correspon-

ding increase in the demand for goods and services that would have increased employers' demand for labor. If so, an asymmetry in the wage effects of relative cohort size would occur, with those born on the "leading edge" of the baby boom benefiting from a more buoyant economy than those born on the trailing edge when entering the labor market. This would explain the failure of young men's relative earnings to recover in the 1980s, after the peak of the baby boom had, in theory at least, finally been absorbed into the labor market.

The term "aggregate demand" refers simply to the sum, at the national level, of all demands for goods and services in the economy. Is there such an effect, and if so, what is its magnitude? Can we measure it? Although many non-economists seem to think such an effect would be obvious, these are not necessarily easy questions to answer.[1]

The assumption in referring to such an aggregate demand effect is that it's important to consider compositional changes in the population: how many are young and how many old—including the ages of the children—and the size of a generation relative to that of its parents. Many macroeconomists still search for effects of what they term the "representative agent," convinced that little significant information will be lost by treating the population as a mass of homogeneous individuals. But anyone in that population knows that his or her own income and consumption patterns vary significantly over the life cycle. We purchase and consume different amounts, of different items, and save different proportions of our income, if we are 24 years old rather than 44, or 64. And we spend vastly different amounts on our children if they are 17 rather than 5, or 12.

Two economic theories that support the idea of age-related patterns of expenditure are often lumped together as the "life cycle"—or "permanent income"—hypothesis.[2] This hypothesis suggests that there are marked age-related fluctuations in the proportion of income consumed and saved over the life cycle. Individuals are hypothesized to gear their consumption expenditures not to current income, which is low at younger ages and rises over time until about age 50, but to their estimate of "permanent income": their expected average annual income over the life cycle.

According to this hypothesis, if we think that our earnings over our lifetime will average, say, $30,000 annually, we will consume roughly that amount each year when we're in our 20s, even if we're paid only $25,000 per year at that age. Like Wimpy in the old Popeye

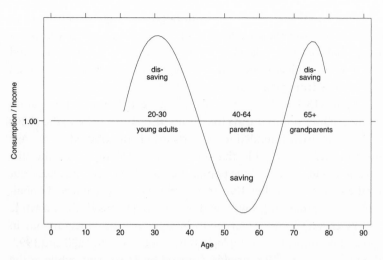

Figure 13.1. The hypothesized life-cycle pattern of personal consumption expenditures as a share of (contemporaneous) personal income, emphasizing the tendency toward "dis-saving" at younger and older ages with saving in between. Applying a strong age-related pattern like this to a dramatic change in age structure like the baby boom is expected to produce measurable fluctuations at the aggregate level.

cartoons, it's assumed that we'll go to the bank manager saying, "I will gladly pay you tomorrow for a hamburger today: loan me $5,000 per year so that I can live in the manner to which I will later become accustomed." This would lead to consumption levels that exceed current income at younger and older ages and fall short of current income during middle age—as depicted in figure 13.1.

Some researchers argue that although we might try Wimpy's tactic, few of us will succeed, because of "imperfect capital markets": the bank manager doesn't know as much about us as we do (or as we *think* we do) and thus is unwilling to accept our own evaluation of our "lifetime earning potential." Others argue that enough of us succeed (given access to credit cards and cooperative older family members) to produce a pattern similar to that in figure 13.1.

It's important to know whether this is a good approximation of our spending and saving behavior, on average—and if so, whether this pattern carries through when the data are aggregated, or whether variations due to changes in one age group are largely offset by changes in another. In a population with a very smooth and stable age distribution, all of these life-cycle differences might cancel out so that we could safely study the "average" or "representative" man. But given the significant fluctuations in population age structure we've experienced over the past century in the United States, it seems unlikely that the effects of such a marked pattern in consumption and savings would disappear at the aggregate level: our "average" man will change from year to year.

Figure 13.2 presents the observed age distribution of population change at four points during the twentieth century. Prior to the 1920s population growth tended to be fairly evenly distributed across age groups, and it's possible that under such circumstances the dissaving in one portion of the population may have been balanced out by the saving in another. But since then we have seen marked imbalances in population growth, with some age groups declining while others grow. It's much harder to imagine a neat canceling-out in those conditions. For example, in the period between 1980 and 1992, the number of 18–19-year-olds dropped by 21 percent, while at the same time the number of under-5s *increased* by 18 percent. That period can't compete with 1964–1966, however, when the number of 18–19-year-olds increased by 33 percent *in just two years!*

Why is this important? If people are fairly homogeneous across age groups in terms of their patterns of expenditure (or if behavior in one group always inexplicably counterbalances that in another), then the marked fluctuations observed in patterns of economic growth through the twentieth century can't have been the result of demographics, since there has never been any actual decline in the overall rate of population growth. We have to look elsewhere for culprits. Similarly, if it's really true that our current level of savings is "disastrously low," we can't expect the nation to "grow out of" the problem as high spenders in the population age into more abstemious patterns: unpleasant policy prescriptions would probably be in order.[3]

Some very great minds—among them, John Maynard Keynes—have attributed these fluctuations to demographics. Keynes suggested that the adverse economic conditions of the 1930s were at least in part due to demographic trends.[4] In both the United Kingdom and the United States, birth rates had begun falling sharply after 1910, a factor that comes across clearly for the United States in the second panel of figure 13.2: note the dramatic drop in the population under 5 years old. And immigration in the United States—demonstrated by Nobel laureate Simon Kuznets to have had a strong positive impact on the economy[5]—had fallen sharply following

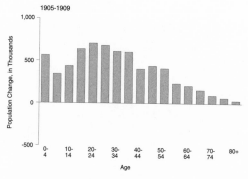

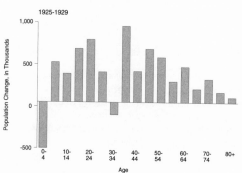

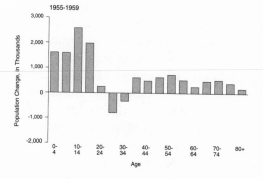

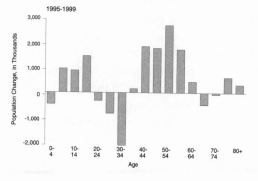

Figure 13.2. Age distribution of population change in the United States at four points during this century: change in thousands within five-year age groups. Whereas growth was fairly evenly distributed across all age groups in 1905–1909, some age groups actually declined in size while others increased in the later periods.

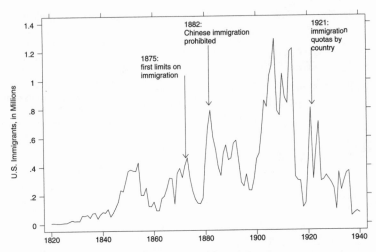

Figure 13.3. Numbers of immigrants to the United States (in millions) in the period prior to 1940. The United States began to restrict immigration in the 1920s, just prior to the nation's first-ever decline in indigenous population growth in the 15–24 age group. This would have had a dramatic (negative) effect on growth in aggregate demand—the demand for goods and services—under the hypothesis presented in this chapter. Source: Unites States Immigration and Naturalization Service 1996, table 1.

reforms in the 1920s, as shown in figure 13.3. Keynes presented a stagnation thesis in which "population growth stimulates investment in factories and machinery; and with population growing, businessmen are more likely to regard their investment misallocations as less serious than when the growth is slow or nil."[6] Nobel laureate Paul Samuelson studied Keynes's hypothesis and concluded that his own "exploration does seem to bear out the correctness of the Keynes-Hansen intuition about growth and unemployment."[7] And Nobel laureate Gary Becker and colleagues recently pointed out the decided benefits they believe are associated with population growth.[8] But these arguments might be thought wide of the mark, focusing as they do on the effects of *overall* population growth rather than differential growth among age groups. (One might question, however, why Keynes thought that fertility declines beginning after 1910 wouldn't have had economic repercussions until 1929: this implies a differential effect on the economy of those in their 20s.)

Researchers have taken two different approaches—micro and macro—in trying to test the sensitivity of aggregate spending patterns to changes in population structure. The microlevel analyses examine the spending patterns of individual households and attempt to identify econometric relationships between household type and consumption, controlling for level of income.

For purposes of illustrating the micro approach, let's say there are just three different types of household in the nation: those with a head aged 30 and two young children, those with a head aged 50 and two teenage children, and those with a head aged 70. In detailed household consumption expenditure surveys, it's determined that the first type spends 95 percent of its income (and thus saves only 5 percent), the second saves 20 percent, and the third saves only 2 percent. Then, if we know the proportion of each type of household in the nation as a whole—let's say 40–40–20, respectively—we can apply those savings rates to those proportions to determine the current overall level of saving (10.4 percent in this example) and how it would differ if the nation comprised different proportions of those household types. (An age composition of 40–20–40, for example, would reduce the overall savings rate to 6.8 percent, without any change in individual behavior.)

The macro approach takes the pattern of spending and saving observed in the nation each year, and the age distribution of the population in each year, and attempts to determine if there's an econometrically significant relationship between the way those two sets of data change from year to year.

The results of these two different approaches? The microlevel studies find no significant effect of changing population age structure (because, they say, the differences among age groups aren't sufficiently large, or they tend to balance each other out in the aggregate, or both). The macrolevel studies, on the other hand, find very strong and significant age structure effects, on a wide range of phenomena from inflation and interest rates to housing and other durable goods expenditures.

How to reconcile these disparate findings? There are several important reasons researchers cite to explain the discrepancies:

1. using inaccurate data on economic performance;[9]
2. using inappropriate econometric techniques;[10]
3. treating the payments retirees receive from pension plans as income rather than the drawing-down of savings, which contributes to the belief that current retirees are saving rather than dis-saving;[11]
4. using inappropriate age groupings in the analyses (as a very simplistic

example, consider the effect, in figure 13.1, of lumping together the age groups 20–40 and 40–60);[12]

5. ignoring cross-generational and cross-household spending in microlevel analyses;[13] and

6. ignoring the presence of or the age differences of children in the households.

The last two are particular hobbyhorses of my own and perhaps bear some elaboration. In terms of the cross-generational effects, imagine, for example, that each of our three household types described above has just spent $500 helping the youngest household set up a nursery for a new baby. Those expenditures were all generated by the presence of one particular age group (a newborn), but in the microlevel analyses we wouldn't know why the older households spent the money—only that they spent it on gifts. Their expenditures would have been observed as behavior related to the age group of their own household head, making all the households appear homogeneous despite age differences, when in fact there was a strong age-related pattern in the expenditure generated, an age-related pattern that *would* have shown up at the macro level.

Similarly, if the period of observation were the 1980s, when the youngest household head was a baby boomer finding it impossible to afford a house, we might observe the two older households spending large amounts as gifts (that were, in fact, going to the youngest, to help them with a down payment on a house). Here again, in the microanalysis we wouldn't know why the two older households spent so much on gifts. Their expenditures (together with whatever the boomer household itself could scrape together) were strongly age related, because the baby boomers were in the household-formation stage, but would have been interpreted as a general decline in the level of savings among all households during the 1980s: a period effect, rather than an age effect.

The Effects of Children and Their Age Distribution

Perhaps the most detailed analyses of the effect of changing age distributions of children have been conducted in recent years by Lazear and Michael (1988) and Lino (1998), using microlevel data from the Consumer Expenditure Surveys conducted regularly by the Bureau of Labor Statistics.

Lazear and Michael addressed first the issue of potential averaging and smoothing of differences across the population, in data reproduced in table 13.1. This table presents some of the results of their analyses of expenditure patterns of husband-wife families by presence and number of children—results that are, effectively, averaged over age groups—and they make the following comments with regard to it: "[O]ne notes very few interesting differences in their demographic descriptions. The income and expenditure levels do rise somewhat with family size, although the average proportion of before-tax income spent on total consumption remains relatively

Table 13.1. Characteristic Spending Patterns of Husband-Wife Families

	Family of 2	Family of 3	Family of 4	Family of 5
	A. Demographic Characteristics			
Education (years)				
Husband	11.9	12.1	12.6	12.4
Wife	12.0	12.2	12.3	12.1
Age				
Husband	46.4	40.5	38.3	39.4
Wife	44.4	37.9	35.5	36.6
Race (% black)	5	7	5	6
Renter (%)	31	32	22	18
	B. Income and Consumption			
Income before tax ($)	14,163	14,026	16,910	17,443
Income after tax ($)	11,160	11,107	13,544	14,096
Total consumption ($)	9,666	10,611	11,737	12,151
	C. Spending Pattern			
Food (%)	19	19	21	23
Housing (%)	29	27	26	24
Clothing (%)	5	6	6	7
Nondurables (%)	7	7	7	7
Durables (%)	16	18	17	17
Transportation (%)	6	6	5	5
Services (%)	18	17	17	18
N	2,461	2,196	1,851	1,078

Note: Families of sizes 3, 4, and 5 have 1, 2, and 3 children of any age, respectively, and no other family members. The spending patterns of families when aggregated like this across age groups show little variation among families by size, but the differences by age group within each family size, and especially by age of child, can be much more substantial. A family with a teenager will tend to spend more, and on different items, than the family of a newborn, as shown in the next two tables. (Use a factor of four to convert these 1972 dollars to year 2000 dollars.) Source: adapted from Lazear and Michael 1988, table 3.1.

stable: 68 percent, 76 percent, 69 percent, and 70 percent, respectively. Likewise the spending pattern, as reflected in the proportion of total consumption spent on each of seven major components, changes very little on average from families of one size to families of another size."[14] This is certainly true: the stability of proportions spent on various categories of consumption across these family sizes is remarkable. Even their average income levels vary only minimally. (Note that these figures from their study were based on the 1972–1973 Consumer Expenditure Survey and are thus expressed in 1972/73 dollars.) More significant for purposes here, however, is another of their observations: "The variation *within a family size* dominates between-group differences. For example, the variation in the proportion spent on food between groups is about 5 percentage points while the variation within a group is 8 or 9 percentage points" (25; emphasis added). That is, the spending patterns of families when aggregated like this across age groups show little variation among families by size—but the differences *by age group within each family size*, and especially by age of child, can be much more substantial. A family with a teenager will tend to spend more, and on different items, than the family of a newborn.

Many researchers tend to assume that these spending differences are simply a reallocation of the same overall total. They assume that if I'm forced to spend more because my child needs expensive orthodontia, I will cut back on my expenditures in other areas, so that my total consumption expenditures remain fairly fixed. Lazear and Michael demonstrate that while there certainly is some reallocation—patterns of expenditure shift radically depending on the age of the child (more on clothing and food and less on housing or transportation, for example)—parents also *increase their total consumption as a proportion of income*, as their children age. And the amounts can be substantial as indicated in tables 13.2 and 13.3, also taken from their book.

These two tables require and merit close attention. Panel A of table 13.2 presents what Lazear and Michael call the "partial effect" of an only child as he or she ages; that is, the redistribution of expenditure that occurs as the child ages *relative to expenditure when the child was 0–5*, but holding total expenditure constant. Thus, for example, even if I were not allowed to spend any more in total when my child reached age 12–17, relative to total spending when he or she was 0–5, I would still shift my patterns of expenditure, taking $401

Table 13.2. Relation of Family Spending Patterns (in 1972 dollars) to Child's Characteristics, Husband-Wife Families with One Child

| | Child's Characteristic | | | | | | |
| | Employment | | | Age | | | |
	Male	Part Time	Full Time	6–11	12–17	18–24	25+
A. Partial Effect							
Redistribution of expenditure ($), total consumption and income held constant							
Food	95	−104	−20	577	567	291	338
Housing	10	−53	−178	−232	−401	−269	−331
Clothing	−44	−44	−12	−24	49	−4	−50
Nondurables	53	62	100	105	52	36	−21
Durables	−53	39	289	−165	−32	−136	46
Transportation	30	21	51	−39	−23	125	51
Services	−91	78	−231	−222	−211	−42	−34
Change in total consumption (%), income held constant	82	979	882	558	484	1505	−96
B. Total Effect							
Food	122	43	112	660	639	516	324
Housing	38	98	−42	−146	−326	−37	−346
Clothing	−32	24	50	15	82	101	−56
Nondurables	63	114	147	135	77	115	−26
Durables	5	352	571	13	123	345	15
Transportation	39	71	96	−11	1	200	47
Services	−53	278	−52	−108	−112	265	−53

Note: Panel A shows the redistribution of expenditure that occurs as a child ages, relative to expenditure when the child was 0–5, holding total expenditure constant. Thus, for example, *even if I were not allowed to spend any more in total* when my child reached 12–17, relative to total spending when he or she was 0–5, I would still shift my patterns of expenditure, taking $401 away from housing and spending an additional $567 on food, for example. The last row in panel A indicates, however, that I would actually spend $484 more in total for a 12–17-year-old (and $1505 more for an 18–24-year-old), even with no increase in income as the child ages. The sum of each column in panel B equals the change in total consumption amount in panel A. (Use a factor of four to convert these 1972 dollars to year 2000 dollars.) Source: adapted from Lazear and Michael 1988, table 3.2.

Table 13.3. Relation of Family Spending Patterns (in 1972 dollars) to Child's Characteristics, Husband-Wife Families with Two Children

| | Child's Characteristic | | | | | | |
| | Employment | | | Age | | | |
	Male	Part Time	Full Time	6–11	12–17	18–24	25+
			A. Partial Effect: Older Child				
Redistribution of expenditure ($), total consumption and income held constant							
Food	81	–181	–179	382	405	363	567
Housing	–51	4	–286	–339	–501	–441	–374
Clothing	–60	–29	43	–18	66	–11	–100
Nondurables	18	27	–9	89	59	127	–123
Durables	78	110	591	–164	19	–67	–318
Transportation	28	–9	36	68	67	179	95
Services	–94	79	–195	–19	–115	–150	7
Change in total consumption ($), income held constant	53	871	–224	630	1044	1505	2597
			B. Partial Effect: Younger Child				
Redistribution of expenditure ($), total consumption and income held constant							
Food	29	–109	–207	179	238	–45	990
Housing	1	–39	–184	1	–68	163	217
Clothing	–42	4	–48	44	102	49	–115
Nondurables	5	13	227	–19	–55	14	27
Durables	112	–36	502	–162	–263	–474	–1483
Transportation	2	68	58	–35	1	71	–19
Services	–107	100	–348	–8	45	222	383
Change in total consumption ($), income held constant	5	876	1225	621	9	2053	–45

Note: As in table 13.2, the last row in panel A shows that I would spend $1505 more on an 18–24-year-old than on a young child, even with a fixed income. The last row in panel B shows away from housing, spending an additional $567 on food (as any parent of a teenager knows!), and so on. (For those who wish to assess these changes in current dollars, multiplying by a factor of four gives a rough translation from 1972 to 2000 dollars.)

The last row in panel A of table 13.2, however, indicates the change in total consumption expenditure that will also occur as the child ages, given an unchanged level of family income. My 12–17-year-old, for example, will induce me to spend an additional $484 (about $1,950 in 2000 dollars, or close to 5 percent of my total consumption expenditures on average) more than I did when he or she was under 6, even with no increase in my total income—and I will distribute this new expenditure as indicated in panel B of table 13.2, with once again the largest share ($639 in 1972/73 dollars) going to food. The impact of an 18–24-year-old is more than three times as large, inducing me to spend close to 15 percent more out of the same income than I otherwise would have. Table 13.3 presents the same type of information, but now for a two-child family since expenditure patterns on first and second children can vary considerably.

These results are supported and even highlighted in a more recent analysis by Lino (1998). Lino estimated, on average, an increase of about 15 percent in two-parent families' expenditure, as a share of income, as children age from 0–2 to 15–17, shown in table 13.4. Much more impressive, however, is the 42 percent increase he found in lower-income, single-parent families. These changes must have had a dramatic effect on per capita (and per dollar of income) aggregate demand and savings rates as the baby boomers grew from infants to teenagers in the late 1960s and 1970s!

The "Dependency Effect" in Developing Countries

Despite these age-related differences, children have been treated as homogeneous across age groups in studies using U.S. data because of a tradition established in analyses of the "dependency effect" in developing countries. Researchers have assumed that economically inactive dependents—those aged 0–14 and 65+—exert a drag on an economy because they force economically active adults to divert income from savings to consumption. Without savings, investment in productivity-enhancing technology is assumed to become difficult or even impossible; but this would be the case only in a closed economy, one in which international investors are prevented from taking

Table 13.4. Estimated Expenditures per Child, by Age Group in 1997, by Type of Family and Before-Tax Income

Age of Child	Husband-Wife Family Income ($)			Single-Parent Family Income ($)	
	<35,500	35,500–59,700	59,700	<35,500	35,500+
0–2	5,820	8,060	11,990	4,900	11,210
3–5	5,920	8,270	12,230	5,510	12,030
6–8	6,070	8,350	12,180	6,230	12,800
9–11	6,090	8,320	12,090	5,820	12,380
12–14	6,880	9,050	12,930	6,270	13,120
15–17	6,790	9,170	13,260	6,970	13,580
Increase in expenditure on 15–17-year-old, relative to child 2 or under, income constant (%)	17	14	11	42	21

Note: Parents spend much more on teenagers than on infants, even if their real income remains the same: an average of 15 percent more in two-parent families and a staggering 42 percent more in lower-income, single-parent families. This change would have had a dramatic effect on per capita (and per dollar of income) aggregate demand and savings rates as the baby boomers grew from infants to teenagers in the late 1960s and 1970s. Source: adapted from Lino 1998, 15, 21.

advantage of the potential profits generated by increases in aggregate demand.

In addition, because of the assumption of homogeneity, many researchers have ignored the fact that changing age distributions among children will cause fluctuations in any dependency effect. Even more important, researchers have tended to ignore the possibility that the dependency effect might change as per capita incomes rise. Parents in developing countries have little or no access to private or public pension funds, so they look to their children for "old-age security": children take the place of saving. But the effect of children in more developed economies is open to question. As material aspirations increase along with economic development, and parents begin to opt for "quality" over "quantity" in children, higher levels of education become mandatory, and parents begin to have more ambitious plans for their children as young adults. This might motivate increases rather than reductions in savings among parents and other relatives.

A New Approach

Three important questions need to be answered. First, do patterns of expenditure and saving vary significantly over the life cycle as suggested in figure 13.1, or are people fairly homogeneous in their needs and their propensity to spend and save? Second, if there are age-related differences, what effect would there be on the macrolevel economy of "the pig passing through the python": the aging of the baby boom? And third, does that hypothesized effect resemble fluctuations the economy has actually experienced in the post-WWII period?

My own analysis, which I'll describe very briefly here, represents a departure from earlier studies in that it uses disaggregated macro data on personal consumption expenditures (PCE) at the state level for five dates (1900, 1929, 1970, 1977, and 1982) in combination with detailed age breakdowns of the population at the state and national levels. The state-level data provide more information than is available at the national level and more accurately represent total expenditures than do typical macrodata, but don't suffer from the masking of cross-generational spending so common at the micro level.[15] And because these data span the entire twentieth century, they permit the analysis of the United States not only as a developed economy, but also as a developing one. U.S. real per capita income in some states was as low as $1,500 in 1900 and as high as $30,000 in 1982, in terms of year 2000 purchasing power. In addition, my approach differs from most previous analyses in its use of age breakdowns by single year of age in the *total population,* including children, rather than just among heads of households or families.

Normally, a model that attempts to include a large number of age-group shares encounters a problem of severe multicollinearity that calls into question the accuracy of any individual coefficient estimates. That is, for example, the change in the share of 5-year-olds in the population each year will tend to be very similar to the change in the shares of 4-year-olds and 6-year-olds, making it impossible to identify which age group is affecting expenditures. This problem can even arise when only a few age groupings are used. My study made use of a mathematical technique that permits the estimation of a large number of age-group coefficients using just a small number of variables—a method that actually *capitalizes* on the multicollinearity.[16]

The results of my analysis suggest pronounced age effects on patterns of expenditure and saving, but also indicate that the dependency effect changes dramatically as national per capita income rises. The overall net effect of children on savings is negative at low

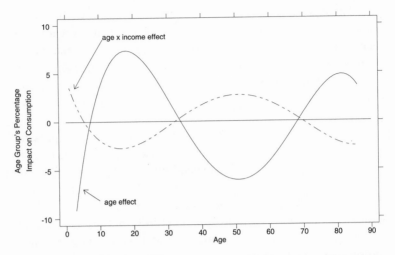

Figure 13.4. Estimated effect of different age groups on consumption expenditure as a share of total income. Points below zero indicate age groups that generate lower than average levels of consumption, while points above zero indicate age groups that generate higher than average consumption as a share of income. The solid line indicates the basic effect of each age group, and the dashed line indicates how that age group's net effect changes with rising per capita income. Source: author's calculations as reported in Macunovich 2002.

levels of real per capita income, but in post-WWII United States, children began to cause a reduction in overall consumption as a share of income, relative to the average, rather than an increase. These effects are demonstrated in figures 13.4 and 13.5.

The results are presented in the same format as figure 13.1: the graphs show what might be thought of as a per adult expenditures as a percentage of income, related to the different age groups in the population. All points below the horizontal line indicate age groups in the population associated with below-average expenditures as a share of income, and all the points above indicate age groups associated with above-average expenditures as a share of income. The solid curve in figure 13.4 traces out the underlying age effect: it exhibits the expected double-humped pattern of age-related coefficients that is consistent with the life-cycle hypothesis presented in figure 13.1. The age groups 15–35 and 60–80 generate above-average demand for goods and services (holding per capita income constant)—the 15–35 age group presumably because they are in the household- and family-formation stage, but earning less than they will during middle age; and the 60+ group because they are (for the most part) retired and living on savings. For those between the ages of 35 and 60, the large negative coefficients on age groups indicate below-average spending as a share of income. The regression results underlying figure 13.4 demonstrate that all of these estimated effects are highly significant.

However, the broken curve in figure 13.4 shows that per capita income works against this basic pattern. As affluence rises, the basic age-related pattern is flattened, and then ultimately reversed. This dynamic effect is best illustrated using simulations, which are presented in figure 13.5. Figure 13.5 combines the two curves in figure 13.4 to show the net effect of different age groups at three alternate levels of real per capita income: $1,000, $10,000, and $35,000 (with year 2000 purchasing power). It suggests that in an affluent society the presence of "dependent" age groups actually motivates increased saving in the economy as a whole. Parents and other relatives are motivated to save for children's college education, to provide a buffer in case of emergencies, and to plan bequests; and as the elderly survive to older and older ages, individuals are given more incentive to

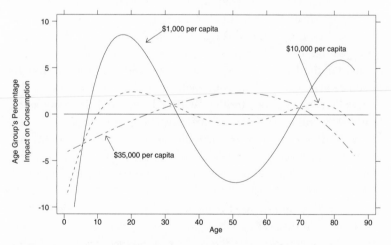

Figure 13.5. Estimated total effect of each age group on aggregate personal consumption expenditure at three different income levels: $1,000/capita, $10,000/capita, and $35,000/capita (in year 2000 dollars). These figures suggest that in high income countries, younger age groups (under about age 25), and age groups over about age 70 actually reduce the share of income devoted to consumption expenditures, while middle age groups increase it. It is important to note that these are not behavioral parameters: they indicate aggregate effects, including all interhousehold and intergenerational spending. Source: author's calculations as reported in Macunovich 2002.

save for their own twilight years. These simulations suggest that in the absence of dependent age groups adults tend to "live for today." They suggest that Americans might be saving less now because they have fewer children to save *for.*

Simulations

How *substantially* significant are the results described here? What is the magnitude of the effect that changing population age structure has exerted on patterns of consumption and saving at the macro level? It's possible to gain some idea of this effect by combining the coefficients estimated in the model described above with the observed U.S. age distribution in each year since 1900 to estimate annual per capita consumption levels in the United States—but holding real per capita income and total population size constant.

This type of simulation is problematic, however, because age structure effects are estimated to vary with level of income: if we hold income constant over a one-hundred-year period, we'll get a very unrealistic picture, as if the economy had stagnated for an inordinate length of time. Holding per capita income constant makes it very difficult to illustrate the full effect of changing age structure, both directly and as it operates through income. In order to address this complication, figure 13.6 presents the results of five different simulations for the United States. In each one, all variables except age structure are held constant, but each at a different level: one at the levels observed in 1900, another at 1925 levels, and three others at 1950, 1975, and 1999 levels, respectively. These simulations trace out an undulating "ribbon" of age structure effects on total personal consumption expenditures over the course of the century, with a maximum range of about 60 percent using the 1900-level characteristics with 1960 to 1980 age profiles.[17]

It's worth emphasizing the meaning of this figure, unrealistic as it actually is: at the average per capita income level observed in 1900, and *holding population size and real per capita income constant* (and thus implicitly assuming perfect capital markets with unrestricted international borrowing), the level of personal consumption expenditures would have been 40 percent higher if the age structure in 1900 had been our "baby boom" structure of 1980, or 20 percent lower given the age structure observed in the United States in the 1950s.

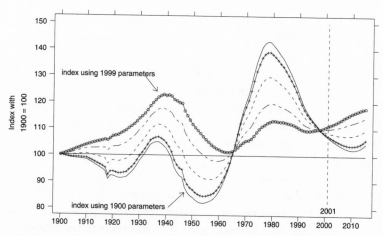

Figure 13.6. Index of the simulated effect of changing age structure on total absolute U.S. personal consumption expenditures at the national level, calculated by applying parameters estimated at the state level at five points during the twentieth century, and varying only the U.S. population age structure over time. The curves are simulated time trends obtained using parameters estimated in Macunovich 2002. Each of the five curves was calculated at a different level of per capita income and total population size, but using the same model and same (actual) variations in age structure over time. They demonstrate the varying effects of age structure at levels of the other variables actually observed in 1900, 1925, 1950, 1975, and 1999. A characteristic pattern emerges in all the curves, regardless of the different levels, with a strong growth period between 1960 and 1980, decline from 1980 to the late 1990s, and recovery thereafter.

Despite the differences in levels among the five curves, they all have in common extremely strong growth between 1960 and 1980, and then decline after 1980, as a result of the baby boom passing from childhood to young adulthood. It's outside the scope of this study to say whether this is a "good" or "bad" effect: it implies strong growth in aggregate demand but could obviously result in declining savings rates unless per capita incomes rise correspondingly. And of course they did rise dramatically in the 1960s and early 1970s, assisted at least in part by the rising domestic aggregate demand. As some researchers have begun to emphasize, in open economies an increase in the share of domestic income devoted to consumption need not result in a decline in overall investment and hence a decline in productivity and real growth. These researchers trace a pattern of increasing age-structure-induced investment supported by an increasingly negative current account balance, culminating in rising productivity and growth in real per capita output (and a reversal to a positive current account balance) as children become productive young adults.[18]

In any event, because real per capita income rose throughout the century, it would be inaccurate to suggest that the wide variations in age-structure-induced demand for goods and services shown in figure 13.6 ever actually occurred in the United States. Real income rose, and the model estimates suggest that as a result our priorities and spending patterns relative to various age groups changed, so that the scale of effects declined and "twisted," until at 1999 income levels the scale of potential age-structure-induced variation is "only" about 20 percent.

To give a more realistic appreciation of the effects of changing age structure that actually occurred throughout the twentieth century, figure 13.7 presents an "amalgamated" index. This index is a composite of the five curves in figure 13.7: it demonstrates 1900-level effects from 1900–1912, 1925-level effects from 1913–1937, 1950-level effects from 1938–1962, 1975-level effects from 1963–1987, and

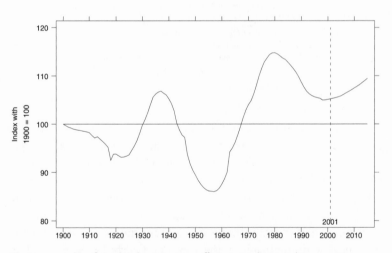

Figure 13.7. Index of simulated age structure effects on total personal consumption expenditures, using an amalgam of the five curves in figure 13.6. The amalgamated index demonstrates 1900-level effects from 1900–1912, 1925-level effects from 1913–1937, 1950-level effects from 1938–1962, 1975-level effects from 1963–1987, and 1999 level effects thereafter. It shows a 25–30 percent overall variation in aggregate demand for consumption goods and services, which was caused solely by changing population age structure during the twentieth century. (Movements after 2001 are based on U.S. Census Bureau forecasts of population age structure.) There is a strong pattern of growth in the 1920s and again in the 1960s and early 1970s, followed by a marked slowdown which then began to turn around after about 1995. If current savings rates are as low as some suggest, this simulation suggests changing population age structure as a significant contributing factor. Source: author's calculations as reported in Macunovich 2002.

1999-level effects thereafter. The widest variation observed in the amalgamated index of age-structure-induced aggregate consumption demand occurs between the 1950s and 1980: an increase of about 25 percent—still substantial, but nothing like the 60 percent swing displayed by the index based on 1900 characteristics.

But despite this shifting scale of effect, the estimates presented here suggest that the baby boom has had a major impact on the U.S. economy, probably contributing a huge boost in the 1960–1980 period but then a considerably weakened effect after 1980. Boomers and their children are likely to exert another strong positive effect in the first part of the twenty-first century, based on the parameters in the model and current Census Bureau population projections.

This analysis is only a beginning, using a new type of data set and a relatively new method of analysis. It suggests a very complex pattern of age structure effects that is consistent with the life-cycle model, but at the same time generates a much wider range of dependency effects and consumption patterns than has been contemplated up to now in the literature.

Summary

In this chapter I have attempted to demonstrate that the baby boom may have played a much more significant role in the U.S. economy's dramatic post-WWII economic fluctuations than is typically acknowledged in the literature. Methodological shortcomings may have contributed to this dismissal of age structure effects—in particular, the miscategorization of cross-generational spending, and the tendency either to omit children from the analyses or to ignore their age distribution. My own analyses have attempted to correct for these problems and suggest that changes in age structure—holding per capita income and total population constant—would have induced swings of up to 25 percent in total consumption demand during the twentieth century. Effects like these would explain the "asymmetry" of relative cohort size effects on male relative income that was described in chapters 5 and 6.

14

Population-Induced Economic Slumps

[B]usiness expectations being based much more on present than prospective demand, an era of increasing population tends to promote optimism, since demand will in general tend to exceed, rather than fall short of, what was hoped for. Moreover a mistake, resulting in a particular type of capital being in temporary over-supply, is in such conditions rapidly corrected. But in an era of declining population the opposite is true. . . . Thus a pessimistic atmosphere may ensue; and, although at long last pessimism may tend to correct itself through its effect on supply, the first result to prosperity of a change-over from an increasing to a declining population may be very disastrous.

John Maynard Keynes, "Some Economic
Consequences of a Declining Population" (1937)

The bankers yielded to the blithe, optimistic, and immoral mood of the times. . . . [O]ne failure led to other failures, and these spread with a domino effect.

John Kenneth Galbraith, *The Great Crash, 1929* (1954)

Of the components of aggregate demand, it is the investment spending by firms and households that is the prime mover in economic fluctuations, being by far the most cyclical and the most volatile. . . . If an economic slow-down reduces profit margins and dims the outlook for profits, the likely reaction of business firms will consist first in cutbacks on decisions to invest, then if matters do not improve, in reductions of inventories, output and employment.

Victor Zarnowitz, "Theory and History behind Business Cycles" (1999)

As demonstrated in the previous chapter, it appears that age structure is very important in national patterns of consumption and savings, and that young adults in the household/family-formation stage contribute strongly to consumption and dis-saving. As a result, one might suppose that changes in the proportion of the population in this stage of the life cycle can have major repercussions on a nation's economy. When their numbers are on the increase, their consumption demands ensure that overall economic growth is strong, but at the same time, aggregate savings rates drop and productivity levels fall.

A strong differential effect of specific age groups on economic performance has been demonstrated in the work of Harvard's Jeffrey Williamson and his colleagues, using the Asian Tigers and also the pre-1914 Atlantic economy. They have shown that the proportion of children relative to working-age adults has dramatic effects on savings rates and the demand for capital—and hence on foreign capital dependence. Theirs are some of the only studies that address distributional effects using detailed age breakdowns throughout the entire age structure, including children, finding a negative effect of population growth per se, but a positive effect of the proportion of the population in the prime working ages. They attribute much of the "Asian miracle," and much of the pre-1914 growth in the Western world, to the entry into prime working ages of these countries' "baby boomers"—those who were part of the population swell produced during the countries' respective demographic transitions.[1]

> [A]s the children of the baby boom became young adults, did the increase in new workers imply the need for investment in infrastructure to get them to work, to equip them while at work, and to house them as they moved away from their parents?
>
> . . . [C]hanging age distributions seem to have had the predicted impact. For East Asia, demographic effects have raised investment shares by 8.8 percentage points since the late 1960s . . . [and] population dynamics account for a substantial share of East Asia's economic miracle. Population dynamics account for somewhere between 1.4 and 1.9 percentage points of East Asia's annual growth in GDP per capita from 1965 to 1990, or as much as one-third of observed economic growth during the period.[2]

Theirs is exciting work in that it finally gives proper credit to changing population age structure in generating strong economic growth. But although these researchers allude to growth slowdowns as populations age, they don't seem to address the potential for economic turmoil created by the transition from high to low growth in specific age groups. This is probably because their models attribute growth to the entire working-age population—the 15–64 age group—and any transition in such a large age group's population share would be very gradual: barely discernable on a year-to-year basis. This would be my one criticism of their work, this failure to differentiate within such a large age group.

Given the life-cycle pattern of expenditure, it seems that changes in the size of the 15–24 age group will have a very different effect on the economy than, say, changes in the numbers of 55–64-year-olds. To the extent that this is the case, when this younger age group's share of population begins to decline, producers will be hit with an unexpected drop in the growth of demand for their products, leading to inventory build-ups and production cutbacks—as Keynes alluded to in the quotation above. Through a chain reaction of similar types of cutback, the economy may tailspin into an economic slump—as the Galbraith quote suggests.

This is not to say that decline in the young adult age group in and of itself is harmful for an economy: it certainly wasn't in the 1950s and early 1960s in the United States, and many have argued eloquently against such a notion, even in the case of population decline generally.[3] Rather, it is the *turning point* from rising to falling proportions of young adults that appears to pose a potential threat to economic stability, and "unexpected" is the key word in the previous paragraph—again, as suggested by Keynes. Producers can in time accommodate themselves to decline, as long as it's expected: it is the unexpected, which occurs at turning points, that "may be very disastrous."[4]

The extent of any economic decline induced by such turning points is undoubtedly a function of many factors in addition to changes in population age structure—most notably, the integrity of the banking system, and the financial sector generally, and the ability of the public sector to prevent escalation. Schumpeter attributed the virulence of the 1929 crash to "supernormal sensitivity of the economic system to adverse occurrences and . . . the weaknesses in the institutional setup."[5] As international trade has grown and strengthened, the integrity and stability of trade partners has become significant, as well.

Thus it appears that a relatively small change in the growth rate of the young adult age group in the United States in 1929, when financial systems were less robust, and major trading partners experienced more severe declines, had significantly greater effects than a much larger change in age structure in 1973, when federal monetary and fiscal policies had a more stabilizing influence and most trade partners had not yet experienced any decline. The point I will stress in this chapter is that unforeseen changes in population age structure have the potential for triggering catastrophic economic turmoil—and virtually always appear to cause at least a degree of economic dislocation.

There appears to be evidence that this process has been at work in the developed nations since at least the turn of the century. Demographers Keyfitz and Flieger provide limited data on population age structure for a handful of the currently developed nations back into the nineteenth century.[6] Figure 14.1 presents graphs of those data that suggest a close correlation between changes in the percentage of the population aged 15–24 and economic performance during the first half of this century.[7]

The vertical bars in figure 14.1 indicate the dates just prior to three major economic downturns in the United States during the first half of this century. The precise identification of these points varies among analysts, but they were roughly 1908–1910, 1929–1930, and 1937–1938.[8] In the United States those dates marked three significant turning points in the percentage of the population aged 15–24, with the severity of the 1938 downturn unique to the United States. In France and Belgium, at least, this proportion actually increased sharply after 1938, rather than declining as it did in the United States. It seems significant then that the United States, alone among its European trading partners, fell back into economic depression again after 1938.

Another significant point is the earlier turning point for the proportion aged 15–24 in France, as compared with the United Kingdom and the United States. The pre-Depression economic peak that occurred in 1929 for the United Kingdom and the United States was experienced in 1926 in France—and by 1930 France was recovered sufficiently to experience another cyclical peak.[9]

In addition, it is worth noting in figure 14.1 the unique increase in the proportion aged 15–24 in the United States in the years just prior to 1929, which undoubtedly contributed to that decade's reputation as the "Roaring Twenties" in the United States (strong economic growth with reduced savings rates), while it "was a time

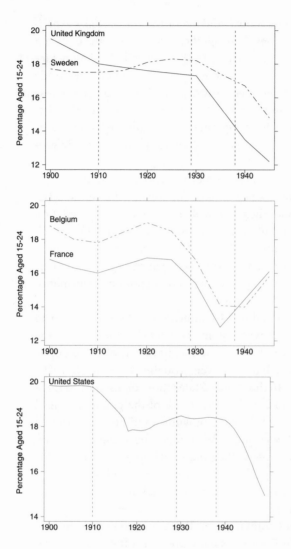

Figure 14.1. Percentage aged 15–24 in some of the currently developed nations during the first half of this century. The vertical bars indicate the dates of the three major economic downturns in the United States during this period: 1910, 1929, and 1938. These downturns seem to be correlated with significant turnaround points in the growth of the population aged 15–24. Source of population data: Keyfitz and Flieger 1968.

of troubles in the major countries of the world economy. In Britain, Scandinavia and Germany (1923–1929) there was an average double-digit unemployment."[10] The increasing proportion aged 15–24 in the United States—an increase in relative cohort size—would also have been a major factor in the fertility decline experienced in the United States during that period.[11]

Declining fertility associated with the demographic transition accounted for much of the longer-term downward trend in the 15–24 age group in figure 14.1, but figure 14.2 illustrates why the drop was

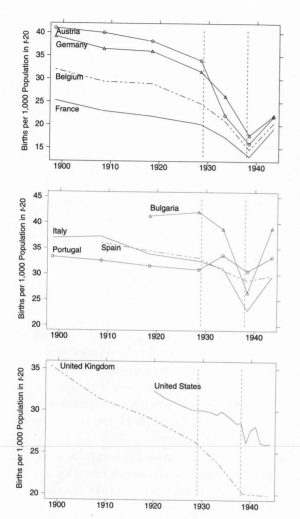

Figure 14.2. Crude birthrates in Europe and the United States, lagged twenty years to correlate with percentage aged 15–24. Here again, note the apparent correlation between changes in population age structure and significant economic downturns. Sources of population data: Rostow 1998 for the European nations; vital statistics and population data from the Bureau of the Census for the United States.

so marked after 1929: falling birthrates during World War I. The data here are taken from Rostow, who provides crude birthrates for many of the European nations during this period.[12] These birthrates are lagged twenty years in figure 14.2, to correlate births with the proportion aged 15–24 twenty years later.

The U.S. decline in births was more limited, and occurred later because of the later U.S. involvement in the war. This later decline in birthrates then contributed to the uniquely sharp drop-off of the proportion of U. S. population aged 15–24 after 1938. The coincidence

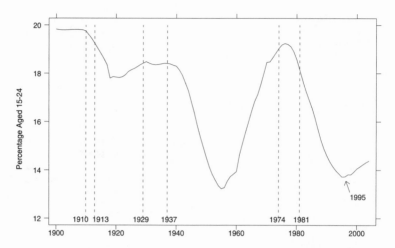

Figure 14.3. Percentage aged 15–24 in the United States, indicating the demographic peaks just prior to major economic downturns (1910, 1913, 1929, 1937, 1974, and 1981). Source of population data: Keyfitz and Flieger 1968 and United Nations 1998a.

of population and economic turning points emerges very clearly in figure 14.3, which illustrates the situation in the United States throughout the twentieth century. It can be seen that all of the population peaks (in the percentage aged 15–24) are associated with major economic downturns. As emphasized earlier, however, it appears to be the *turning point* in the proportion aged 15–24, rather than its actual decline, which is associated with economic difficulties—and the magnitude of the decline in that proportion appears to be virtually unrelated to the depth of the associated economic recession. It's also worth noting, in figure 14.3, the turning point in 1995 that coincides with our most recent economic *upturn.*

The halting progress of world economies throughout the 1980s and 1990s becomes more understandable, then, in light of the trends in percentage aged 15–24 across nations, as shown in figure 14.4. Panel *a* illustrates the sharp declines experienced after 1980 in the proportion aged 15–24, which coincide with economic slowdowns in all English- and German-speaking countries. Growth in the percentage aged 15–24 ceased in the United States and Canada after 1975, and then plummeted after 1980, but sharp declines were not experienced by the United Kingdom, Germany, Austria, and Switzerland until after 1985 (panel *b*). Norway, Denmark, the Netherlands, Italy, Portugal and Spain were similarly late in experiencing the turning

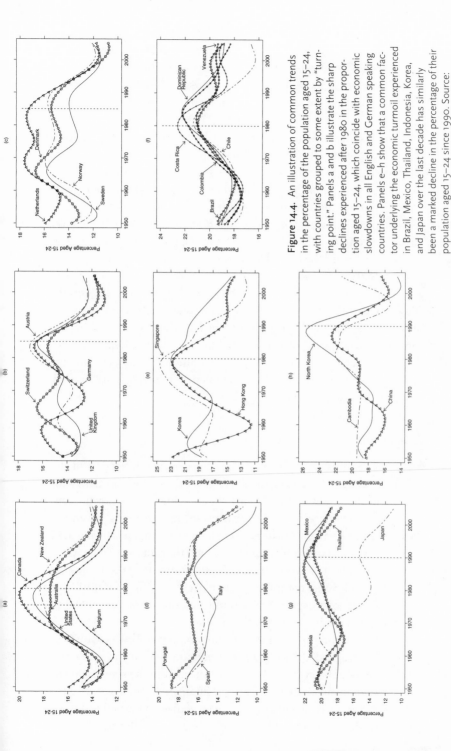

Figure 14.4. An illustration of common trends in the percentage of the population aged 15–24, with countries grouped to some extent by "turning point." Panels a and b illustrate the sharp declines experienced after 1980 in the proportion aged 15–24, which coincide with economic slowdowns in all English and German speaking countries. Panels e–h show that a common factor underlying the economic turmoil experienced in Brazil, Mexico, Thailand, Indonesia, Korea, and Japan over the last decade has similarly been a marked decline in the percentage of their population aged 15–24 since 1990. Source: United Nations 1998a.

point in percentage aged 15–24, as shown in panels *c* and *d* of figure 14.4. In addition the percentages drop further in those countries, and stay down longer there. These patterns are all consistent with the differing economic trends in these countries during the 1980s and 1990s.

Panels *e–h* of figure 14.4 suggest that a common factor underlying the economic turmoil experienced in Brazil, Mexico, Thailand, Indonesia, Korea, and Japan over the last decade has similarly been a marked decline in the percentage of their population aged 15–24 since 1990—in this case a legacy of the demographic transition they experienced in the post-WWII period. Such declines have been fairly widespread in the Third World, possibly explaining the weakness in global markets in the late 1990s despite the booming economy in the United States.

And finally, figure 14.5 demonstrates that not even the former Eastern Bloc countries have been immune to such fluctuations, although they appear to have marched to the tune of a different drummer. Bulgaria, Romania, Hungary, the Czech Republic, and Yugoslavia experienced a decline earlier and were in a period of recovery while the Western nations declined, but during the 1990s they entered another period of decline.

Summary

There have been pronounced fluctuations in the proportion of the population aged 15–24 across all nations during the twentieth century, and these fluctuations appear to coincide with major fluctuations in economic activity. This hardly seems surprising, given the strong age patterns in consumption and savings that were indicated in the previous chapter. It is consistent with the findings of a long line of researchers who have examined age structure effects on economic growth in individual countries[13], and it accords with the intuition of some of the most respected voices in economics, as attested by the quotations at the beginning of this chapter.

A cursory analysis such as this one cannot be taken as statistical "proof" that age structure plays a dominant role in the economic cycles that have been studied over the century. But the speculation in this chapter seems supported by the findings of other researchers who have found strong effects of age structure changes that follow countries' demographic transitions.[14] Research is called for that will

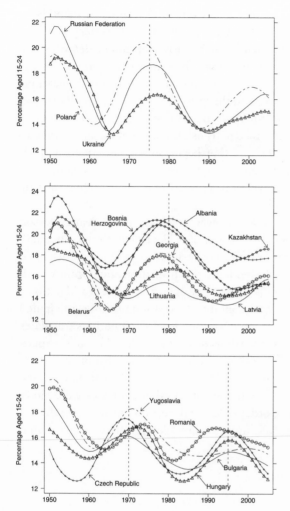

Figure 14.5. Trends in the percentage aged 15–24 in several former Eastern Bloc countries. Strong cyclic patterns have occurred in these countries as well. Source: United Nations 1998a.

refine their work, to focus more on the effects of the 15–24 age group, to identify an appropriate model, and test that model using relevant economic (and institutional) variables. Even then it seems unlikely that the full strength of the relationship will be estimated because of the discontinuity of the "trigger" effect that occurs at downturns, and the many factors that play a role in determining the breadth, depth, and length of any economic downturn that is induced by turning points in age structure.

But the evidence presented in this and the previous chapter provides an explanation for the "asymmetry" observed in the effects of relative cohort size on relative income and fertility. It identifies a powerful negative force that counters the beneficial effect of declining relative cohort size, at least in the early years after a demographic turning point. Since younger, less-skilled workers are more susceptible in economic downturns, they are hit harder by the dislocations brought about by changes in the growth rate of relative cohort size. The United States has experienced only one episode of declining relative cohort size that seemed to translate almost immediately into increases in fertility—the one that began in the late 1930s and extended into the 1950s—and there it seems likely that the effects of wartime expenditures will prevent us from ever unraveling the true effects of changing cohort size.

There is another area, however, in which we can learn a lesson from the recent experience of countries like Brazil, Korea, Thailand, and Indonesia, some of the first countries to experience the dramatic fertility reductions of the demographic transition after World War II, as well as from the 1930s' experience of current First World nations. It seems likely that some economic dislocation *must* be anticipated once the fertility decline in currently developing nations translates into a decline in the proportions of young adults. They may experience booming growth prior to that point, as demonstrated by Williamson and his colleagues, but perhaps "the bigger they are, the harder they fall." Perhaps the lesson of other countries will help to adjust expectations in order to lessen the economic impact of this inevitable—but historically unforeseen—"delayed effect" of the demographic transition.

Macroeconomic Correlations: GDP Growth, Inflation, Savings Rates, and the Stock Market

> If demographic forces are allowed to have their way, capital flows over Asia borders will be very different three decades from now.
>
> Higgins and Williamson, "Age Structure Dynamics in Asia and Dependence on Foreign Capital" (1997)

There is a widely shared belief among analysts that in 1973 the United States entered a "new era" of low productivity and sluggish real growth. Theories abound regarding the cause of the changes that occurred at that time, with the oil price shock a leading contender. And in the latter half of the 1990s, there was increasing talk of yet another "new era": this time an era of growth and prosperity with low inflation and unemployment. If we go back in history we can find similar allusions to major structural changes, around the turn of the last century and again in the 1930s. Although historically there was in each case some discussion of potential demographic influences operating at the time of these rifts, demographics are rarely mentioned in current analyses. Yet if the results in the previous chapters have any validity whatsoever, there is a strong possibility that demographics at least played a role.

Another common feature that's apparent when one looks back through the history of our economy is the tendency at the dawn of each "new era" to assume a linear trend: to assume that long-term forecasts should be based on the new parameters. But this type of linear approach could be very misleading if the underlying forces are in fact—like the pattern of population change—highly nonlinear. The attempt in this chapter is to conduct a very simple analysis using time series of macroeconomic and population data to explore the possibility of correlations between population age structure and economic performance. It is hoped that the relationships demonstrated here will motivate further study.

Theoretical Considerations

The theoretical reasons for expecting a significant relationship between population age structure and savings rates were discussed in chapter 13. They are based on the life-cycle hypothesis of spending and saving: it's assumed that individuals attempt to smooth consumption over their lifetime, and that attempt in combination with the lifetime pattern of earnings (low initially, rising to a peak in middle age and then declining before retirement) causes them to dis-save at younger ages, then save (which will include paying down credit card debt!) in middle age, and finally dis-save again in retirement as they draw on accumulated savings. And my own analyses described in chapter 13 suggest an additional component in that life-cycle model, associated with children as they age: parents' expenditures tend to be U shaped in relation to the age of their children, with heavy spending on under-5s and older teens but much lower levels of expenditure (holding income constant) or even net saving in between.

Given this sinusoidal pattern of saving over the life cycle, then, it's simply an empirical question whether there is any net effect of changing population age structure on the overall saving rate, or whether the accumulated increases and decreases associated with each age group simply balance each other out at any point in time. To the extent that there is any effect of age structure on savings rates, GDP growth will be negatively affected, in the short term at least, in the sense that saving defers consumption. Some economists maintain, however, that since saving provides funds for investment in productivity-enhancing capital equipment, it has the potential to raise per capita income and thus consumption. Here again, the extent of the net effect is simply an empirical question.

But there will be a direct effect of population growth and change on GDP growth, in addition to the productivity-enhancing effects of saving. Although it's assumed that individuals smooth consumption over their lifetimes, their purchasing patterns tend to be "lumpy": the purchase of a house is treated in economic terms as the purchase of a smooth flow of "housing services" over many years, but the full effect of that purchase on the housing market and on the economy will be felt in the year of purchase. As a result, young people in the household- and family-formation stage are expected to have an inordinately strong effect on GDP growth, as mentioned in earlier chapters.

But what about the stock market? To the extent that the 15–24 age group has a disproportionate effect on consumption demand, investors will view the prospect of growth in that key age group as an indicator of future growth in profits, and this will tend to push up share prices prior to the emergence of a population bulge in that age group (price to earnings ratios will rise). However, once that age group actually begins to grow, firms will need to invest heavily in new plant and equipment in order to increase output to realize those increased profits. Funds will thus be diverted from the stock market and share prices will fall (price to earnings ratios will fall).

In addition, there's the "one more sucker" argument: the idea that an excess of population in the age group saving for retirement will tend to push up share prices. This has been a common refrain among analysts since the baby boom entered middle age. And the flip side of this argument is that share prices will fall whenever there's an excess of retirees cashing in on their savings, creating the possibility of an "asset meltdown" sometime in the first quarter of this century.

The combination of these two arguments produces a sinusoidal pattern of age structure effects, with positive forces generated by teenagers (as investors anticipate a consumer buying spree when the teens leave home), negative forces generated by young adults (as producers divert funds to investment in plant and equipment for expansion), positive forces exerted by prime-age adults (as they save for retirement, and negative forces exerted by retirees (as they begin to live off of their pensions).

Preliminary Analysis

The first part of this analysis was carried out in 1997 as background for a discussion paper at a conference organized by the Federal Reserve Bank of Boston. It tests for correlations using a fairly common approach with population data: taking just a few population age group shares as indicative of the overall age distribution. Thus, for example, if figure 13.1 is a true representation of life cycle differences in spending and saving, with a shift from dis-saving to saving as individuals move from their twenties into middle age, and then a shift back into dis-saving in retirement, then one might use as explanatory variables, the proportion of the population each year aged 20–39, 40–64, and 65+.

A significant shortcoming of this approach is the danger that boundaries will be mis-defined. If those aged 40–44 in fact exhibit behavior more like those aged 20–39 than those aged 45–64, erroneously including them in with the 45–64 age group will "dilute" any results obtained, with the behavior of the 40–44-year-olds canceling out the behavior of some of those aged 45–64 in the data. Another problem with this approach is that there tends to be a great deal of similarity between the behavior of adjacent groups—we don't expect to see a major discontinuity when people move from age 39 to 40, for example—and among the movements of almost all population age groups. This makes it difficult for econometric techniques to identify which group was most responsible in generating a particular effect, and analyses using too many age groups will get results saying that *no group* was responsible, even if some were.

As a result, these preliminary analyses identified a few narrowly defined age groups within which individuals might exhibit very similar behavior, but between which they might be very different.[1] Econometric analyses using those explanatory variables demonstrate strong and significant correlations between age-group shares and trends in four macroeconomic variables: the real GDP growth rate, the savings rate, inflation, and the annual percentage change in the Dow Jones Industrial Average (DJIA). For each of these macroeconomic indicators two regressions were estimated: one using all available years of data, and the other using only data through 1985 (through 1976 for the DJIA). The coefficients estimated in the latter set were then used to "predict" trends in the following years through 1995. The results of this exercise are presented in figure 15.1, together with the actual observed values for comparison. In all cases the models based on data excluding information on the latest period did a very respectable job of predicting the actual performance in the excluded period.

An Update for the DJIA

Theoretically it's difficult to justify the choice of such narrowly defined age groups, however. Any choice might be questioned: why 25–29 rather than 26–30, and why 9 rather than 10? In addition, while the estimated coefficients from the regressions for GDP, the savings

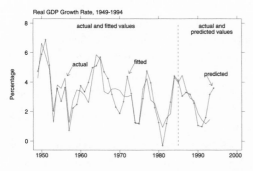

Real GDP Growth Rate, 1949-1994

Personal Savings Rate, 1947-1994

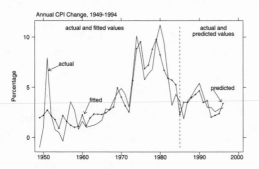

Annual CPI Change, 1949-1994

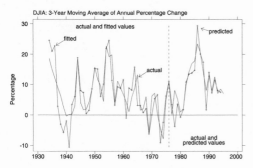

DJIA: 3-Year Moving Average of Annual Percentage Change

Figure 15.1. Predicting real GDP growth, savings, and inflation from 1985–1995, and the DJIA from 1976–1995, using population-based models fitted on data for 1949–1985 (1949–1976 for the DJIA) based on models reported in Macunovich 1997b, 2002. Values after 1985 predicted using data from previous years.

rate and inflation are arguably consistent with the life-cycle hypothesis and the results in chapter 13 (with those age 48–65 estimated to reduce inflation, and those age 24–35 exerting a positive effect, for example) the estimated coefficients in the regressions for the DJIA are harder to justify. This latter is probably not surprising: analyses show that there is as expected a high degree of multicollinearity among the age groups used.

A better approach would be to include a comprehensive set of controls for the population at all ages, and two researchers in 1991 suggested a method of doing so without encountering the problems mentioned above.[2] I've described the methodology in detail elsewhere:[3] it was used in the analyses reported in chapter 13. Here I simply present the results of an analysis using that methodology with the DJIA.

But before looking at the results, it's informative to look at the data: what sort of pattern, if any, is apparent in the historic path of the DJIA throughout the twentieth century? At first glance, looking at figure 15.2, the answer might seem to be "Not much!" That figure presents the monthly closing levels of the Dow, with no adjustment for inflation, and then adds a correction for inflation (using the Producer Price Index) which brings out a bit more pattern—but a proper analysis requires rates of change, which are presented in figure 15.3.

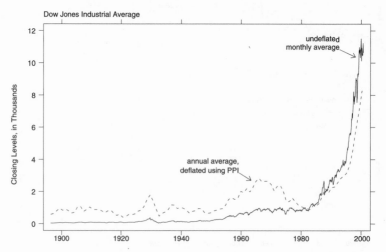

Figure 15.2. Closing levels of the DJIA as observed and deflated using the Producer Price Index.

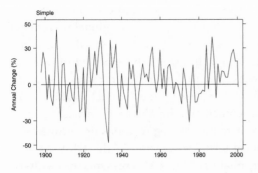

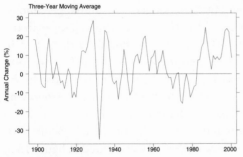

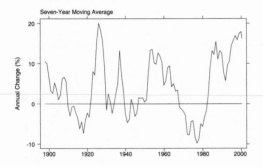

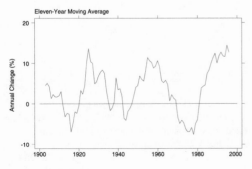

Figure 15.3. Smoothing the DJIA by taking successively longer moving averages of the annual percentage change in the deflated index. An apparent longer-term cyclical trend begins to emerge, moving from the top panel (simple annual percentage change) to the bottom panel (eleven-year moving average). The choice of eleven years might seem odd: why not ten? Moving averages are typically calculated only in odd numbers because the average is centered on the reported year: an eleven-year moving average for 1990, for example, includes the five years prior to 1990 and the five succeeding years, as well as 1990 itself.

An underlying cyclical regularity in the DJIA begins to emerge from successively longer moving averages of the annual percentage change in the deflated index, as in figure 15.3. It's this underlying longer-term pattern, if any, that would be expected to respond to demographic influences. Day-to-day and even month-to-month changes are too strongly influenced by the "animal spirits" of investors, to use the phrase coined by John Maynard Keynes.

And there does appear to be a strong relationship between age structure and these longer-term movements in the DJIA, as suggested by my preliminary analysis. Figure 15.4 presents the results of a three-step exercise: First, I fitted a model of the annual percentage change in the DJIA on a set of variables measuring changes in the population age distribution (using the methodology described in Macunovich 2002). Second, I used the estimated coefficients from step one to "predict" movements that would have occurred in the DJIA during the observed period, 1900–2000, as well as the following fifty-year period—based just on changing age distribution in the population.[4] Third, I compared the model's "predicted" values with the eleven-year moving average of the DJIA presented in figure 15.3,

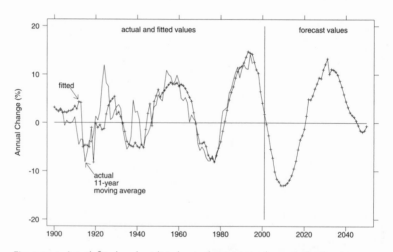

Figure 15.4. Actual, fitted, and predicted annual percentage change in the Dow Jones Industrial Average, using regressions reported in Macunovich 2002. The fitted and predicted values are based on a regression of the annual percentage change in the DJIA between 1900 and 2000, on annual changes in population age shares. The fitted values correspond very closely to the eleven-year moving average of annual changes in the DJIA: a model based just on changing population age structure appears to explain most of the longer-term variation in the index.

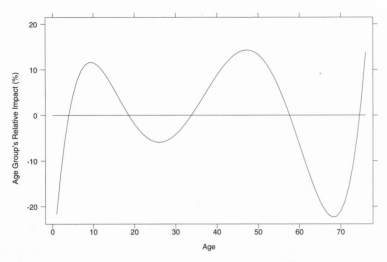

Figure 15.5. Pattern of estimated coefficients on population age shares from a regression of the annual percentage change in the DJIA between 1900 and 2000 on annual changes in population age shares—in a model presented in Macunovich 2002 and in figure 15.4.

to see if population effects can explain the longer-term movements in the market.

Figure 15.4 demonstrates that the model does an astonishingly good job of "predicting" the actual long-term fluctuations in the DJIA's movements. And based on these historic patterns, the model predicts another cycle in the first half of the twenty-first century—a cycle on which we are, apparently, already embarked.

Sensitivity analyses have demonstrated that this is a very robust result.[5] And the pattern of estimated coefficients on age groups conforms with the assumptions described earlier in this chapter, as demonstrated in figure 15.5. The market experiences a "rush" in response to growth in the under-20 age group, then regroups when that growth hits the 20–35 age group and producers expand their production capacity. Growth among prime-age adults (the 35–60 age group) pushes up share prices, and then when that group hits retirement age, share prices are depressed. Interestingly, the model estimates that in the absence of changing population age distribution during the twentieth century the stock market would have simply experienced an average annual real increase of 2 to 3 percent per annum.

The results of a similar type of analysis using the S&P 500

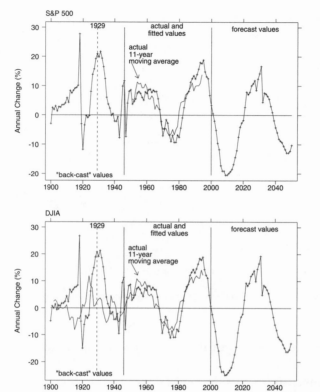

Figure 15.6. Actual, fitted, predicted, and "back-cast" annual percentage change in the S&P 500 and the DJIA, using regressions reported in Macunovich 2002. The fitted, predicted, and back-cast values are based on a regression of the annual percentage change in the DJIA between 1946 and 2000 on annual changes in population age shares. The back-cast values suggest that there was a demographic basis—which peaked in 1929—for the "irrational exuberance" in the stock market in the 1920s, as well as for the troughs during the two World Wars.

Index—which has only been available since 1946—are presented in figure 15.6. There I've prepared "predicted" values not just for the observed period and for 2001–2050: I've also used the model to "back-cast" values for the period prior to 1946. And in a third exercise, also presented in figure 15.6, I've done the same thing with the DJIA: fitted the model just on data for 1946–2000, then back-cast for the 1900–1945 period and forecast for 2001–2050. The patterns estimated here are very similar to that presented in figure 15.4, and they suggest two rather startling conclusions: (1) the "irrational exuberance" that drove the market up in the 1920s was apparently demographically induced: a strong cycle was initiated in 1920, which peaked in 1929; and (2) the two wartime troughs, around WWI and WWII, could also have been predicted on the basis of contemporaneous population change—although in this case at least some of the population change may have itself been war-induced.[6] In particular, an examination of the data suggests that the sharp dislocation in

1918–1920 is due to age structure effects of the flu epidemic at that time, in combination with war-time losses and drastic reductions in immigration.

Summary

The results presented here demonstrate a strong correlation between the age structure of the population and longer-term change in measures of macroeconomic performance: GDP growth, the savings and inflation rates, and the rate of increase in two stock market indices. They suggest that changes in the age structure of the population might have been responsible for the marked cyclicality in the underlying patterns of longer-term change in these measures during the twentieth century. Although the results for the Dow Jones support the notion of an "asset meltdown" in the first quarter of this century, they hold out the promise that if population continues to play a role similar to that played in the twentieth century, changing age structure will contribute to a subsequent strong recovery in the second quarter of the twenty-first century.

In addition, analyses of the Asian Tigers and other South and Southeast Asian countries have demonstrated that many of these countries will be emerging from demographically induced periods of low savings, to periods of high savings during the next twenty-five years (as did Japan in the 1980s, when it appeared as though that country was buying up of our most prestigious real estate).[7]

South Asia will graduate from its current heavy dependence on foreign capital to complete independence by 2025. The CAB [current account balance] in Bangladesh will switch from –8.2 percent of GDP in 1990–92 to +1.4 percent in 2025, a total change of 9.6 percentage points, almost identical with the impact of the fall in the dependency rate recorded by Japan between 1950–54 and 1990–92. India will undergo a similar trend, although the total impact will not be as great (a 7.9 percentage point drop in CAB share). Pakistan and Sri Lanka will closely replicate the case of Bangladesh. The experience in East Asia will be similar (Japan aside), with the CAB share rising by about 10 percentage points for China and Korea.

Nevertheless, the movement toward net capital export positions will be most pronounced in Southeast Asia. Between 1990–92 and 2025, the CAB share will rise by 10.4 percentage points in Indonesia, by 11.3 in

Malaysia, by 10.5 in the Philippines, by 9.5 in Singapore, and by 11.7 in Thailand.

If demographic forces are allowed to have their way, capital flows over Asia borders will be very different three decades from now.[8]

It seems likely that these excess savings will not only cross internal Asian boundaries. These countries will be looking for places to invest just at the point when American baby boomers are cashing in for retirement. Thus, while the long-term pattern of change in the DJIA may have been almost solely a function of indigenous population age structure during the twentieth century, it will likely become a function of global population age structure in the twenty-first.

Conclusion

> We are passing . . . over a divide which separates [us from] the great era of
> growth and expansion of the nineteenth century. . . . The great transition, in-
> cident to a rapid decline in population growth and its impact on capital for-
> mation.
>
> Alvin Hansen, presidential address, Fifty-first Annual Meeting of the
American Economic Association (1938).

The focus throughout this book has been on the socioeconomic effects of changing demographics—particularly the effects of a
dramatic upheaval or "birth quake" like the post-WWII baby boom.
But it would be naive to suggest that this has been the sole cause of
the disruptions we've observed over the past century. Rather, the attempt here has been to demonstrate that demographics have played
a very significant role—so much so that models and explanations developed without controls for population change are almost certain to
produce biased results.

An excellent example of this type of bias can be seen in the economic projections used most recently by the Social Security Administration. These projections were based on relatively simple extrapolations of past trends seventy-five years into the future—but what *are*
the past trends? Real wages, for example, are projected to increase at
a rate of only about 1 percent per annum for the next seventy-five
years, largely because that was the rate of growth observed during
the "productivity slowdown" between 1973 and the late 1980s. But
what about the 2.6 percent-per-year growth we experienced between

1948 and 1973? If the baby boom did have significant effects on the economy as it entered the labor force during the 1970s and 1980s, any linear extrapolation should assume for the future a growth rate that averages over the entire postwar period, rather than one based only on the anomalous period most negatively influenced by baby boom effects. The strong growth we've observed in recent years—in excess of 3 percent per year—suggests the need to view the 1970s and 1980s as the declining portion of a baby boom-induced cycle, rather than as indicative of a long term trend.

Acknowledging baby boom effects need not negate the existence of underlying long-term trends. Fertility rates may indeed be declining slowly over the years, as women move into careers and children become more expensive, but the point stressed here is that the baby boom's effect exaggerated our measures of the rate of decline. Similarly, women's college enrollment and labor force participation rates must certainly have been on a slow upward trend since WWII, just as they were throughout the first half of the twentieth century. But the baby boom accelerated the pace of change. That in turn accelerated the rate at which we inexorably progressed from an industrial to a service economy—which in turn may have exerted an unacceptable strain on our methods of measuring economic growth. One might argue that a very gradual "commoditization" of household services need not bias significantly our perceptions of the growth rate of real GDP—but the rate of growth we experienced in market-based services, induced by women's very rapid entry into the labor market, must certainly have biased that measure.

Similarly, rampant corruption, unsound banking practices, and the pressures created by changes in international trade and financial markets—to name but a few of the factors cited by the press and by financial experts—have been highly significant in the currency crises in various Latin American and Southeast Asian countries in the last few decades. But this book poses the question, Why *then*? What caused the crises to occur when they did? and suggests that unanticipated population-induced changes in aggregate demand might conceivably have played a role, by disrupting investor expectations. In addition, evidence has been presented that those changes in population age structure echoed fertility transitions approximately twenty years earlier in each country, transitions which were triggered by perceived economic hardships among increasing proportions of young relative to prime-age men. If these speculations have any merit, we should anticipate further "crises" in developing countries, since that fertility transition and its subsequent effects on population age structure are common patterns experienced by all nations as they develop economically.

Effects of Changing Age Composition versus Changing Age-Specific Effects

The primary focus in this book has been on the effects of changing demographics on *age-specific rates* of behavior—the idea that a cohort which is particularly large relative to its parental cohort might actually exhibit lower marriage and fertility rates and higher crime, suicide, female labor force participation, and divorce rates than a smaller cohort at any given age. This is an explanation of *behavioral* change. But topics like those mentioned in the previous paragraph—effects on aggregate demand, savings, inflation, and general economic performance—involve changes that might be observed, given a "birth quake," even if no behavioral changes occur. If behavior varies over the life cycle—crime rates and fertility rates are much higher for those in their early 20s than for those in their 40s, for example—then the movement of the "pig through the python" will produce changes in the incidence of that behavior *per capita in the total population* even in the absence of any behavioral change at the individual level.

Some have questioned my inclusion of such compositional effects in a study that focuses primarily on age-specific behavioral change. I have done so in order to counter a very common tendency among social scientists to attribute behavioral change not to cohort size effects, but rather to what are called "period effects." It's very popular to "blame" many of the behavioral changes observed among members of the baby boom on "the economy." When economic times are as difficult as those in the 1970s and 1980s, it's argued, young people are forced to make adjustments. My point in attempting to demonstrate an apparent link between demographics and the economic turmoil of the past few decades, is to suggest that what many term "period" effects might in fact be "cohort" effects—that no matter how you slice it, we have been observing the impact of changing demographics.

Historical Peculiarity or Recurring Cycle?

The Easterlin hypothesis as originally proposed was thought to imply the potential for recurring cycles. Each baby boom would generate a baby bust twenty-five years later, which would in turn create a baby boom after yet another twenty-five years, and so on. The realization documented here, however, suggests asymmetries which may dampen that effect leaving only a late twentieth century historical peculiarity—a one-off occurrence. If that is indeed the case why should we be concerned about the demographic effects discussed throughout this book? The reasons are twofold, with the first being the argument presented in the previous paragraphs: we ignore this historical peculiarity, if such it is, at our peril, because its effects confound any attempts to estimate models of other factors using twentieth century data. We cannot disentangle all of the relevant factors in our own history without acknowledging significant demographic effects.

The second reason is equally significant, if the speculative hypotheses in the latter part of this book have any merit. The demographic transitions we're observing in the Third World echo the experience of First and Second World countries a century earlier. The developing countries have been moving from high fertility and high mortality with little growth, to high fertility with declining mortality and increasing growth, and ultimately to the pattern of low mortality and low fertility with little or no growth seen in the more developed nations today. In the process their declining mortality and then fertility will inevitably generate a period some twenty years later when the proportion of young adults in the population first increases and then declines dramatically.

Based on the effects illustrated in this book, such a pattern of change in the population age structure of developing countries will first create forces favoring rapid economic expansion, followed by a fairly abrupt reduction in the growth rate of aggregate demand, which will strain these countries' financial institutions as investors default on loans taken out at the height of growth-induced speculation. Will these countries' eventual recovery following their financial crises then generate mini baby booms, when young people raised during the crisis with reduced expectations find themselves pleasantly surprised by their relative earnings in recovering economies? In this sense, then, even a historical peculiarity could be recurring—not within any one economy, but across countries as they develop.

The Significance of the Relative Income Concept

In addition, it should be noted that even as a mere historical peculiarity the baby boom has provided us with a laboratory for testing the
effects of changes in young men's relative economic status—what
has been referred to throughout this book as "relative income." It is
likely that all economists would acknowledge the relativity of income
measures—the fact that a given income will be perceived very dif-
ferently by different individuals, because they all assess that income
relative to different standards regarding an acceptable style of living.
But most economists feel that we have no way of quantifying individuals' material aspirations.

Because young men's wages plummeted relative to those of
prime-age workers (their fathers), and because this decline appears
to have triggered a large number of behavioral changes, our society's
experience over the past three decades suggests that we do have at
least one method of quantification. It implies that one of the key factors for young people in assessing the acceptability of a given level of
income is the standard of living experienced in their parents' homes.
Many other groups probably affect the standards individuals internalize—peer groups, older siblings, the media, and society as a
whole, to name a few—but measures of parental income give us a
starting point for analysis. This underlines the importance of data
sources describing not just young adults' own economic status, but
also that of the families in which they were raised. For young married couples we need that information for both partners. At present,
social scientists in the United States have no source of such comprehensive information. We can only approximate it with aggregate
data.

It has been fairly common since the 1980s for social scientists to
downplay the significance of the relative economic status hypothesis, because of unsupportive results obtained from a small number
of studies that attempted to measure and test the impact of internalized standards, particularly those based on parental affluence. But a
detailed review of that literature has demonstrated significant shortcomings, either in the methodology or in the types of measures formulated and tested, and points out that two-thirds of the forty-plus
micro- and macrolevel analyses based on North American data produced results supportive of either the relative cohort size, relative income concepts, or both as they relate to fertility.[1] The review empha-

sizes the need for more research both on the formation of, and on the formulation of, proper measures of individuals' material aspirations.

Where Do We Go from Here?

I have tried to emphasize throughout this book that I see the work presented here as only a crude beginning. The baby boom and its potential effects drew me away from consulting and into graduate studies, but I was dismayed to find so little interest in these questions among fellow economists. Because I seemed to be headed against the current, I felt that I needed to compile as much evidence as possible, as quickly as possible, in order to test for myself whether this is an area that deserves further research at a more detailed level, with more microlevel data. For myself, at least, it has passed that test.

My attempt has been to make use of readily available sources of data, applying a consistent set of definitions in a wide range of areas. This meant defining early on my measures of relative income and relative cohort size, and then sticking with them in order not to fall into the trap of "data mining" (an econometrician's term for the process of "torturing the data until it confesses"). But this was constraining, and I recognize that many will want to test my definitions.

Similarly, despite the fact that I am testing hypotheses concerned with behavior at the individual level, many of my analyses have been conducted using aggregate data because of the absence of appropriate information at the micro level. In order to establish for myself that the aggregate results do appear to hold at the micro level, I have thus far made two forays into the world of more disaggregated data: the first my analysis of the effects of demographics on the wage structure, and the second my use of regional data to test the effects of male relative income on patterns of fertility, marriage, and divorce.[2] The most important contribution of the first of these was to demonstrate strong effects of cohort size on the wage structure at all ages, and in the absence of any preconceptions about the "proper" definition of relative cohort size. The second study confirmed that the effect I had observed at the aggregate level, of changing male relative income on marriage, appears to hold as we move into more disaggregated data. The task now is to apply the same (regional) technique in tests of female labor force behavior as well as, perhaps, college enrollment.

Perhaps an even more interesting question though, is whether these same effects appear in other national settings. The analyses presented in chapter 12 suggest that they do, but to date studies of the Easterlin hypothesis in other Western nations have produced only mixed results.[3] My suspicion is that the problem here lies in the form of the tests that have been conducted. In the absence of age-specific wage data (for formulating measures of male relative income to test its effect on fertility behavior) researchers have looked for the "reduced form" relationship: does fertility behavior respond to changing relative cohort size? But this approach makes two very fundamental and restrictive assumptions: that the effects of relative cohort size on relative income are symmetric (so that fertility should rise as soon as relative cohort size begins to decline) and that institutional differences across countries have no effect either on the relationship between relative cohort size and relative income, or on the effect of relative income on fertility. But the prevalence of international migration within the European Union must dampen any effects of domestic cohort size on wages, for example, just as "family friendly" policies and differing cultural norms might dampen the effect of changes in relative income on fertility. Japan, for example, is currently experiencing extremely low levels of relative cohort size, which have never been translated into high male relative income and fertility. Why? Because they have a rigid wage structure that rewards experience and tenure regardless of changing relative supplies of older and younger workers. And because their social structure has imposed such restrictive marital roles on women that once they're given some economic independence they choose not to marry at all. This is especially the case given that parents seem to be content to let these young women continue residing at home. Marriage and fertility rates plummet, along with aggregate consumption demand in an economy bereft of the needed stimulus provided by young adults setting up new households on their own. There are very few young adults, relatively speaking, and even fewer of them are striking out on their own.

So where does that leave us? In need of a great deal more research—but research with a more "holistic" approach. These demographic effects appear to be so pervasive that it may well be possible that the standard academic approach—examining one specific relationship while holding all others constant—might miss the forest for the trees. The effects operating through just one channel may appear fairly minor; it's only when all the effects are taken into account that we identify a pervasive and highly significant effect. When we examine effects of demographics on the wage structure, for example, and dismiss effects of unemployment on young men's wages as "business-cycle effects" we may in fact be missing a very significant effect of changing relative cohort size. Unfortunately the holistic approach is strongly discouraged in academia.

15–24: Science or Witchcraft?

The population age group 15–24 has been referred to in many instances throughout the preceding chapters. Is there something special about that particular definition of the age group of young adults? In a word, no—apart from the fact that it is a standard grouping available in many data sources, and the one that most closely corresponds with the hypotheses presented here about age structure effects on aggregate demand. The early portion spans the period during which we know that parents tend to spend most heavily on their children (and during which children have enjoyed the highest spending power themselves, in recent years), while the later portion spans the period when most young people incur the major expenditures associated with higher education and setting up their own households. This age group marks the emergence of new consumers into the national economy. But analyses spanning the twentieth century in the United States lead me to believe that the appropriate age grouping may be country and period specific: In 1900 few young adults even completed high school, much less college, so they would have had an impact on the economy at a much younger age than in recent years. For example, graphical analyses like that presented in figure 14.3, when based on 17–19-year-olds or 20–22-year-olds rather than on 15–24-year-olds, display a remarkable virtual year-to-year correspondence between changes in the age group and short-term economic fluctuations (including the 2001 downturn)—but this correspondence occurs with 17–19-year-olds prior to World War II and with 20–22-year-olds in recent years.

But here as in so many other areas a great deal of additional research is required in order to confirm or refute the age structure effects, as identified in earlier chapters, on the demand for goods and services in the economy. Research is needed on the overall structure of effects, using data that account for all consumption expenditures, not just the fraction covered in the official Consumer Expenditure

Surveys. In addition, the data must account for all age groups including children, and recognize the potential for interhousehold age-related expenditures—spending, for example, by baby boomers' parents to help them purchase their own homes. Such spending is generated by the children's needs and ages, rather than the parents', but traditional household surveys have missed this connection.

There is nothing sacrosanct about the 15–24 age grouping—and sensitivity analyses, wherever possible, indicate that results are not overly affected by modifications within the spirit of the general hypothesis. A related issue, which was addressed more specifically in chapter 3, is the definition of relative cohort size using the number of 20–22-year-olds relative to those aged 45–49. This is a much less critical definition, since it was never actually used in econometric analyses: it was used only to demonstrate the close similarity between current population ratios and the general fertility rate twenty-some years earlier, that was presented in chapter 3. The aggregate econometric analyses used the exogenous measure of cohort size: the lagged general fertility rate. The subsequent microlevel analysis of the wage structure imposed no constraint whatsoever on the concept of relative cohort size: it simply assigned to each worker his birth cohort size and allowed the econometric analysis to determine which age groups were complements and which substitutes. But this, too, is an obvious area for future research.

Effect of Changing Age Structure on Investors' Expectations

The formation of producers' and investors' expectations is a related area in which considerable research is needed to assist in testing the hypotheses covered in this book. It has been hypothesized here that unanticipated downturns in the growth rate of teenagers and young adults—those in one of the most consumption-intensive portions of the life cycle—might undermine investors' expectations regarding the growth of aggregate demand, leading to cutbacks in production and employment that might snowball throughout the economy.

To what extent do producers and investors—like many researchers—project short-term economic activity based on linear extrapolations of recent trends and use these projections in their new venture and production decisions? And to what extent are these projections—like those of many researchers—made without reference to foreseeable changes in population age structure? How sensitive are their investment decisions to fluctuations in aggregate demand that might be triggered by unanticipated slowdowns in the growth rates of key age groups, like those aged 15–24—and how sensitive are general economic conditions to the withholding of investment resulting from such slowdowns? To what extent are loan defaults by producers, investors, and developers correlated with such slowdowns? To what extent are business cycles correlated with these demographic turning points?

The five-year growth rate in the percentage of the population aged 15–24, as shown in figure 1.2 (page 45), indicates an unusually strong coincidence between changes in this demographic indicator and economic performance during the twentieth century. The periods of decline in the proportion aged 15–24 (1929–1932, 1934–1954, and 1974–1994) coincide with eras of slow economic growth, while the periods prior to 1929, between 1954 and 1974, and since 1994 have all been characterized by growth in both spheres.

Asymmetry across the Twentieth Century

Another tantalizing question addresses interactions between real economic effects (changes in aggregate demand that might be demographically induced) and effects caused by stock market fluctuations. The analyses in chapter 13 suggested that a period of renewed age-structure-induced growth in aggregate demand began around 1995 and continues at least into the early part of the twenty-first century (figures 13.6 and 13.7, pages 217 and 218). But the analyses in chapter 15 (figures 15.4 and 15.6, pages 238 and 240) suggested hard times in the stock market beginning around 2001. It seems to me possible that future analyses will have to consider feedback effects between these two sectors, in order to arrive at more realistic projections of future economic activity.

Figure 3.6 (page 69) contrasted the patterns of fertility rates and births in the United States during the twentieth century. Very obvious there is the correspondence between the two series until about 1975, with marked divergence thereafter. My suspicion is that this is yet another reason why a relatively minor demographic shift caused such a major dislocation in 1929, but a much larger shift caused a more manageable one in the 1980s. Certainly monetary and fiscal policies and controls have played a significant role in buffering shocks in recent years, but in addition the patterns of positive and negative correlations among different age groups has changed in the past twenty-five years, so that age group effects which may have cancelled each other historically will now be reinforced—or vice versa. Some of these age groups have a stronger influence on the stock market, and others on real aggregate demand. Again, we need to take all of these into account in a more holistic analysis.

Are the Effects of a Birth Quake Permanent?

But the issues I find most fascinating—the ones I will be addressing most often in the future—are those related to behavioral change among young adults. Having ended up on a career path myself, despite early intentions to be a stay-at-home mom, and having watched my daughter and five younger baby boomer siblings deal with the tectonic shifts of the birth quake, one of my primary interests is in the relationship between demographics and attitudinal change, operating through economic effects.

To what extent would our attitudes toward work and family have changed regardless of demographically induced economic changes? And even more important, can these attitudinal changes be undone by further demographic and economic events? Even if male relative income had increased again in the 1980s as Easterlin expected, would it have been possible to generate a recurring baby boom cycle? Would our change in attitudes and expectations regarding "women's role" simply slow down any move by women back to more domestic roles, or would it prevent movement altogether? And do we need a reversal of women's roles to produce another baby boom: will young parents, feeling relatively affluent as they become increasingly scarce, procreate regardless of career commitments? If we knew the answers to these questions, we would also know whether below-replacement fertility is an end state or simply a passing phenomenon.

Expectations in the Williams College Class of 1999

How traditional—or untraditional—are Williams College students? This is a question that students in my classes have asked four times between 1990 and 1995 and have attempted to answer using sample surveys. In each survey, over two hundred students, selected at random, were asked a series of questions about their expectations regarding family and career after Williams. The results of these surveys have been surprisingly consistent over the years—and may surprise some of you!

The latest survey was conducted in November 1995 and was restricted to 228 students (116 male and 112 female) in the class of 1999.[1] Because these were all first-year students, their responses can be compared to those of all U.S. high school seniors in 1976 and 1986.[2]

Traditional Family Values?

Ninety-one percent of women students and 96 percent of men expect to marry, with 26.7 the average expected age at marriage for both sexes. Approximately 3 percent expect to marry right after graduation. By comparison, surveys of all American high school seniors in 1976 and 1986 indicated that only about 75 percent expected to marry.

Ninety-six percent of both men and women expect to have children: 50 percent want two children, and 38 percent of both men and women want to have *more* than two children. The average desired number of children is 2.39 for men and 2.31 for women, and the first of these is expected on average by the age of 27.7 years. 6 percent want to have their first child by age 25.

Here again the Williams class of 1999 demonstrates stronger family aspirations than the average American high school senior in 1976 and 1986, when only about 80 percent expected to have children. But Williams students are pretty much on target in terms of number of children desired: the average in 1976 was 2.63, and in 1986 it was 2.37—although in the general population in these earlier years women wanted more children, on average, than men. This situation is reversed at Williams in the class of 1999.

Richard Easterlin stated that "a notable consensus exists on two, three, and four child families. This is shown by surveys of American women conducted between 1936 and 1972 on their ideal family size—throughout this period, the proportion favoring two to four children is always 85 percent or more."[3] In the class of 1999, this proportion is 85 percent for men, and 86 percent for women. So far a pretty traditional picture.

But Who Will Look After the Children?

Women in the class of 1999 are strongly career oriented: they expect to work an average of forty-three hours per week before starting a family. Less surprisingly, the men expect to work forty-six hours per week. Among both men and women, none expect *not* to be working outside the home, and only 2 percent expect to work twenty hours per week or less. For women, this is a marked departure from earlier generations: among women aged 21–24 in 1975, only 56 percent felt that they would be working outside their homes at age 35 (when supposedly their children would have been grown).

Interestingly, however, 6 percent of the men expect to have stay-at-home wives (even when there are no children in the family), and 13 percent expect their wives to work twenty hours or less per week: they'll have to find partners from outside the circle of Williams alumnae.

But given this strong work orientation, who will care for the children? Members of the class of 1999 were asked to rank the following possible career arrangements for parents when they have young children: *(a)* both parents work full time outside the home; *(b)* both parents work part time; *(c)* wife full time and husband part time;

(d) husband full time and wife part time; (e) husband full time and wife at home; (f) wife full time and husband at home. Men ranked (d) and (e) highest and (a) lowest, while women ranked (b) highest, (d) second highest, and (a) lowest. The area of convergence here is category (d)—husband works full time and wife works part time—and respondents' answers to questions about their own career plans are consistent with this. Women indicate that they will drop to about twenty-two hours per week outside the home when they have children under 3 years old, while they expect their husbands to reduce their work hours only minimally, to about thirty-seven hours per week. The men's expectations conform closely to this: they expect that their wives will work only about twenty-three hours per week outside the home, while they themselves work about forty hours per week. Interestingly, however, while only 17 percent of women expect to drop out of the work force altogether when they have young children, 29 percent of the men expect to have stay-at-home wives during this period.

In this area—gender roles while raising young children—Williams students appear to be much more "progressive" than high school seniors back in 1977. In that year, 70 percent considered (a)—both partners work full time—to be unacceptable, while only 28 percent of Williams students found this unacceptable. However, both in 1977 and in the class of 1999 about three-quarters of respondents rated the traditional arrangement (e.g., husband full time and wife at home) as either "desirable" or "acceptable." Many fewer Williams women than men found this arrangement "desirable," however: only 8 percent of women as compared to 23 percent of men.

The full set of responses from the class of 1999 regarding expected work arrangements appears in table A.1. It shows, for both men and women in the class of 1999, how many hours per week they expect to work outside the home, depending on whether or not they have children at home. None of the men, when they have no children, expect to forgo work entirely, 2 percent expect to work from 1 to 20 hours per week, 4 percent expect to work from 21 to 35 hours per week, and 47 percent expect to work from 36 to 44 hours per week, while 39 percent expect to work more then 45 hours per week. On average, they expect to work 46.3 hours per week, while the women on average expect to work 42.9 hours per week, when they have no children. By comparison, only 34 percent of the women expect that their husbands will work 45 or more hours per week, and that on average

Table A.1. Expected Work Arrangements, Williams College Class of 1999 Survey

| | Expected Work Hours per Week | | | | | | | | | | | |
| | Men | | | | | | Women | | | | | |
Age of Children	0	1–20	21–35	36–44	45+		0	1–20	21–35	36–44	45+	
No children												
For self (%)	0	2	4	47	47	(46.3)	0	2	6	58	34	(42.9)
By spouse (%)	0	1	4	62	34	(43.1)	6	7	14	51	23	(38.9)
Children under 3												
For self (%)	0	6	28	39	27	(39.6)	17	35	30	14	5	(22.5)
By spouse (%)	0	10	25	45	20	(37.6)	29	21	22	17	10	(22.9)
Children 3–4												
For self (%)	0	4	21	44	31	(41.1)	10	20	34	30	6	(28.1)
By spouse (%)	0	2	19	57	22	(39.7)	17	26	23	22	11	(26.6)
Children 5–13												
For self (%)	0	1	9	55	35	(43.5)	3	10	25	42	20	(36.2)
By spouse (%)	1	1	12	60	26	(41.0)	13	11	24	36	16	(33.1)

Note: Numbers in parentheses are the average responses in hours.

they expect that their husbands will work 43.1 hours per week, while men on average expect that their wives will work, on average, 38.9 hours per week.

Even a cursory examination of this table shows a high degree of correspondence between men's and women's expectations for themselves and for their spouses. The area of greatest disagreement is for women when children aged 3–4 are present: men expect women to quit the labor market (17 percent) or to work twenty hours or less (43 percent) in much larger proportions than women themselves expect to do so (10 percent and 30 percent, respectively). Perhaps surprisingly, this discrepancy even shows up when there are no children present (6 percent of men expect to have stay-at-home wives, while no women expect to stay at home in this situation) and when children are school age (13 percent of men expect to have stay-at-home wives, while only 3 percent of women expect this). More men expect to have their wives work twenty hours or less in these situations, as well.

And How Altruistic Are the Class of 1999?

In 1976 and 1986, American high school seniors were asked to rate a series of life goals as either "not important," "somewhat important," "quite important," or "extremely important." We asked the respondents in the Williams study to rank these same goals for the purposes of comparison. The proportions of men and women indicating "quite or extremely important" in each survey year are indicated in table A.2. Perhaps the most dramatic differences here between Williams students in the class of 1999 and the average high school senior in earlier years are in the lower proportions who see "having lots of money" as important and the higher proportions hoping to "work to correct social and economic inequalities." In addition, there has been a progressive increase over the years in the proportions of men hoping to have a good marriage and family life, and Williams students—both men and women—rate "time for recreation and hobbies" higher than students in earlier surveys, while they see less need to give their children "better opportunities." These findings, consistent with the class of 1999's membership in a small cohort, are supported by survey findings reported in "Graduates Pledge to Lead Ethical Careers," *Syracuse Herald-American*, on May 5, 1999. The article describes a biannual survey conducted by

Table A.2. Priorities Compared across Surveys

| Life Goal | Percentage Responding "Quite or Extremely Important" | | | | | |
| | 1976 | | 1986 | | Class of 1999 | |
	Men	Women	Men	Women	Men	Women
Having lots of money	55	35	68	57	33	31
Giving my children better opportunities than I had	83	83	88	88	74	63
Time for recreation and hobbies	69	60	75	66	88	86
Working to correct social and economic inequalities	29	37	30	34	46	56
Having a good marriage and family life	84	91	86	93	94	92
Finding purpose and meaning in life	84	93	80	90	83	90

Don Nagy among MBAs at Duke University, which showed that "students' attitudes have taken a 180-degree turn over the past decade. In 1989, students responding to the survey ranked power, prestige and money near the top of their lifetime goals. Beginning in 1991, successful relationships, a balanced life and more leisure time became more important, and in the last survey the list was topped by marriage, health and ethics." Commentators like David Frum (2000) have attributed the "selfishness" of baby boomers to the "impossible hopes" and "belief in the limitless potential of their societies, their governments and themselves" that were generated by liberal politicians and their generous social programs in the 1960s. But I am suggesting that the real culprit was relative cohort size with its impact on male relative income.

What Is the Family Background of the Class of 1999?

Fifteen percent of the class have no siblings, while 45 percent come from two-child families and 40 percent have two or more siblings. Mothers of the majority of students (67 percent of men and 51 percent of women) stayed at home full time when their children were under 5 years old. This proportion drops to about one-third when children were 5–9, and to about one-fifth when they were 10–17. The mothers of Williams women tended to work full time in higher pro-

Table A.3. Fathers' Share of Housework, Williams College Class of 1999 Survey

	Men's Fathers		Women's Fathers	
	Housework	Child Care	Housework	Child Care
Percentage spending no time	9	4	17	9
Percentage spending up to 25 percent of time	45	39	56	41
Percentage spending up to 50 percent of time	84	84	81	78

portions (30–50 percent higher) than the mothers of Williams men, with this difference most pronounced when the Williams students were 5–9 years old: 39 percent of the women's mothers worked full time outside the home, while only 25 percent of the men's mothers did.

Approximately 11 percent of the women's fathers stayed home full time at some point when they were young, while only 7 percent of the men's fathers were at least temporary "house husbands." Overall, the proportions of housework and child care performed by Williams students' fathers are indicated in table A.3. Of note is the fact that men whose fathers stayed at home full time intend to stay at home more with their own children, on average: they intend to work about ten hours per week less than men whose fathers did not act as "house husbands." Perhaps this is an indication of gradual change over the generations, in the acceptance of "nontraditional" gender roles.

Tinker, Tailor, Soldier, Spy?

The intended fields of specialization in the class of 1999 (table A.4) show some strong similarities between men and women, but also a number of notable differences. The latter are in the areas of business and finance (29 percent of men, but only 7 percent of women), elementary and secondary school teaching (12 percent of women, but only 5 percent of men), social services (8 percent of women, but no men), law (9 percent of women, but only 6 percent of men) and journalism (7 percent of women, but only 3 percent of men). The most popular field overall is medicine (21 percent of both men and women), with business and finance in second place, and science and engineering in third (14 percent of men and 12 percent of women).

Table A.4. Career Plans, Williams College Class of 1999 Survey

	Percentage Intending to Enter	
	Men	Women
Field of Specialization		
law	6	9
medicine	21	21
education (K–12)	5	12
education (college)	9	11
business and finance	29	7
homemaking	—	—
government	5	3
social services	—	8
journalism	3	7
science and engineering	14	12
other	7	11
Occupation		
manager	19	7
researcher	18	13
consultant	10	3
nurse	—	—
market researcher	3	2
personnel	1	2
sales	1	1
service	—	3
technical	2	—
manual	—	—
teaching	16	22
clerical	—	—
professional	26	39
other	5	9

Nine percent of men and 10 percent of women intend to teach at the college level.

When the focus switches to occupations, we see a much larger proportion of men expecting to become managers, researchers, or consultants (47 percent, as opposed to only 23 percent of women). Women, on the other hand, expect to go into professional occupations (doctor, dentist, lawyer, artist, etc.) at much higher rates than men (39 percent as opposed to 26 percent). Neither men nor women indicate any intention to be homemakers, nurses, manual laborers, or clerical workers.

Data for Figure 4.1

Table B.1. Expected Male Relative Income, by Race and Educational Attainment.

	White Males				African American Males			
	all	16+	12	<12	all	<16+	12	<12
1968	0.412	0.672	0.387	0.222	0.489	1.114	0.578	0.304
1969	0.431	0.694	0.400	0.232	0.493	1.107	0.559	0.310
1970	0.432	0.689	0.394	0.232	0.521	1.127	0.571	0.331
1971	0.422	0.680	0.374	0.224	0.521	1.147	0.564	0.325
1972	0.409	0.663	0.362	0.212	0.505	1.174	0.546	0.297
1973	0.400	0.640	0.353	0.205	0.472	1.137	0.520	0.261
1974	0.379	0.600	0.334	0.192	0.436	1.080	0.478	0.224
1975	0.360	0.579	0.312	0.176	0.396	0.992	0.432	0.193
1976	0.352	0.568	0.307	0.170	0.374	0.917	0.399	0.175
1977	0.341	0.549	0.297	0.162	0.348	0.843	0.357	0.159
1978	0.331	0.532	0.289	0.154	0.325	0.800	0.315	0.154
1979	0.330	0.532	0.291	0.152	0.314	0.773	0.300	0.144
1980	0.331	0.526	0.297	0.153	0.312	0.761	0.294	0.138
1981	0.324	0.521	0.289	0.148	0.299	0.716	0.275	0.127
1982	0.316	0.523	0.277	0.139	0.282	0.677	0.254	0.117
1983	0.301	0.519	0.259	0.125	0.260	0.607	0.235	0.095
1984	0.289	0.516	0.239	0.116	0.234	0.615	0.202	0.074
1985	0.287	0.524	0.227	0.112	0.221	0.610	0.188	0.063
1986	0.293	0.537	0.224	0.109	0.220	0.636	0.189	0.062
1987	0.303	0.552	0.228	0.114	0.233	0.665	0.208	0.060
1988	0.316	0.565	0.236	0.122	0.249	0.731	0.221	0.058
1989	0.321	0.570	0.238	0.126	0.260	0.690	0.236	0.062
1990	0.315	0.558	0.235	0.121	0.260	0.675	0.231	0.070
1991	0.300	0.533	0.225	0.115	0.248	0.634	0.225	0.061
1992	0.283	0.506	0.211	0.106	0.234	0.628	0.202	0.055
1993	0.269	0.488	0.197	0.097	0.215	0.571	0.177	0.050
1994	0.259	0.467	0.187	0.089	0.206	0.545	0.161	0.042
1995	0.260	0.465	0.183	0.092	0.208	0.537	0.162	0.029
1996	0.266	0.471	0.184	0.097	0.221	0.587	0.159	0.033
1997	0.277	0.488	0.190	0.103	0.222	0.590	0.164	0.031
Maximum drop (%)	40	33	54	62	61	54	72	91

Note: Numerator is a five-year moving average of real annual earnings of all unenrolled males in their first five years of work experience, multiplied by their activity rate (the proportion of the unenrolled population actually employed). Denominator is a five-year moving average of real annual income in all families with children, with head of either sex aged 45–54 in year t –5.

Overview

1. Replacement-level fertility—approximately 2.1 births per woman, on average—is the level needed in order for each generation to replace itself, and thus maintain a constant level of population.

2. All three of the fertility rates mentioned thus far—the total fertility rate (TFR: total births per woman if she experienced current age-specific rates throughout her lifetime), crude birth rate (CBR: births per 1,000 total population), and general fertility rate (GFR: births per 1,000 women of childbearing age)—followed very similar patterns over the past century. The CBR is most easily calculated from readily available data, but is more subject to distortionary effects when population age structure is changing, than is the GFR. For a visual comparison of these three measures, see figure 3.2.

3. "Earnings" refers to annual income received as compensation for work performed in the labor market, while "total income" includes not just earnings but also "non-earned" income in a given year from all other sources, such as interest and dividends. Chapter 3 describes in more detail the measures underlying figure 2.

4. It is interesting to note that the "echo baby boom," as it enters school age, appears to be encountering many of these same effects—even though it is simply the result of increasing *numbers* of births, rather than increasing *birth rates*. In the fall of 1994, the *New York Times* reported overcrowding in kindergartens in New York City due to "unforeseen" increases in enrollments (D. Martin, "The Great Kindergarten Shuffle Succeeds," *New York Times*, October 10, 1994). In a 1996 article on school overcrowding in the 1990s, the school closures of the 1970s were named as the root cause (P. Belluck, "Roots of School Overcrowding Stretch Back Two Decades," *New York Times*, Sunday, 8 September 1996, Metro section, p. 41).

5. Welch 1979.

6. Unless otherwise specified, all discussions are presented in terms of constant or "real" dollars—that is, after the effects of inflation have been removed.

7. See, for example, Welch 1979 and Berger 1984, 1985.

8. Macunovich 1999a.

9. Higgins and Williamson (1999) have documented this effect of relative cohort size on inequality in countries around the globe.

10. Solnick and Hemenway 1998.

11. Zizzo and Oswald 2000.

12. McBride 2001.

13. L. Uchitelle, "The American Middle, Just Getting By," *New York Times*, August 1, 1999.

14. Easterlin 1987.

15. Easterlin 1987.

16. See, for example, Easterlin, Macdonald, and Macunovich 1990a,b; Easterlin, Macunovich, and Crimmins 1993; Easterlin, Shaeffer, and Macunovich 1993; Macunovich and Easterlin 1990.

17. Easterlin 1987.

18. The share of employed young women aged 25–29 in what are typically considered "male" occupations peaked between 1980 and 1990, with only about 3 percent in engineering, science, and math and 4 percent in "male" skilled blue collar occupations. And only about 12 percent of young women held positions as executives, administrators, doctors, or lawyers in the late 1990s. (See chapter 7.)

19. Findings by Rindfuss, Brewster, and Kavee 1996 support the idea that attitudes regarding women's roles changed *in response to* changed behavior, rather than the other way around.

20. Ahlburg and Schapiro 1984.

21. Grogger 1998.

22. Easterbrook 1999; Whitman 1999; Zinsmeister, Moore, and Bowman 1999.

23. Zinsmeister, Moore, and Bowman 1999.

24. This "cluttered nest" phenomenon is not unique to North America, as evidenced by current experience in Italy and in Japan.

25. Macunovich et al. 1995.

26. Macunovich and Easterlin 1990.

27. One recent study, for example, found that Social Security and pensions could explain only about one-quarter of the reduction in full-time work among those in their early sixties, and none of the reduction among those aged 65 and over (Anderson, Gustman, and Steinmeier 1999).

28. Social Security Administration actuarial study no. 108, p. 20.

29. The trend in increased "commoditization" of home-produced goods and services appears to follow the trend in female labor force participation,

though lagging slightly behind because of the time it takes for attitudes to change regarding the social acceptability—especially among mothers and wives—of letting others perform these services for us.

30. For an excellent discussion, see Goldin 1990.

31. See, for example, Becker 1981; Fuchs 1989.

32. For example, the work of sociologist Talcott Parsons (1949, 1956) presented the basic concept of productivity-enhancing specialized gender roles later elaborated by economist and Nobel laureate Gary Becker (1981).

33. Schoeni 1995.

34. Blackburn and Korenman 1994.

35. Keith Bradsher, "Young Men Pressed to Wed for Success," *New York Times*, December 13, 1989.

36. Goldin 1990.

37. Mankiw and Weil 1989.

38. Fair and Dominguez 1991.

39. McMillan and Baesel 1990.

40. Schieber and Shoven 1994.

41. Bloom and Williamson 1998; Higgins and Williamson 1997; Williamson 1998.

42. Miles 1999.

43. Lindh and Malmberg 1998.

44. This analysis was suggested by Easterlin, Wachter, and Wachter (1978).

45. The discussion in chapter 3 explains this choice of age group in more detail. It's a common grouping that has been used in cross-national analyses presented in chapters 12 and 14, and supported by findings reported in chapter 13.

Chapter One

1. Smith 1937.

2. Hardin 1972; Ehrlich 1978.

3. The idea of growth-induced technological innovation originated with Ester Boserup (1965a,b). For a general summary of Julian Simon's work, see, for example, Simon 1996.

4. See, for example, Keynes 1937; Hansen 1939; Barber 1978.

5. See Hicks 1939; Simon 1994; Habakkuk 1971.

6. Auerbach and Kotlikoff 1992; Bloom and Williamson 1998; Higgins and Williamson 1997; Williamson 1998. Kelley (1988) presents an excellent discussion of the literature on the role of population in economic development.

7. Easterlin published various aspects of his theories beginning in the 1960s, but the first full statement appeared in Easterlin 1978, and its most complete presentation appears in Easterlin 1987.

8. See Galbraith 1958; Brown 1987.

9. It should be pointed out in Malthus's favor that a later version of his *Treatise* emphasized the strong likelihood that people's desire to better their living conditions—a "relative income" concept—would probably make them strive to limit family size.

10. But there are important exceptions to each of these statements. For example, Evans (1990) included a control for cohort size in an analysis of racial fertility differentials, while Maxwell (1991) attempted to control for material aspirations. With regard to the use of demographic measures in U.S. economic models, see, for example, Mankiw and Weil 1989; Fair and Dominguez 1991; and McMillan and Baesel 1990. And as mentioned in an earlier note, one group of researchers has found strong age structure effects among the Asian economies (Bloom and Williamson 1998; Higgins and Williamson 1997; and Williamson 1998) and in the pre-1914 Atlantic economy (Auerbach and Kotlikoff 1992 and Williamson 1998). There is also an extremely large and diverse literature on the effects of dependency rates (the proportion of the population aged 1–15 and 65+ relative to the working-age population) on savings rates in developing economies, which I cite extensively in material related to chapter 13 in Macunovich 2002. In addition, for cutting-edge explorations in quantifying and determining the significance of consumption aspirations, see the work of van Praag (1993) and van de Stadt, Kapteyn, and van de Geer (1985).

11. Macunovich 1999a.

12. See Macunovich 1998a for a detailed review of the literature on the relationship between fertility and relative cohort size/relative income.

Chapter Two

1. Duesenberry 1949. Also highly influential at this time were Modigliani 1949 and Leibenstein 1950.

2. Solnick and Hemenway 1998.

3. Zizzo and Oswald 2000.

4. MacDonald and Douthitt 1992; van Praag 1993; van de Stadt, Kapteyn, and van de Geer 1985.

5. Pollak 1976; Ahlburg 1984.

6. See Macunovich 1998a for a review of studies testing the strength of various potential reference groups in affecting fertility decisions.

7. *The New Palgrave: A Dictionary of Economics*, s.v. "Easterlin hypothesis."

8. Easterlin 1978; Ahlburg 1984.

9. Easterlin 1987.

10. Ex ante: based on predicted or expected results; forecast, anticipated. Literally "from before." Ex post: based on or determined by actual results rather than forecasts of expectations (*Oxford Encyclopedic English Dictionary*, 2d ed.).

11. T. Lewin, "Men Whose Wives Work Earn Less, Studies Show," *New York Times*, October 12, 1994.

12. Smock and Manning 1997, 331.

13. The figures reported here are taken from a survey of 228 first-year students (116 male and 112 female) in November 1995. A full report of survey results is presented in appendix A.

14. Easterlin 1987, 11.

15. Crimmins, Easterlin, and Saito 1991.

16. Although I have not yet conducted formal surveys in my new position at Barnard College, informal surveys of Barnard and Columbia students in my classes support this hypothesis. Students consistently predict a significantly higher number of children for themselves, on average, than they predict for their cohort, and a higher proportion of them expect to marry than they predict for their cohort. In addition, both the women and the men expect the women to move to part-time work to care for young children.

17. Smock and Manning 1997.

Chapter Three

1. For a more extensive discussion of this topic, see Macunovich 1998a.

2. The variable definitions presented here, and used throughout my analyses, were developed in 1992 when I first began this work and have been held constant since then in order to maintain consistency across all of the analyses and avoid any temptation to "data mine."

3. The term "wage" is used to refer to hourly remuneration and "earnings" to refer to annual remuneration for work in the labor market, unless otherwise specified. A "permanent or lifetime" measure of earnings would be an average of real (i.e., adjusted for inflation) annual earnings over an individual's working lifetime. "Income" unless otherwise specified includes not just annual earnings, but also nonearned income from sources such as interest and dividends.

4. Korenman and Okun 1992.

5. See, for example, Olneck and Wolfe 1978, which compares the fertility of brothers (assuming that the number of children for each would be the same if their earnings are the same) on the assumption that the parental reference group in setting material aspirations is the same for both brothers, ignoring any input their wives may have in the decision-making process. See also Mac-Donald and Rindfuss 1978.

6. Easterlin addressed this problem in the following way: "Two young adults contemplating marriage come, of course, from two different families. To predict their material aspirations would require, one might suppose, combining the incomes in their respective families of origin and averaging them, perhaps in proportion to the male's and female's respective weights in shopping decisions. But because people generally find mates from within the same economic class, the income of either family usually approximates the average

of the two. For this reason, and to simplify matters, I shall confine myself to the family of origin of the prospective husband" (1987, 41).

7. "The pressure or absence of numbers is likely to be felt more in the early years of adulthood, but the effect, good or bad, is likely to follow a generation throughout its existence. In this sense, year of birth marks a generation for life" (Easterlin 1987, 4–5).

8. Many critics have expressed concern about the fact that other forces also influence material aspirations. However, one is really concerned only with the *trend* in these aspirations, and to the extent that other forces may not change as rapidly or as systematically as the economic forces exerted by cohort size, these other forces may be ignored without incurring any significant bias.

9. Easterlin 1987, 43.

10. Easterlin 1987, table 3.1.

11. In subregional analyses described in chapters 9 and 11, where I calculate marriage, divorce, and fertility measures using Current Population Survey microdata, I extend the focus to include all unenrolled men and women in their first fifteen years out of school.

12. Alternative choices of age groups in the more specific male age ratio—say, plus or minus five years in either direction—produce roughly interchangeable measures, given the fairly smooth pattern of births over the years.

13. Welch 1979; Freeman 1979; Ahlburg, Crimmins, and Easterlin 1981; Berger 1983, 1984, 1985; Dooley and Gottschalk 1984.

14. Wachter and Wascher (1984) were the first to question this aspect of Easterlin's hypothesis, in an article about schooling choices: they opened up a veritable Pandora's box of hypotheses about asymmetric effects and whether these would tend to smooth or exaggerate the cycles of the baby boom. See Alsalam 1985; Falaris and Peters 1985; Nothaft 1985; Connelly 1986; Stapleton and Young 1988; Berger 1989.

15. This cohort position variable is calculated as the rate of growth of relative cohort size in a five-year "window" around the cohort's year of entry into the labor market: the value at $t + 2$ divided by the value at $t - 2$.

16. See, for example, Easterlin 1987, 32–33, and 1968, 13.

17. See, for example, Johnson 1980; Wachter 1980; Houston 1983.

18. Fair and Macunovich 1996.

19. Ermisch 1979, 1980.

20. Welch 1979.

21. Potential experience is calculated as an individual's age minus reported years of education minus six.

22. This is consistent with the argument presented by Oppenheimer (1976).

23. Behrman and Taubman 1990.

24. Macunovich 1996a.

Chapter Four

1. Corresponding graphs by race and level of education, showing virtually identical time trends, are presented in Macunovich 2002.

2. These alternative measures of male relative income are illustrated in Macunovich 2002.

3. Fair and Macunovich 1996.

Chapter Five

1. The work presented here is based on more comprehensive analyses in Macunovich 1998b, 1999a, and 2000a,c.

2. Fair and Macunovich 1996.

3. Freeman 1979.

4. Smith and Welch 1981.

5. Berger 1984, 1985.

6. Bloom, Freeman, and Korenman 1987; Murphy, Plant, and Welch 1988; among others.

7. Karoly and Klerman 1994, 205.

8. Bluestone 1994, 335.

9. For example, Mincer 1991; Berger 1989.

10. This is a concept first introduced by Wachter and Wascher (1984) in relation to the effect of cohort size on schooling choice.

11. McMillan and Baesel 1990.

12. Mankiw and Weil 1989.

13. Fair and Dominguez 1991.

14. Ellwood 1985, 9.

15. The size of the active military excluding males aged 20–24 has been relatively constant in the United States since about 1952, at a level of about 1.5 million. It was only during WWII that this portion of the military increased along with the number of males aged 20–24.

16. Murphy and Welch 1992; Borjas and Ramey 1994, 1995.

17. The results of these models are available in Macunovich 2002. I used the lagged general fertility rate, as described in chapter 3, as the measure of relative cohort size in all of the models reported here.

18. Opportunity cost of any action is the value to an individual of his or her next best alternative. Someone in school loses out on potential earnings, so the total of those forgone earnings would be the opportunity cost of attending college.

19. These changes are discussed in more detail in Macunovich 2002.

20. These estimates were developed as part of an analysis of female labor force participation. See Fair and Macunovich 1996.

Chapter Six

1. As measured by the Gini coefficient for family income, a statistic that indicates how far a society is from perfect equality. This figure is taken from Ryscavage 1995, 51.

2. About one-third, according to Karoly and Burtless 1995.

3. Income or earnings quintiles are groupings of individuals based on the level of their (annual) income or earnings. Those in the bottom quintile earn wages that put them among the 20 percent of the population with the lowest earnings. Table 6.1 presents data for such quintiles, except that it reports figures for those in the eleventh to twentieth and eighty-first to nineti-eth percentiles—rather than the first to twentieth and eighty-first to one hun-dredth—because it is often felt that there are distortions in the estimates for those in the very top or bottom of the income distribution.

4. Standard deviation is an indicator of the amount of variation in a measure like earnings, observed among members of a group—the spread between those at the bottom and those at the top.

5. Blau and Kahn 1996, 806.

6. Macunovich 1999a.

7. Macunovich 1999a focuses on younger workers, and Macunovich 2002 extends the analysis to the full labor force.

8. These 150,000 observations represent over 650,000 individual obser-vations, grouped by education, race, state, and experience. When the model was estimated on the fully disaggregated data, it explained over 27 percent of the variance in the data.

9. Similar graphs for other age groups, and by education level, are pre-sented in Macunovich 1999a and 2002. These demonstrate the model's ability to explain wage movements throughout the labor force.

10. Although figures 6.1–6.3 illustrate the situation only for younger workers, Macunovich 2002 contains similar results for workers at all educa-tion and experience levels.

11. McCall (2000, 426) finds that "high rates of joblessness, immigration and casualization (part-time work, temporary work, and unincorporated self-employment) exert significant positive effects on the level of residual wage inequality within labor markets."

12. These results are reported in Macunovich 1999a and 2002.

13. I say this from firsthand experience after trying—and failing—to convince some fellow members of the 1994–1995 Social Security Technical Panel that the economy could be expected to rebound again, despite its performance since the mid-1970s.

14. Higgins and Williamson 1999.

Chapter Seven

1. The work presented here is based on more comprehensive analyses in Fair and Macunovich 1996 and Macunovich 1995, 1996a,b,c; 1999a, 2002.

2. Smith and Ward 1985.

3. See, for example, Bergman 1986.

4. See, for example, Brown 1987.

5. See, for example, the work of Cramer (1979, 1980) and an excellent summary of this literature in Lehrer and Nerlove 1986.

6. This position is presented in Goldin and Katz 2000.

7. Sanderson (1987, 307) reports that "[t]he availability of modern coitus-independent means of fertility control played no role in producing below-replacement fertility in the United States in the late nineteenth century. Such means of fertility control were not available in the late nineteenth century. Even without these modern methods, ever-married urban white women of native parentage born in 1846–55 and living in the Northeast in 1900 had an average of 3.0 live births over their reproductive span." There are costs associated both with having children, and with preventing pregnancy (whether psychic or monetary or simply those associated with the inconvenience of using various contraceptive methods). The Pill simply reduced the latter costs, but if the costs associated with children (net of perceived benefits) are perceived to be sufficiently low, the relatively small cost reduction afforded by the Pill will not play a significant role in fertility and labor force participation decisions.

8. Rindfuss, Brewster, and Kavee 1996.

9. Macunovich 1996a; Fair and Macunovich 1996.

10. Documentation on this phenomenon is provided in Macunovich 2002.

11. The decline in the ratio of observed hourly wages—that is, not controlling for occupational change—was even more dramatic than indicated in figure 7.7, declining from a 20 percent premium to a 10 percent penalty. This is another demonstration of the extent to which women's occupational shifts were driven by this ratio: when part-time wages were high, those who could chose to work in the occupations with the highest part-time wages. Then, in moving to full-time work, they changed occupations.

12. More detailed figures not presented here demonstrate that there is a continuous change from the bottom to the top quintile—but here for the sake of brevity I present just the top and bottom.

Chapter Eight

1. The work presented here is based on more comprehensive analyses in Macunovich 1997a and 2002.

2. Steelman and Powell 1991 present an excellent analysis of parents' motivation in funding higher education for their children.

3. Jones (1980, 57–58) states that in 1952, for example, "the nation still wound up short 345,000 classrooms despite frantic construction of new ones. Classrooms with 45 students to a single teacher were not uncommon, and three out of every five classrooms across the country were considered overcrowded. Upwards of 78,000 makeshift classrooms sprang up in churches and

vacant stores across the country, and students found themselves sharing both books and desks." He goes on, "The teacher shortage hit 72,000 in the early 1950s and, by 1959, nearly 100,000 of the nation's 1.3 million public school teachers were working with substandard credentials. In states like New Jersey, where the school population increased by 62 percent from 1950 to 1960, some 57,000 students were crowded into half-sessions and 48,000 were being taught by underqualified teachers."

4. Ahlburg, Crimmins and Easterlin 1981; Wachter and Wascher 1984.

5. They both controlled for the Vietnam draft for the period 1960–1972, on the assumption that draft deferments allowed during most of this period for those in school would have caused increased enrollments. Both used the annual number of inductees relative to the number of males aged 16+. In addition, WW included a second military measure: the absolute number of young men in the military in a given year in the relevant age group (18–19 and 20–24).

6. Model predictions for women aged 20–24, and for both men and women aged 18–19, follow the patterns shown in figure 8.2. They are presented in full in Macunovich 1997a and 2002.

7. The same model was used to explain both men's and women's enrollment rates. Although it's unconventional to include a draft variable in an enrollment equation for young women, it is assumed that the pronounced increases in the enrollment rates of young men induced by the draft would have had a positive influence on young women's enrollment rates—both because of a "role model" effect and because with large numbers of men serving in Vietnam or in school, young women would anticipate higher levels of labor force participation for themselves and would therefore choose to invest in higher education.

Chapter Nine

1. The work presented here is described in more detail in Macunovich 2002.

2. No, that's not a typo! "Posslq" (pronounced "possle-q") is a term coined by Statistics Canada in its 1981 census to describe unmarried "Persons of the Opposite Sex Sharing Living Quarters."

3. The proportion ever married is used here, rather than the proportion currently married, to allow for the fact that individuals can move out of the married state, as well as in—through divorce, separation, or death of a partner.

4. Some of these age-specific rates calculated from the March CPS are presented in Macunovich 2002.

5. Cherlin 1992.

6. MacDonald and Rindfuss 1981, 123.

7. Ibid., 131.

8. Schoen, Urton, Woodrow, and Baj 1985.

9. Lestaeghe and Surkyn 1988. Their position is presented primarily in terms of fertility, but is extended to the full range of family change.

10. These positions are nicely summarized in Preston 1986 and Westoff 1986.

11. Glick, Beresford, and Heer 1963.

12. Guttentag and Secord 1983.

13. For theories regarding the impact of absolute male earnings and the female wage, see Oppenheimer, Kalmijn, and Lew 1993; Oppenheimer, Blossfeld, and Wackerow 1995; Oppenheimer, Kalmijn, and Lim 1997.

14. The results described here are presented in more detail in Macunovich 2002.

15. The regions used in the analyses described here are twenty-one state groupings that can be identified consistently across the entire period covered by the CPS.

16. The data set used in the analyses contained more than 23,000 (13,000) observations of young men (women) one to five years out of school and more than 76,000 (48,000) in their first fifteen years out.

17. These econometric analyses also contained full sets of controls for education, race, years out of school, and region, as well as a time trend.

18. In "matching up" young men's and women's characteristics, a two-year age difference was assumed between men and women. That is, the characteristics of young women x years out of school were paired with those of young men $x + 2$ years out of school.

19. T. Lewin, "Next to Mom and Dad: It's a Hard Life (or Not)," *New York Times*, November 17, 1999.

20. The disaggregated marriage model (dependent variable: proportion ever married) was first estimated for unenrolled full-time male workers one to fifteen years out of school, where the t-statistic on relative income (F-statistic for the full regression) was 27.3 (515.14 [23,113]) for young men in the first five years out of school, rising to 35.4 (748.9 [34,648]) for those one to seven years out. The corresponding $t(F)$ statistics for "parental" income when the numerator and denominator of relative income were entered separately were –5.4 (485.7) and –5.4 (699.52). These results are presented and described more fully in Macunovich 2002.

The model was then estimated for all unenrolled young men (not just full-time workers) one through fifteen years out of school, in regressions which used deviation from mean proportion married as the dependent variable to correct for potential correlation between wages and proportion married. In the regressions for young men in their first five years out of school, the t-statistic for male wages (parental income) was 3.7 (–5.2) with an overall F-statistic of 223.23 (14,589) and an adjusted R^2 of 0.37. These results, together with corresponding ones for (deviation from mean) proportion married and divorced, both male and female, are presented and described more fully in Macunovich 2002.

21. This finding of a positive effect of the female wage on marriage propensities is consistent with findings in a large number of microlevel analyses, such as Cherlin 1980; Goldscheider and Waite 1986; Mare and Winship 1991; McLoughlin and Lichter 1993; Oppenheimer, Blossfield and Wackerow 1995; and Teachman, Polonko, and Leigh 1987.

22. Oppenheimer, Kalmijn, and Lew 1993; Oppenheimer, Blossfield, and Wackerow 1995; Oppenheimer, Kalmijn, and Lim 1997.

23. Bumpass and Sweet 1991, 913.

Chapter Ten

1. Hill 1979; Schoeni 1995.

2. Duncan and Holmlund 1983; Hersch 1991.

3. Estimates of wage premiums paid to married men vary widely, depending on the period studied and the econometric techniques used. The highest premiums seem to be those associated with older married men in the mid-1970s. For example, Bartlett and Callahan (1984) found that married men aged 55–64 in 1977 earned 20–32 percent more than otherwise comparable unmarried men, while Siebert and Sloane (1981) found unadjusted wage differentials of 15–50 percent, and Nakosteen and Zimmer (1987) estimated a 41 percent premium in a model that controlled for endogeneity, although with a large standard error.

4. Blackburn and Korenman 1994. One published study does maintain that the marital wage premium disappears after controlling for other observed differences between married and unmarried men (Cohen and Haberfeld 1991), and another concludes that the premium is due simply to a selection of higher-earning men into marriage (Nakosteen and Zimmer 1987). Both of these studies, however, made use of problematic subsets of the same data set, the University of Michigan Panel Survey of Income Dynamics (PSID), which introduced two sources of bias into their analyses. First, both included males aged 18–24 (Nakosteen and Zimmer looked *only* at this younger age group, while Cohen and Haberfeld included them along with older males) without excluding those currently enrolled in school. Because married men in this age group tend to be those not enrolled in school, the higher earnings of the married men will tend to be highly correlated with lower educational status, so that controlling for education will remove the significance of (inversely correlated) marital status. That both of these studies found a highly unusual *negative* effect of education on earnings supports this hypothesis. Second, because full labor force data are available in the PSID only for heads of household, both of these studies omitted males who were not heads of household, thus placing a probable upward bias on the earnings of unmarried men in the sample. The proportion married among 18–24-year-olds in the Nakosteen and Zimmer sample was an unusually high 66 percent due to this elimination of lower-earning single males.

5. Ester Boserup 1965a,b.

6. Daniel 1995.

7. Daniel 1995; Kenny 1983; Korenman and Neumark 1991; Gray 1997.

8. For example, Bellas 1992; Pfeffer and Ross 1982.

9. A rash of reports on the marriage wage premium appeared in the popular press in 1994 (T. Lewin, "Men Whose Wives Work Earn Less, Studies Show," *New York Times,* October 12; "A Working-Wife Penalty?" *Washington Post,* September 11; "A Big Hand from the Little Lady?" *Business Week,* August 1) in response to a management survey by researchers at Loyola and Northwestern (reported in Stroh and Brett 1995)—all pointing to strong positive effects of stay-at-home wives on their husbands' earnings. However, the Stroh and Brett study also failed to control for endogeneity of wives' labor force participation.

10. Loh 1996.

11. Korenman and Neumark 1991.

12. Daniel 1995; Gray 1997.

13. Gray 1997. Gray restricted his NLS and NLSY data sets to white men initially aged 24–31 and calculated weeks of work experience for each respondent only "during years in which school was not reported as his primary activity."

14. Gray used an instrumental variables (IV) technique to control for the potential endogeneity of wives' labor force participation. His principal instrument was a variable measuring gender role attitudes: a four-point categorical response, ranging from "strongly agree" to "strongly disagree," to the statement that men should share housework responsibilities with women.

15. Grossbard-Shechtman 1986.

16. Pfeffer and Ross 1982.

17. Broehl 1995. Her work was a very interesting extension of Blackburn and Korenman 1994.

Chapter Eleven

1. The work presented here is based on more comprehensive analysis in Macunovich 1995, 1996a, 1998a, 1998b. Detailed regression results are available in Macunovich 2002.

2. Two very readable summaries are Bean 1983 and Bouvier 1980. One well-known theory not included in those summaries, however, is described in Butz and Ward 1979a,b.

3. These issues are addressed well in Davis, Bernstam, and Ricardo-Cambell 1986 and, especially, in Preston 1986 and Westoff 1986.

4. A notable exception here is the work of Lestaeghe and Surkyn (1988), who suggest that economic fluctuations may arise out of ideational and institutional changes.

5. There have been several critical reviews of articles testing the Easterlin model, such as Olsen 1994 and Pampel and Peters 1995—although most of the studies reviewed tested the relationship between fertility and relative cohort size, rather than male relative income. My own review (Macunovich 1998a) discusses this issue.

6. It's necessary to speculate about women's wages because we don't have any detailed information on them during the 1950s and early 1960s, and for the entire period up to 1976 it's difficult to identify an hourly wage, which is needed to estimate "price of time" effects.

7. This model is described and tested in Butz and Ward 1979a,b.

8. Macunovich 1996a.

9. Numerous studies have demonstrated that availability of affordable child care is an important factor in determining the labor force participation rates of mothers with young children: see, for example, Berger and Black 1992 and Presser 1989. Although most of the analyses look at the effect of child care on labor force participation, one might assume that there would be a corresponding effect on fertility. There is no consensus on this point, however. It *is* generally recognized that social acceptability is an important factor in the use of paid child care to permit young career-oriented women to become mothers, as discussed by Preston (1986) and Ryder (1990).

10. See, for example, Ermisch 1980, Ohbuchi 1982, Serow 1980, and studies comparing own income with the average in one's peer group, such as Thornton 1979, and Reed, Udry, and Rupert 1975. The dates on these studies are old because little research has been done on this topic in recent decades!

11. Macunovich 2002.

12. Macunovich 1996a, 1998c.

13. The aggregate models and their results are reported in greater detail in Macunovich 1996a, 1998c.

14. It has been suggested that membership in a minority racial group will have differential effects on fertility because of the desire for upward mobility and the belief that limiting family size will assist in achieving this goal. The results described here are consistent with those of several other researchers. See, for example, Goldscheider and Uhlenberg 1969; Reed, Udry, and Ruppert 1975; and Boyd 1994.

15. These results are available in Macunovich 2002.

16. The data set used in the analyses contained more than 23,000 (13,000) observations of young men (women) one to five years out of school, and more than 76,000 (48,000) in their first fifteen years out.

17. In "matching up" young men's and women's characteristics, a two-year age difference was assumed between men and women. That is, the characteristics of young women x years out of school were paired with those of young men $x + 2$ years out of school.

18. The proportion of young women with children must be expected to grow with progressive years out of school and will thus be naturally correlated with male earnings. This is controlled for to a great extent by including "years out of school" dummy variables. However, to ensure that any such age-related correlation is removed from the results, in addition to the single year out of school dummy variables, the regressions reported here all used as the dependent variable, in place of the actual proportion, the cell deviation from the mean within each level of "years out of school."

19. The disaggregated fertility model (dependent variable: cell deviation from group mean percentage of women with at least one own child) was estimated for women one through fifteen years out of school, in five-year groupings. In addition to the variables of interest, it contained full sets of controls for education, race, years out of school, and region, as well as a time trend.

In the model for women one to five years out of school, with 19,388 observations, an F-statistic of 124.91, and an R^2 of 0.2188, the estimated (standardized) coefficient on a female wage $\times$ quintile interaction fell from 0.04 ($t = 4.0$) for women in the lowest relative income quintile to –0.01 ($t = 1.3$) for those in the highest. The standardized coefficient on "parental" income was –0.118 ($t = 7.4$) and on male earnings was 0.084 ($t = 5.6$).

Unstandardized, the full estimated coefficient on the female wage (the sum of the basic effect plus the interaction effect) fell from 1.04 in the first quintile to 0.11 in the fifth. These results are presented and described more fully in Macunovich 2002.

Chapter Twelve

1. I conducted the global study in response to that researcher's use of my analyses of male relative income effects (Macunovich 1999b, 2000b) to support the argument that all aid should be withdrawn from developing countries (and our borders closed to immigration), since increased income results in increased fertility.

2. The literature exploring causes of the demographic transition is described in Szreter 1993, and two of the leading researchers in the field have recently summed up the present state of knowledge regarding the fertility portion of that transition in Caldwell and Caldwell 1997.

3. Rostow 1998.

4. Macunovich 2000b, 2002.

5. See, for example, Lavely and Freedman 1990.

6. These additional graphs appear in Macunovich 2002.

7. Even more detailed econometric results than presented in the published articles appear in Macunovich 2002.

8. Keyfitz and Flieger 1968.

Chapter Thirteen

1. The work presented here is based on a more comprehensive analysis presented in Macunovich 2002.

2. Modigliani 1949 and Friedman 1957.

3. I present this concept of "disastrously low" saving more as question than fact because many reputable analysts feel that it results simply from errors of measurement. Savings are officially calculated as the residual when consumption is subtracted from income—but our measurements of both are subject to a wide margin of error. Since saving even historically represents a relatively small proportion of total income, any measurement errors are mag-

nified in percentage terms, when transferred from the larger to the smaller proportion of income.

4. Keynes 1937.

5. Kuznets 1958, 1961.

6. This summary of Keynes's hypothesis is taken from Espenshade 1978, 147.

7. Samuelson 1988, 14.

8. Becker, Glaeser, and Murphy 1999, 149.

9. Slesnick 1992.

10. Stoker 1986.

11. Miles 1999.

12. Lazear and Michael 1988.

13. Weil 1994.

14. Lazear and Michael 1988, 27.

15. These are new data, made available recently by Stanley Lebergott (1996) at Wesleyan University: see Macunovich 2002 for a more detailed description.

16. The method was suggested in this type of analysis by Fair and Dominguez (1991) and is in turn similar to Almon's distributed lag technique (1965). It was subsequently used by Higgins and Williamson (1997) in an analysis of age structure effects on capital flows in Southeast Asia: an analysis that also incorporated age structure among children. This methodology is described in more detail in Macunovich 2002, but in general terms is one that allows the estimation of coefficients on single year population age shares, by constraining them to lie along a polynomial, with the degree of that polynomial determined theoretically and tested empirically. Fair and Dominguez applied this technique in their own analyses, but excluded age groups under 16.

17. The unweighted average per capita real income in the data set in 1900 is about $5,000 in year 2000 dollars. Unweighted per capita personal consumption expenditure in the same year is about $4,900, also in year 2000 dollars. The actual levels in 1900 are immaterial to this analysis, however, in terms of the 60 percent swing—aside from their impact on age structure effects—since the effects displayed here are elasticities.

18. Higgins and Williamson 1997; Higgins 1998.

Chapter Fourteen

1. See, for example, Bloom and Williamson 1998; Higgins and Williamson 1997; and Williamson 1998.

2. Bloom and Williamson 1998, 449–50.

3. See, for example, Easterlin 1996.

4. Keynes 1937.

5. Schumpeter 1946.

6. Keyfitz and Flieger 1968.

7. The age group 15–24 is used here because it can be identified in a number of data sets across nations and across time periods.

8. All except the 1937–1938 economic turning point indicated in this and other figures were selected because they preceded contractions of longer than average duration. The National Bureau of Economic Research provides "official" statistics on the timing of business cycles (www.nber.org): they identify the average length as twenty-two months in the period up to 1919, twenty months between 1919 and 1945, and eleven months since 1945. In the period between 1907 and 1914, there were three contractions: May 1907 to June 1908 (thirteen months), January 1910 to January 1912 (twenty-four months), and January 1913 to December 1914 (twenty-three months). Although analysts tend to place more emphasis on the crash of 1907–1908 because it was a spectacular one—at least for financial institutions—in fact the duration of the following two contractions was nearly twice that of the 1907–1908 contraction. I have included the 1937–1938 contraction despite its shorter length (thirteen months) because it seems reasonable to assume that in the absence of World War II it would probably have gone on much longer. The 1929–1933 contraction continued for forty-three months.

9. Rostow 1998, 104.

10. Rostow 1998, 84.

11. Michael Edelstein (Queens College), who was kind enough to read and provide comments on an earlier version of this manuscript, has urged me to acknowledge the role of immigration in the aggregate demand shifts experienced in the first three decades of the twentieth century. As indicated in figure 13.3, there were massive influxes during this period, which, as Edelstein emphasizes (in private correspondence dated March 28, 2001) "are much larger than any domestically generated birthrate effects. Indeed, the immigrant population consisting of younger men and women, single and in their early parenting years are a demographic force unto themselves. Then, in 1914, immigration comes to a virtual standstill until 1919 *but* the usual housing investment effects from the pre-WWI immigration are deflected by the need for funds to finance the export boom of 1915–1917 and then the war effort. High levels of immigration immediately return with peace in 1919 until legislation cuts the inflow in the early 1920s. Note, too, that the delayed housing boom from the pre-war years and the usual housing response to the post-WWI immigration are a major part of the 1920s boom until around 1927; the abating immigration is influential here." This is all certainly true, and as Edelstein reminded me in further comments, Richard Easterlin did an excellent job of tracing these effects in his first book (1968). However, these immigrants are fully represented in my analyses, in terms of their effects on the resident U.S. age structure. As Edelstein points out, immigrants tend to be concentrated in the younger adult age groups, and to the extent that they were in the beginning of the twentieth century, they first ameliorated (in the first few decades) and then exacerbated (in the late 1920s) the effects of declining U.S. birth rates. Only the "bunching" effects around WWI, in terms of their housing demands, are not accounted for in a pure age-structure analysis.

12. Rostow 1998.

13. See, for example, Easterlin 1968; Kuznets 1958; Kelley 1969; Mankiw and Weil 1989; McMillan and Baesel 1990; Fair and Dominguez 1991; and Malmberg 1994.

14. Bloom and Williamson 1998; Higgins and Williamson 1997; and Williamson 1998.

Chapter Fifteen

1. The age groups used, and their definitions, are set out in the full write-up of this analysis (Macunovich 1997b), together with the results of simple regressions.

2. Fair and Dominguez 1991. Higgins and Williamson (1997) have since used the method, as well.

3. Presented in Macunovich 2002.

4. The 2001–2050 forecast is based on the Census Bureau's middle population projection for that period.

5. The results of these sensitivity analyses, together with the basic model estimation, are presented in Macunovich 2002.

6. The population data used in the analysis are counts of the total U.S. population including armed forces overseas.

7. Bloom and Williamson 1998; Higgins and Williamson 1997; and Williamson 1998.

8. Higgins and Williamson 1997, 284.

Chapter Sixteen

1. This review of over 185 books and articles is presented in Macunovich 1998a. The reader is directly particularly to section 10 of that review.

2. Macunovich 1999a and the analysis described in chapters 9 and 11.

3. For a full review, see Macunovich 1998a.

Appendix A

1. This survey was conducted by the twenty-five members of the Williams College class of 1999 First Year Residential Seminar.

2. Comparison figures from earlier years are drawn from Easterlin 1987 and Crimmins, Easterlin, and Saito 1991.

3. Easterlin 1987, 52.

References

Ahlburg, D. A. 1984. Commodity Aspirations in Easterlin's Relative Income Theory of Fertility. *Social Biology* 31 (3/4): 201–207.

Ahlburg, D. A., E. M. Crimmins, and R. A. Easterlin. 1981. The Outlook for Higher Education: A Cohort Size Model of Enrollment of the College Age Population, 1948–2000. *Review of Public Data Use* 9:211–227.

Ahlburg, D. A., and M. O. Schapiro. 1984. Socioeconomic Ramifications of Changing Cohort Size: An Analysis of U.S. Postwar Suicide Rates by Age and Sex. *Demography* 21 (1): 97–108.

Almon, S. 1965. The Distributed Lag between Capital Appropriations and Expenditures. *Econometrica* 33 (January): 178–196.

Alsalam, N. 1985. The Dynamic Behavior of College Enrollment Rates: The Effects of Baby Booms and Busts. Working Paper 21, University of Rochester, Rochester, NY.

Anderson, P. M., A. L. Gustman, and T. L. Steinmeier. 1999. Trends in Male Labor Force Participation and Retirement: Some Evidence on the Role of Pensions and Social Security in the 1970s and 1980s. *Journal of Labor Economics* 17 (4, pt. 1): 757–783.

Auerbach, A. J., and L. J. Kotlikoff. 1992. The Impact of the Demographic Transition on Capital Formation. *Scandinavian Journal of Economics* 94 (2): 281–295.

Barber, C. L. 1978. On the Origins of the Great Depression. *Southern Economic Journal* 44 (January): 432–456.

Bartlett, R., and C. Callahan. 1984. Wage Determination and Marital Status: Another Look. *Industrial Relations* 23 (1): 90–96.

Bean, F. D. 1983. The Baby Boom and Its Explanations. *Sociological Quarterly* 24 (summer): 353–365.

Becker, G. S. 1981. *A Treatise on the Family.* Cambridge, MA: Harvard University Press.

Becker, G. S., E. L. Glaeser, and K. M. Murphy. 1999. Population and Economic Growth. *American Economic Review* 89 (2): 145–149.

Behrman, J. R., and P. Taubman. 1990. A Comparison and Latent Variable Test of Two Fertile Ideas. *Journal of Population Economics* 3:19–30.

Bellas, M. L. 1992. The Effects of Marital Status and Wives' Employment on the Salaries of Faculty Men: The (House)wife Bonus. *Gender and Society* 6 (4): 609–622.

Berger, M. C. 1983. Changes in Labor Force Composition and Male Earnings: A Production Approach. *Journal of Human Resources* 18:177–196.

———. 1984. Cohort Size and the Earnings Growth of Young Workers. *Industrial and Labor Relations Review* 37 (4): 582–591.

———. 1985. The Effect of Cohort Size on Earnings Growth: A Reexamination of the Evidence. *Journal of Political Economy* 93:561–573.

———. 1989. Demographic Cycles, Cohort Size, and Earnings. *Demography* 26 (2): 311–321.

Berger, M. C., and D. A. Black. 1992. Child Care Subsidies, Quality of Care, and the Labor Supply of Low-Income, Single Mothers. *Review of Economics and Statistics* 74 (4): 635–642.

Bergman, B. 1986. *The Economic Emergence of Women.* New York: Basic Books.

Blackburn, M., and S. Korenman. 1994. The Declining Marital-Status Earnings Differential. *Journal of Population Economics* 7:247–270.

Blau, F., and L. Kahn. 1996. Wage Structure and Gender Earnings Differentials: An International Comparison. *Economica* 63:S29–S62.

Bloom, D. E., R. Freeman, and S. Korenman. 1987. The Labour-Market Consequences of Generational Crowding. *European Journal of Population* 3:131–176.

Bloom, D. E., and J. G. Williamson. 1998. Demographic Transitions and Economic Miracles in Emerging Asia. *World Bank Economic Review* 12 (3): 419–455.

Bluestone, B. 1994. Old Theories in New Bottles: Toward an Explanation of Growing World-Wide Income Inequality. In *The Changing Distribution of Income in an Open U.S. Economy,* ed. J. H. Bergstrand, T. F. Cosimano, J. W. Houck, and R. G. Sheehan, 286–309. New York: North-Holland.

Borjas, G., and V. Ramey. 1994. Time-Series Evidence on the Sources of Trends in Wage Inequality. *American Economic Review* 84 (2): 10–16.

———. 1995. Foreign Competition, Market Power, and Wage Inequality. *Quarterly Journal of Economics* 110 (4): 1075–1110.

Boserup, E. 1965a. *The Conditions of Economic Growth.* London: Allen and Unwin.

———. 1965b. *The Conditions of Agricultural Growth: The Economics of Agrarian Change under Population Pressure.* Chicago: Aldine.

Bouvier, Leon F. 1980. America's Baby Boom Generation: The Fateful Bulge. *Population Bulletin* 35 (1).

Boyd, R. L. 1994. Educational Mobility and the Fertility of Black and White Women. *Population Research and Policy Review* 13 (1): 275–281.

Broehl, J. R. 1995. For Richer and for Poorer: The Declining Marital Status Wage Premium. B.A. thesis, Department of Economics, Williams College, Williamstown, MA.

Brown, C. 1987. Consumption Norms, Work Roles, and Economic Growth, 1918–80. in Gender in the Workplace, ed. C. Brown and J. A. Pechman, 13–58.

Bumpass, L. L., J. A. Sweet, and A. Cherlin. 1991. The Role of Cohabitation in Declining Rates of Marriage. *Journal of Marriage and the Family* 53 (4): 913–927.

Butz, W. P., and M. P. Ward. 1979a. The Emergence of Counter-Cyclical U.S. Fertility. *American Economic Review* 69 (3): 318–328.

———. 1979b. Baby Boom and Baby Bust: A New View. *American Demographics* 1 (September): 1–17.

Caldwell, J. C., and P. Caldwell. 1997. What Do We Now Know about Fertility Transition? In *The Continuing Demographic Transition*, ed. G. W. Jones, R. M. Douglas, J. C. Caldwell, and R. M. D'Souza, 15–25. Oxford: Clarendon Press.

Cherlin, A. J. 1980. Postponing Marriage: The Influence of Young Women's Work Expectations. *Journal of Marriage and the Family* 42:355–65.

———. 1992. *Marriage, Divorce and Remarriage.* Revised and enlarged ed. Cambridge, MA: Harvard University Press.

Cohen, Y., and Y. Haberfeld. 1991. Why Do Married Men Earn More Than Unmarried Men? *Social Science Research* 20:29–44.

Coleman, D. 1996. New Patterns and Trends in European Fertility: International and Sub-national Comparisons, In *Europe's Population in the 1990s*, ed. D. Coleman 1–61. Oxford: Oxford University Press.

Connelly, R. 1986. A Framework for Analyzing the Impact of Cohort Size on Education and Labor Earnings. *Journal of Human Resources* 21:543–562.

Cramer, J. C. 1979. Employment Trends of Young Mothers and the Opportunity Costs of Babies in the United States. *Demography* 16 (2): 177–197.

———. 1980. Fertility and Female Employment: Problems of Causal Direction. *American Sociological Review* 45 (April): 167–190.

Crimmins, E., R. Easterlin, and Y. Saito. 1991. Preference Changes among American Youth: Family, Work, and Goods Aspirations, 1976–86. *Population and Development Review* 17 (1): 115–133.

Daniel, K. 1995. The Marriage Premium. In *The New Economics of Human Behavior*, ed. M. Tommasi and K. Ierulli, 113–125. Cambridge: Cambridge University Press.

Davis, K., M. S. Bernstam, and R. Ricardo-Cambell. 1986. Below-

Replacement Fertility in Industrial Societies. *Population and Development Review* 12 Suppl.

Dooley, M. D., and P. Gottschalk. 1984. Earnings Inequality among Males in the U.S.: Trends and the Effect of Labor Force Growth. *Journal of Political Economy* 92:59–89.

Duesenberry, J. S. 1949. *Income, Saving, and a Theory of Consumer Behavior.* Cambridge, MA: Harvard University Press.

Duncan, G. J., and B. Holmlund. 1983. Was Adam Smith Right after All? Another Test of the Theory of Compensating Wage Differentials. *Journal of Labor Economics* 1 (4): 366–379.

Easterbrook, G. 1999. America the O.K. *New Republic,* January 4 and 11, 19–25.

Easterlin, R. A. 1968. *Population, Labor Force, and Long Swings in Economic Growth: The American Experience.* New York: Columbia University Press.

———. 1978. What Will 1984 Be Like? Socioeconomic Implications of Recent Twists in Age Structure. *Demography* 15 (4): 397–432.

———. 1987. *Birth and Fortune.* 2d ed. Chicago: University of Chicago Press.

———. 1996. *Growth Triumphant: The Twenty-First Century in Historical Perspective.* Ann Arbor: University of Michigan Press.

Easterlin, R. A., C. Macdonald, and D. J. Macunovich. 1990a. How Have the American Baby Boomers Fared? Earnings and Economic Well-Being of Young Adults, 1964–1987. *Journal of Population Economics* 3 (4): 277–290.

———. 1990b. Retirement Prospects of the Baby Boom Generation. *Gerontologist* 30 (6): 776–783.

Easterlin, R. A., D. J. Macunovich, and E. M. Crimmins. 1993. Economic Status of the Young and Old in the Working Age Population, 1964 and 1987, *The Changing Contract across Generations,* ed. Vern L. Bengtson and W. Andrew Achenbaum, New York: Aldine DeGruyter.

Easterlin, R. A., C. M. Shaeffer, and D. J. Macunovich. 1993. Will the Baby Boomers Be Less Well Off Than Their Parents? Income, Wealth and Family Circumstances over the Life Cycle, *Population and Development Review* 19 (3): 497–522.

Easterlin, R. A., M. L. Wachter, and S. M. Wachter. 1978. Demographic Influences on Economic Stability: The United States Experience. *Population and Development Review* 4 (1): 1–22.

Ehrlich, P. 1978. *The Population Bomb.* New York: Ballantine Books.

Ellwood, D. T. 1985. Youth Unemployment. *NBER Reporter,* fall:3–4.

Ermisch, J. F. 1979. The Relevance of the "Easterlin Hypothesis" and the "New Home Economics" to Fertility Movements in Great Britain. *Population Studies* 33:39–58.

———. 1980. Time Costs, Aspirations, and the Effect of Economic Growth on German Fertility. *Oxford Bulletin of Economics and Statistics* 43:125–143.

Espenshade, T. J. 1978. How a Trend towards Stationary Population Affects Consumer Demand, *Population Studies*, 32(1): 147–158.

Evans, M. D. R. 1990. Cohort Size and Fertility among Blacks and Whites: U.S. Cohorts Born between 1905 and 1954. *International Review of Modern Sociology* 20 (Spring): 89–104.

Fair, R. C., and K. Dominguez. 1991. Effects of the Changing U.S. Age Distribution on Macroeconomic Equations. *American Economic Review* 81 (5): 1276–1294.

Fair, R. C., and D. J. Macunovich. 1996. Explaining the Labor Force Participation of Women 20–24. Cowles Foundation discussion paper no. 1116 (March), Yale University, New Haven, CT.

Falaris, F. M., and H. E. Peters. 1985. The Effect of the Demographic Cycle on Schooling and Entry Wages. Working paper 85–6, National Opinion Research Center, Chicago, IL.

Freeman, R. B. 1979. The Effect of Demographic Factors on Age-Earnings Profiles. *Journal of Human Resources* 14:289–318.

Friedan, B. 1963. *The Feminine Mystique*. New York: Laurel Books.

Friedman, M. 1957. *A Theory of the Consumption Function*. Princeton, NJ: Princeton University Press.

Frum, D. 2000. *How We Got Here: The 70's, the Decade That Brought You Modern Life (for Better or Worse)* New York: Basic Books.

Fuchs, V. 1989. Women's Quest for Economic Equality. *Journal of Economic Perspectives* 3 (1): 25–42.

Galbraith, J. K. 1958. The Dependence Effect. In *The Affluent Society.* Boston: Houghton Mifflin.

Glass, D. V. 1967. *Population: Policies and Movements in Europe.* London: Frank Cass.

Glick, P., J. Beresford, and D. Heer. 1963. Family Formation and Family Composition. In *Sourcebook on Marriage and the Family,* ed. Marvin Sussman. Boston: Houghton Mifflin.

Goldin, C. 1990. *Understanding the Gender Gap: An Economic History of American Woman.* New York: Oxford University Press.

Goldin, C., and L. F. Katz. 2000. The Power of the Pill: Oral Contraceptives and Women's Career and Marriage Decisions. http://www.ssrn.com/link/labor-human-capital.html.

Goldscheider, C., and P. R. Uhlenberg. 1969. Minority Group Status and Fertility. *American Journal of Sociology* 74:361–372.

Goldscheider, F. K., and L. J. Waite. 1986. Sex Differences in the Entry into Marriage. *American Journal of Sociology* 92:91–109.

Gottschalk, P., and M. Joyce. 1998. Cross-National Differences in the Rise in Earnings Inequality: Market and Institutional Factors. *The Review of Economics and Statistics* 80 (4): 489–502.

Gray, J. S. 1997. The Fall in Men's Return to Marriage: Declining Productivity

Effects or Changing Selection? *Journal of Human Resources* 32 (3): 481–504.

Grogger, J. 1998. Market Wages and Youth Crime. *Journal of Labor Economics* 16 (4): 756–791.

Grossbard-Shechtman, A. 1986. Marriage and Productivity: An Interdisciplinary Analysis. In *Handbook of Behavioral Economics*, vol. A, ed. Benjamin Gilad and Stanley Kaish, 289–302. Greenwich, CT: JAI Press.

Guttentag, M., and P. F. Secord. 1983. *Too Many Women?: The Sex Ratio Question.* Beverly Hills: Sage.

Habakkuk, H. J. 1971. *Population Growth and Economic Development since 1750.* New York: Humanities Press.

Hansen, A. H. 1939. Economic Progress and Declining Population Growth; Presidential Address Delivered at the Fifty-First Annual Meeting of the American Economic Association, Detroit, Michigan, December 28, 1938. *American Economic Review* 29 (1, pt. 1): 1–15.

Hardin, G. 1972. *Exploring the New Ethics for Survival: The Voyage of the Spaceship* Beagle. New York: Penguin Books.

Hersch, Joni. 1991. Male-Female Differences in Hourly Wages: The Role of Human Capital, Working Conditions, and Housework. *Industrial and Labor Relations Review* 44 (4): 746–759.

Hicks, J. R. 1939. *Value and Capital.* Oxford: Clarendon Press.

Higgins, M., and J. G. Williamson. 1997. Age Structure Dynamics in Asia and Dependence on Foreign Capital. *Population and Development Review* 23 (2): 262–293.

———. 1999. Explaining Inequality the World Round: Cohort Size, Kuznets Curves, and Openness. Working paper no. 7224. NBER, Cambridge, MA.

Hill, M. S. 1979. The Wage Effects of Marital Status and Children. *Journal of Human Resources* 14 (4): 579–594.

Houston, M. F. 1983. Aliens in Irregular Status in the United States: A Review of Their Numbers, Characteristics, and Role in the U.S. Labor Market. *International Migration* 21:131–146.

Johnson, G. E. 1980. The Labor Market Effects of Immigration. *Industrial and Labor Relations Review* 33 (3): 331–341.

Jones, L. 1980. *Great Expectations: America and the Baby Boom Generation.* New York: Ballantine Books.

Juhn, C., and K. Murphy. 1995. Inequality in Labor Market Outcomes: Contrasting the 1980s and the Earlier Decades. *Federal Reserve Board of New York Economic Policy Review* January.

Karoly, L., and G. Burtless. 1995. Demographic Change, Rising Earnings Inequality, and the Distribution of Personal Well-Being, 1959–1989. *Demography* 32 (3): 379–405.

Karoly, L., and J. Klerman. 1994. Using Regional Data to Reexamine the Contribution of Demographic and Sectoral Changes to Increasing U.S. Wage

Inequality. In *The Changing Distribution of Income in an Open U.S. Economy*, ed. J. H. Bergstrand, 132–157. New York: North-Holland.

Kelley, A. C. 1969. Demographic Cycles and Economic Growth: The Long Swing Reconsidered. *Journal of Economic History*, 29 (4): 633–656.

———. 1988. Economic Consequences of Population Change in the Third World. *Journal of Economic Literature* 26 (December): 1685–1728.

Kenny, L. W. 1983. The Accumulation of Human Capital during Marriage by Males. *Economic Inquiry* 21 (April): 223–231.

Keyfitz, N., and W. Flieger. 1968. *World Population: An Analysis of Vital Data*. Chicago: University of Chicago Press.

Keynes, J. M. 1937. Some Economic Consequences of a Declining Population. *Eugenics Review* 29 (1): 13–17.

Korenman, S., and D. Neumark. 1991. Does Marriage Really Make Men More Productive? *Journal of Human Resources* 26 (2): 282–307.

Korenman, S., and B. S. Okun. 1992. Recent Changes in Fertility Rates in the United States: The End of the "Birth Dearth"? Typescript.

Kuznets, S. 1958. Long Swings in the Growth of Population and in Related Economic Variables. *Proceedings of the American Philosophical Society* 102:25–52.

———. 1961. *Capital and the American Economy: Its Formation and Financing*. Princeton, NJ: Princeton University Press.

Lavely, W., and R. Freedman. 1990. The Origins of the Chinese Fertility Decline. *Demography* 27 (3): 357–367.

Lazear, E. P., and R. T. Michael. 1988. *Allocation of Income Within the Household*. Chicago: University of Chicago Press.

Lebergott, S. 1996. *Consumer Expenditures: New Measures and Old Motives*. Princeton, NJ: Princeton University Press.

Lehrer, E., and M. Nerlove. 1986. Female Labor Force Behavior and Fertility in the United States. *Annual Review of Sociology* 12:181–204.

Leibenstein, H. 1950. Bandwagon, Snob, and Veblen Effects in the Theory of Consumers' Demand. *Quarterly Journal of Economics* 64:183–207.

Lestaeghe, R., and J. Surkyn. 1988. Cultural Dynamics and Economic Theories of Fertility Change. *Population and Development Review* 14 (1): 1–45.

Lindh, T., and B. Malmberg. 1998. Age Structure and Inflation: A Wicksellian Interpretation of the OECD Data. *Journal of Economic Behavior and Organization* 36:19–37.

Lino, M. 1998. *Expenditures on Children by Families: 1997 Annual Report*. Miscellaneous publication no. 1528–1997, United States Department of Agriculture, Center for Nutrition Policy and Promotion, Washington, DC. http://www.usda.gov/fcs/cnpp/using2.htm.

Loh, E. S. 1996. Productivity Differences and the Marriage Wage Premium for White Males. *Journal of Human Resources* 31 (3): 566–589.

MacDonald, M., and R. A. Douthitt. 1992. Consumption Theories and Consumers' Assessments of Subjective Well-Being. *Journal of Consumer Affairs* 26 (2): 243–261.

MacDonald, M. M., and R. R. Rindfuss. 1978. Relative Economic Status and Fertility: Evidence from a Cross-Section. In *Research in Population Economics*, vol. 1, ed. J. Simon, 291–307. Greenwich, CT: JAI Press.

———. 1981. Earnings, Relative Income, and Family Formation. *Demography* 18 (2): 123–136.

Macunovich, D. J. 1995. The Butz-Ward Fertility Model in the Light of More Recent Data. *Journal of Human Resources* 30 (2): 229–255.

———. 1996a. Relative Income and Price of Time: Exploring Their Effects on U.S. Fertility and Female Labor Force Participation. *Population and Development Review* 22 (suppl.): 223–257.

———. 1996b. A Review of Recent Developments in the Economics of Fertility. In *Household and Family Economics*, ed. P. Menchik, 91–150. Boston: Kluwer Academic.

———. 1996c. Social Security and Retirees: Two Views of the Projections—An Economist's Perspective. In *Social Security: What Role for the Future?* ed. P. Diamond, D. Lindeman, and H. Young, 43–67. : Washington, DC: National Academy of Social Insurance.

———. 1997a. An Impending Boom in the Demand for U.S. Higher Education among 18–24 Year Olds? *Change* (Heldref Publications) May/June: 34–44.

———. 1997b. Discussion Comments Related to "Social Security: How Social and How Secure Should It Be?" by Steven Sass and Robert Triest. In *Social Security Reform: Links to Saving, Investment, and Growth*, ed. S. A. Sass and R. K. Triest, 64–73. Conference series no. 41, Federal Reserve Bank of Boston, June.

———. 1998a. Fertility and the Easterlin Hypothesis: An Assessment of the Literature, *Journal of Population Economics* 11:53–111.

———. 1998b. Relative Cohort Size and Inequality in the U.S. *American Economic Review* (Papers and Proceedings) 88 (2): 259–264.

———. 1998c. Race and Relative Income/Price of Time Effects on U.S. Fertility. *Journal of Socio-Economics* 27 (3): 365–400.

———. 1999a. The Fortunes of One's Birth: Relative Cohort Size and the Youth Labor Market in the U.S. *Journal of Population Economics* 12:215–272.

———. 1999b. The Role of Relative Income and Relative Cohort Size in the Demographic Transition. *Population and Environment* 21 (2): 155–192.

———. 2000a. Why the Baby Bust Cohorts Haven't Boomed Yet: A Re-examination of Cohort Effects on Wage Inequality in the U.S. In *Back to Shared Prosperity*, ed. Ray Marshall, 145–157. Armonk, NY: M. E. Sharpe.

———. 2000b. Relative Cohort Size: Source of a Unifying Theory of Global Fertility Transition? *Population and Development Review* 26 (2): 235–261.

———. 2002. Additional data and analyses supporting the arguments presented in *Birth Quake: The Baby Boom and Its Aftershocks.* Available from the author: http://www.columbia.edu/~dm555/birthquake/appendices.html.

Macunovich, D. J., and R. A. Easterlin. 1990. How Parents Have Coped: The Effect of Life Cycle Demographic Decisions on the Economic Status of Pre-School Age Children, 1964–1987. *Population and Development Review* 16 (2): 299–323.

Macunovich, D. J., R. A. Easterlin, C. M. Shaeffer, and E. M. Crimmins. 1995. Echoes of the Baby Boom and Bust: Recent and Prospective Changes in Intergenerational Living Arrangements of Elderly Widows in the United States, *Demography* 32 (1): 17–28.

Malmberg, B. 1994. Age Structure Effects on Economic Growth: Swedish Evidence. *Scandinavian Economic History Review* 42:279–295.

Malthus, T. R. 1798. *An Essay on the Principle of Population, As It Affects the Future Improvement of Society, with Remarks on the Speculations of Mr. Godwin, M. Condorcet, and Other Writers.* London: J. Johnson.

Mankiw, N. G., and D. N. Weil. 1989. The Baby Boom, the Baby Bust, and the Housing Market. *Regional Science and Urban Economics* 19:235–258.

Mare, R. D., and C. Winship. 1991. Socioeconomic Change and the Decline of Marriage for Blacks and Whites. In *The Urban Underclass,* ed. C. Jencks and P. E. Peterson, 175–202. Washington DC: Brookings Institution.

Maxwell, N. L. 1991. Individual and Aggregate Influences on the Age at First Birth. *Population Research and Policy Review* 10:27–46.

McBride, Michael. 2001. Relative-Income Effects on Subjective Well-Being in the Cross-Section. *Journal of Economic Behavior and Organization* 45: 251–278.

McCall, L. 2000. Explaining Levels of Within-Group Wage Inequality in U.S. Labor Markets. *Demography* 37 (4): 415–430.

McLaughlin, D., and D. Lichter. 1993. Economic Independence, Marriage Markets, and Marital Behavior among Low-Income Women. *The 1993 Proceedings of the American Statistical Association,* 484–493.

McMillan, H. M., and J. B. Baesel. 1990. The Macroeconomic Impact of the Baby Boom Generation. *Journal of Macroeconomics* 12 (2): 167–195.

Miles, D. 1999. Modeling the Impact of Demographic Change upon the Economy. *Economic Journal* 109 (January): 1–36.

Mincer, J. 1991. Human Capital, Technology, and the Wage Structure: What Do Time-Series Show? Working paper no. 3581, NBER, Cambridge, MA.

Modigliani, F. 1949. Fluctuations in the Saving-Income Ratio: A Problem in Economic Forecasting. In *Studies in Income and Wealth,* vol. 11, 371–443. New York: NBER.

Murphy, K., M. Plant, and F. Welch. 1988. Cohort Size and Earnings in the United States. In *The Economics of Changing Age Distributions in Developed Countries,* ed. R. D. Lee, W. B. Arthur, and G. Rodgers, 39–58. Oxford: Clarendon Press.

Murphy, K., and F. Welch. 1992. The Structure of Wages. *Quarterly Journal of Economics* 62 (1): 285–326.

Nakosteen, R. A., and M. A. Zimmer. 1987. Marital Status and the Earnings of

Young Men: A Model with Endogenous Selection. *Journal of Human Resources* 22 (2): 248–268.

National Center for Health Statistics. 1964, 1965, 1966, 1967, 1968, 1969, 1986. *Vital Statistics: Nuptiality.*

———. 1991a. Advance Report of Final Divorce Statistics, 1988. *Monthly Vital Statistics Report* 39 (12, suppl. 2).

———. 1991b. Advance Report of Final Marriage Statistics, 1988. *Monthly Vital Statistics Report* 40 (4, suppl.).

———. 1995a. Advance Report of Final Divorce Statistics, 1989 and 1990. *Monthly Vital Statistics Report* 43 (9, suppl.).

———. 1995b. Advance Report of Final Marriage Statistics, 1989 and 1990. *Monthly Vital Statistics Report* 43 (12, suppl.).

———. 1995c. Annual Summary of Births, Marriages, Divorces, and Deaths: United States, 1994. *Monthly Vital Statistics Report* 43 (13).

———. 1997a. Births, Marriages, Divorces, and Deaths for 1996. *Monthly Vital Statistics Report* 45 (12).

———. 1997b. *Vital Statistics: Volume 1 Natality,* U.S. Department of Health and Human Services: Hyattsville, MD.

———. 1998. Births, Marriages, Divorces, and Deaths for 1997. *Monthly Vital Statistics Report* 46 (12).

———. 1999. Births: Final Data for 1997, *National Vital Statistics Reports* 47(18).

———. 2001a. Births: Final Data for 1999, *National Vital Statistics Reports* 49(1).

———. 2001b. Births: Preliminary Data for 2000, *National Vital Statistics Reports* 49(5).

Nothaft, F. F. 1985. The Effect of Cohort Size on Human Capital Investment and Earnings Growth. Working paper 42, Board of Governors of the Federal Reserve System, Washington, DC.

Ohbuchi, H. 1982. Empirical Tests of the Chicago Model and the Easterlin Hypothesis: A Case Study of Japan. *Journal of Population Studies (Jinkogaku Kenkyu)* 5 (May): 8–16.

Olneck, M. R., and B. L. Wolfe. 1978. A Note on Some Evidence on the Easterlin Hypothesis. *Journal of Political Economy* 86 (5): 953–958.

Olsen, Randall J. 1994. Fertility and the Size of the U.S. Labor Force. *Journal of Economic Literature* 32 (1): 60–100.

Oppenheimer, V. K. 1976. The Easterlin Hypothesis: Another Aspect of the Echo to Consider. *Population and Development Review* 2:433–457.

Oppenheimer, V. K., H. Blossfield, and H. Wackerow. 1995. New Developments in Family Formation and Women's Improvement in Educational Attainment in the United States. In *Family Formation in Modern Societies and the New Role of Women,* 150–173. Boulder: Westview Press.

Oppenheimer, V. K., M. Kalmijn, and V. Lew. 1993. Men's Transition to Work and Marriage Timing. Typescript.

Oppenheimer, V. K., M. Kalmijn, and N. Lim. 1997. Men's Career Development and Marriage Timing during a Period of Rising Inequality. *Demography* 34 (3): 311–330.

Oppenheimer, V. K., and V. Lew. 1995. Marriage Formation in the Eighties: How Important Was Women's Economic Independence?" In *Gender and Family Change in Industrialized Countries*, ed. K. O. Mason and A. Jensen, 105–138. Oxford: Clarendon Press.

Pampel, F. C., and H. E. Peters. 1995. The Easterlin Effect. *Annual Review of Sociology* 21:163.

Parsons, T. 1949. The Social Structure of the Family. In *The Family: Its Function and Destiny*, ed. R. N. Ashen. New York: Harper and Brothers.

———. 1956. *Economy and Society: A Study in the Integration of Economic and Social Theory.* Glencoe, IL: Free Press.

Peters, K. D., J. A. Martin, S. J. Ventura, and J. D. Maurer. 1997. Births and Deaths: United States, July 1995–June 1996. *Monthly Vital Statistics Report* 45 (10, suppl. 2).

Pfeffer, J., and J. Ross. 1982. The Effects of Marriage and a Working Wife on Occupational and Wage Attainment. *Administrative Science Quarterly* 27:66–80.

Pollak, R. A. 1976. Habit Formation and Long-Run Utility Functions, *Journal of Economic Theory* 13:271–297.

Presser, H. B. 1989. Can We Make Time for Children? The Economy, Work Schedules, and Child Care. *Demography* 26 (4): 523–543.

Preston, S. H. 1986. Changing Values and Falling Birth Rates. *Below-Replacement Fertility in Industrial Societies, Population, and Development Review* 12 (suppl.):176–195.

Reed, F. W., J. R. Udry, and M. Ruppert. 1975. Relative Income and Fertility: The Analysis of Individuals' fertility in a Biracial Sample. *Journal of Marriage and the Family* November: 799–805.

Rindfuss, R. R., K. L. Brewster, and A. L. Kavee. 1996. Women, Work, and Children in the U.S. *Population and Development Review* 22:457–482.

Rostow, W. W. 1998. *The Great Population Spike and After: Reflections on the 21st Century.* Oxford: Oxford University Press.

Ryder, N. B. 1990. What Is Going to Happen to American Fertility? *Population and Development Review* 16 (3): 433–454.

Ryscavage, Paul. 1995. A Surge in Growing Income Inequality? *Monthly Labor Review* August: 51–61.

Samuelson, P. 1988. The Keynes-Hansen-Samuelson Multiplier-Accelerator Model of Secular Stagnation. *Japan and the World Economy* 1:3–19.

Sanderson, Warren. 1987. Below-Replacement Fertility in Nineteenth Century America. *Population and Development Review* 13 (2): 305–313.

Schieber, S. J., and J. B. Shoven. 1994. The Consequences of Population Aging on Private Pension Fund Saving and Asset Markets, Working paper no. 4665. NBER, Cambridge, MA.

Schoen, R., W. Urton, K. Woodrow, and J. Baj. 1985. Marriage and Divorce in Twentieth-Century American Cohorts. *Demography* 22 (1): 101–114.

Schoeni, R. F. 1995. Marital Status and Earnings in Developed Countries. *Journal of Population Economics* 8:351–359.

Schumpeter, J. A. 1946. The American Economy in the Interwar Period: The Decade of the Twenties. *American Economic Review* 36:1–10.

Serow, W. J. 1980. Economic Aspects of Recent Changes in Dutch Marital Fertility. *Genus* 36 (December): 189–202.

Siebert, W. S., and P. J. Sloane. 1981. The Measurement of Sex and Marital Status Discrimination at the Workplace. *Economica* 48 (190): 125–141.

Simon, J. L. 1994. The Demographic Causes and Consequences of the Industrial Revolution 23 (1): 141–158.

———. 1996. *The Ultimate Resource 2.* Princeton, NJ: Princeton University Press.

Slesnick, D. T. 1992. Aggregate Consumption and Saving in the Postwar U.S. *Review of Economics and Statistics* 74 (4): 585–597.

Smith, A. 1937. *The Wealth of Nations.* New York: Modern Library.

Smith, J. P., and M. P. Ward. 1985. Time-Series Growth in the Female Labor Force. *Journal of Labor Economics* 3 (1, pt. 2): S59–S90.

Smith, J. P., and F. Welch. 1981. No Time to Be Young: The Economic Prospects for Large Cohorts in the United States. *Population and Development Review* 7 (1): 71–83.

Smock, P. J., and W. D. Manning. 1997. Cohabiting Partners' Economic Circumstances and Marriage. *Demography* 34 (3): 331–341.

Social Security Administration. 1994. Unpublished tabulations from the March Current Population Survey prepared by the Division of Economic Research, Office of the Actuary, July 6.

———. 1992. Economic Projections for OASDI Cost and Income Estimates: 1992. Actuarial study no. 108, SSA pub. no. 11–11551, U.S. Department of Health and Human Services.

Solnick, S. J., and D. Hemenway. 1998. Is More Always Better? A Survey on Positional Concerns. *Journal of Economic Organization and Behavior* 37:373–383.

Stapleton, D. C., and D. J. Young. 1988. Educational Attainment and Cohort Size. *Journal of Labor Economics* 6 (3): 330–361.

Steelman, L. C., and B. Powell. 1991. Sponsoring the Next Generation: Parental Willingness to Pay for Higher Education. *American Journal of Sociology* 96 (6): 1505–1529.

Stoker, T. 1986. Simple Tests of Distributional Effects on Macroeconomic Equations. *Journal of Political Economy* 94 (4): 763–795.

Stroh, L. K., and J. M. Brett. 1995. The Dual-Earner Dad Penalty in Salary Progression. Typescript.

Szreter, S. 1993. The Idea of Demographic Transition and the Study of Fertility Change: A Critical Intellectual History. *Population and Development Review* 19 (4): 659–701.

Teachman, J. D., K. A. Polonko, and G. K. Leigh. 1987. Marital Timing: Race and Sex Comparisons. *Social Forces* 66:239–268.

Thornton, A. 1979. Fertility and Income, Consumption, Aspirations, and Child Quality Standards. *Demography* 16 (2): 157–175.

United Nations. 1998a. *World Population Prospects, the 1998 revision.* Population Studies no. 145. New York: United Nations.

————. 1998b. Age Specific Fertility. gopher://gopher.undp.org:70/00/ungophers/popin/wdtrends.

————. 1999. *World Population 1950–2050 (the 1998 Revision).* Diskette, United Nations, New York.

United States Bureau of the Census. 1975. *Historical Statistics of the United States, Colonial Times to 1970.* Washington, DC: U.S. Government Printing Office.

United States Immigration and Naturalization Service. 1996. *Statistical Yearbook.* Washington, DC: U.S. Government Printing Office.

van de Stadt, H., A. Kapteyn, and S. van de Geer. 1985. The Relativity of Utility: Evidence from Panel Data. *The Review of Economics and Statistics,* 67 (2): 179–187.

van Praag, B. M. S. 1993. The Relativity of the Welfare Concept. In *The Quality of Life,* ed. M. Nussbaum and A. Sen, 362–385. Oxford: Clarendon Press.

Ventura, S. J., S. C. Curtin, T. J. Mathews. 1998. Teenage Births in the United States: National and State Trends, 1990–96. *National Vital Statistics System,* DHHS pub. no. (PHS) 98–1019, 8–0426 (4/98), U.S. Department of Health and Human Services, Centers for Disease Control and Prevention, National Center for Health Statistics, Washington, DC.

Ventura, S. J., J. A. Martin, T. J. Mathews, and S.C. Clarke. 1997. Advance Report of Final Natality Statistics, 1994. *Monthly Vital Statistics Report* 44 (11, suppl.)

Wachter, M. L. 1980. The Labor Market and Illegal Immigration: The Outlook for the 1980s. *Industrial and Labor Relations Review* 33 (3): 342–354.

Wachter, M. L., and W. L. Wascher. 1984. Leveling the Peaks and Troughs in the Demographic Cycle. *Review of Economics and Statistics* 66:208–215.

Wattenberg, B. J. 1987. *The Birth Dearth: What Happens When People in Free Countries Don't Have Enough Babies?* New York: Pharos Books.

Weil, D. N. 1994. The Saving of the Elderly in Micro and Macro Data. *Quarterly Journal of Economics* 109 (1): 55–81.

Welch, F. 1979. Effects of Cohort Size on Earnings: The Baby Boom Babies' Financial Bust. *Journal of Political Economy* 87 (5, pt. 2): S65–S97.

Westoff, C. F. 1986. Perspective on Nuptiality and Fertility. In *Below-Replacement Fertility in Industrial Societies, Population and Development Review* 12 (suppl.): 155–170.

Whitman, D. 1999. More Moral: America's Moral Non-Decline. *New Republic,* February 22, 18–19.

Williamson, J. G. 1998. Growth, Distribution, and Demography: Some Lessons from History. *Explorations in Economic History* 35:241–271.

Zinsmeister, K., S. Moore, and K. Bowman. 1999. Is America Turning a Corner? *American Enterprise* 10 (1): 36–60.

Zizzo, D. J., and A. Oswald. 2000. Are People Willing to Pay to Reduce Others' Incomes? Typescript.

Author Index

Numbers in parentheses indicate the pages on which the endnote references appear.

Subject Index

Page numbers for figures are in italic. Numbers in parentheses indicate the pages on which the note references appear.

France
  crude birth rate, *225*
  economic depression, timing of, 223
  historic vital rates, *193–194*
  population age structure, *224*

Gambia, fertility transition in, 190, 192
GDP growth
  econometric results, 233–234
  female labor force participation, effect of, 17–18, 244
  population age structure effects, *235*
  savings, effect of, 239
  See also aggregate demand effects; economic conditions
gender roles
  1995 Gallup Poll results, 52
  attitudinal change, 14, 167–168
  college enrollment of women, effect on, 139
  dampen population cycles, 42
  future changes, 14, 253
  Japan's limited cohort size effects, 249
  marriage wage premium, estimating, 276n. 14 (165)
  and relative income, 11, 71, 139
  specialization and marriage wage premium, 162
  among Williams students, 53, 255–256, 261
  women as secondary workers, 72
general fertility rate
  change in, *68*
  contrasted with CBR, *64*
  contrasted with population age ratio, *41, 66*
  crude birth rate, better than, 63, 64
  definition, 3n. 2 (265)
  measure of cohort size and position, 108
  used in econometric analyses, 64, 65, 251, 271n. 17 (94)
General Social Survey, 8
Georgia (nation), proportion aged 15–24, *227*
Germany
  crude birth rate, *225*
  guest workers in, 189
  proportion aged 15–24, *227*
  unemployment in 1923–1929, 224
  West, population decline in, 184

GI Bill, 168
globalization
  inequality, effect on, 105
  wage structure, effect on, 92
government policy. *See* institutional factors
Guinea-Bisseau, fertility transition in, 190

holistic approach, 249
Hong Kong
  proportion aged 15–24, *227*
  vital rates, *191*, 192
housing market, 22
Hungary, proportion aged 15–24, *229*

immigration
  aggregate demand, effect on, 281n. 11 (224)
  calls to end in U.S., 279n. 1 (184)
  historic pattern in U.S., *204*
  illegal, effect on relative income, 71
  potential for masking cohort size effects, 42
  relative income, effect on, 70
imperfect substitutes
  age group definitions, 65
  definition, 5–7, 38
  in developing economies, 186, 188
  in Easterlin hypothesis, 38
income distribution, trends in, 104, 105
Indiana, male relative income in, *84*
Indonesia, proportion aged 15–24, *227*
Industrial Revolution, and feedback effects, 37
industrial structure, 18–19
inequality
  suggested causes, 105, 106, 272n. 11 (112)
  trends, 7, 104, 105
  trends vs. Easterlin hypothesis, 88
  Welch's estimates, 87
  within-cell variance, effect of, 109
inflation
  econometric results, 233–234
  hyperinflation, 25
  population age structure, effect of, *22, 24–26, 235*
institutional factors
  barriers to cohort size effects, 189, 192, 249